The Imperfect Revolution

to JEAN, a great colleague, Union
President & former history
Chair

with much APPRECIATION

GORDON

AMERICAN ABOLITIONISM AND ANTISLAVERY
John David Smith, series editor

*The Imperfect Revolution: Anthony Burns and the
Landscape of Race in Antebellum America*
Gordon S. Barker

The Imperfect Revolution

Anthony Burns and the Landscape of Race in Antebellum America

GORDON S. BARKER

The Kent State
University Press
Kent, Ohio

© 2010 by The Kent State University Press, Kent, Ohio 44242
ALL RIGHTS RESERVED
Library of Congress Catalog Card Number 2010020012

ISBN 978-1-60635-069-0
Manufactured in the United States of America

Library of Congress Cataloging-in-Publication Data
Barker, Gordon S., 1952–
    The imperfect revolution : Anthony Burns and the landscape of race in antebellum America /
Gordon S. Barker.
        p. cm. — (American abolitionism and antislavery)
Includes bibliographical references and index.
ISBN 978-1-60635-069-0 (hardcover : alk. paper) ∞
    1. Burns, Anthony, 1834–1862.
    2. Burns, Anthony, 1834–1862—Trials, litigation, etc.
    3. Fugitive slaves—United States—Biography.
    4. Fugitive slaves—Legal status, laws, etc.—United States.
    5. Fugitive slaves—Legal status, laws, etc.—Massachusetts.
    6. Antislavery movements—United States—History—19th century.
    7. Antislavery movements—Massachusetts—Boston—History—19th century.
    8. United States. Fugitive slave law (1850)
    9. United States—Race relations.
    I. Title.
    E450.B93B37 2010
    973.7'115092—dc22
    [B]

                        2010020012

British Library Cataloging-in-Publication data are available.
14 13 12 11 10   5 4 3 2 1

For Christiane

Contents

Preface
First Reflections

A lmost ten years ago, reflecting on the outpouring of literature following the publication of Gordon S. Wood's *The Radicalism of the American Revolution* and the famous debate between James M. McPherson and Ira Berlin about "Who Freed the Slaves," I became curious about how nineteenth-century blacks viewed the American Revolution. In particular, I wondered whether blacks in antebellum America considered the American Revolution over, and their ongoing struggle independent of that which their white neighbors had waged in the late eighteenth century, or if they believed the Revolution was still raging. I wondered whether Gordon Wood, defining the Revolution as a deep-rooted political and cultural transformation that spanned nearly one hundred years, ending in Jacksonian America, had stopped his periodization a little too soon. When I came upon Anthony Burns embracing Patrick Henry's legendary words "Give me Liberty or Give me Death," a philosophy that some 180,000 black Americans also embraced when they took up arms in the American Civil War and transformed it from a war for the Union into a war of liberation, I had my answers.

Many people have helped me in the realization of this project, which had its genesis in a graduate research seminar at the College of William and Mary taught by Carol Sheriff, a brilliant professor who encouraged me to follow my curiosity and who became the second reader on a dissertation committee that most graduate students can only dream of having. Melvin Patrick Ely also provided much encouragement and lent his immeasurable talent and great wisdom as chair of the dissertation committee; Ronald Schechter and Kris Lane provided insights that strengthened the final product; and Robert A. Gross of the University of Connecticut, the external reader, identified key issues for me to explore and incorporate into this book. This work would not have been realized without the support of these remarkable scholars and wonderful individuals.

I have received valuable assistance from librarians and support staff at the Earl Gregg Swem Library of the College of William and Mary, the Bishop's University Library, the James A. Gibson Library of Brock University, the Massachusetts Historical Society, the Boston Public Library, the St. Catharines Public Library, and the St. Catharines Museum. Bishop's University also provided funding for additional research and prepublication expenses. Marjorie Dawson, Wilma Morrison, and Maggie Parnall, who shared with me their interest in imprinting Anthony Burns in our collective memory, provided me with inspiration and strengthened my determination to bring this project to fruition. Cheryl Porter helped me put together the final manuscript. Lastly, without the support of my family, who patiently put up with a scholar who must, at times, have seemed to be living in nineteenth-century America, this project never would have seen the light of day. My brother George listened to me for hours discussing antebellum race relations; my daughter Nadine spent much time doing research with a historian, dusting off old newspapers and other materials—hours that she might have spent with friends. Christiane, the love of my life, shared all my ups and downs throughout this project. To her I dedicate this work.

Prologue
Remembering Anthony Burns

Boston never before was so deeply moved [as during the Burns rendition]. . . .
In all her revolutionary experience she never presented such a spectacle.
    —Boston Daily Evening Transcript, *June 2, 1854*

Faneuil Hall is the purlieus of the Court House . . . where the children of
Adams and Hancock may prove that they are not bastards. Let us prove that we
are worthy of liberty.
    —*Wendell Phillips*

I may show the world that the work of 1854 is not in vain.
    —*Anthony Burns*

On a beautiful but cold, windy day in Boston in the spring of 2005, I
found myself alone with the two historical interpreters on duty in
the Visitor Information Center adjacent to Faneuil Hall. In that venerable
building, known also as the "cradle of liberty," Boston's leading antislavery
activists harangued a boisterous crowd in 1854 two days after the capture of
Anthony Burns, soon to be Virginia's most famous fugitive slave. Denouncing the South's peculiar institution and the Fugitive Slave Law of 1850, the
abolitionists called for the rescue of Burns from the "iron house of bondage."[1]
They asked Bostonians to remember their heritage of 1776 and demonstrate
their commitment to the principles that had been so valiantly defended by
their forefathers.

Having just visited the Great Hall, imagining the excitement that must
have filled the air as the likes of Theodore Parker, Wendell Phillips, and
Samuel Gridley Howe called for the extension of American liberties to Burns,
I asked the first interpreter, an efficient-looking woman busily organizing
pamphlets on the counter, "Could you tell me about Anthony Burns and
what happened here in 1854?" She gave me a blank, how-dare-you stare;
motioned toward her colleague; and said to me, "You will have to ask him.
I don't know anything about Anthony Burns." Somewhat taken aback, I

hesitantly turned to her serious-looking middle-aged colleague, also white, and said, "I would like information on Anthony Burns." He responded curtly, "We have no printed material on Burns; the only information on him that we have here is in my head, and about all I know is that Burns was a fugitive slave returned from Boston."

Recognizing my disappointment and obviously seeing a need to put me on the right path, the interpreters immediately told me about the Freedom Trail. They politely advised me to forget about Burns. "The Freedom Trail," they stressed, "was much more important." They told me that Paul Revere was a particularly interesting figure and said that I should follow the trail of red bricks, which would lead me to the legendary night rider's house in the North End. I knew about Paul Revere—his story was one that even my high school history teacher, a man who always spoke in a monotone, could not make dull. But I kept thinking about Anthony Burns.

I left the Visitor Information Center with mixed emotions. I knew that in late May and early June of 1854, placards and handbills about Burns covered Boston. I also knew that day after day the Burns drama occupied the front pages of the city's newspapers. The affair also made headlines in the newspapers of other cities throughout the North and the South. Burns's fate engaged hundreds of thousands—perhaps millions—of Americans, black and white, rich and poor. President Franklin Pierce's administration regarded the Burns crisis as a national priority and allocated substantial resources to deal with it. The name of Virginia's suddenly famous fugitive slave was on the lips of all Bostonians—legislators, leading lawyers, businessmen, women, shopkeepers, artisans, laborers, students, and the so-called lowlife about the wharves. That day in 2005, I had the uneasy feeling that this history was being forgotten, and that the national memory had become badly skewed. In the following pages, my first objective is to help ensure Anthony Burns his rightful place in both mainstream American history and our collective memory.

As a drama in the American struggle for freedom, Anthony Burns's story easily ranks with Paul Revere's ride in April 1775. Like Revere, Burns was a remarkable man who demonstrated strength of character, ingenuity, and agency. He searched for his own "Freedom Trail"; tragically, he found it only very late in his short life. Despite being born a slave, separated early in life from his mother and other family members, mistreated—even disfigured— by cruel masters, and deprived of access to education, Burns persevered in his search for a better life. He learned to read and write and became an outstanding preacher and a devoted teacher who ran a clandestine school for blacks in Richmond, Virginia, before his courageous flight north in search of liberty. He experienced the misfortune of recapture on free soil, endured a trial in which the odds seemed to be against him, and then found himself returned to bondage before thousands of onlookers.

His spirit unbroken, Burns survived a period of solitary confinement in Robert Lumpkin's infamous slave jail in Richmond before his master sold him to a North Carolina slave trader known for reaping huge profits by selling human property to the Deep South. Burns eventually gained his freedom as a result of the efforts of the Reverend Leonard A. Grimes and other members of Boston's Twelfth Baptist Church, who had been deeply moved by his misfortune. They persisted in their efforts to locate him and purchased his liberty. Once free, Burns attended Oberlin College and, after a brief period in Indianapolis, became the beloved pastor of a Baptist church in St. Catharines, Ontario. Many members of his congregation were fugitive slaves and free blacks who fled to the region that was then called Canada West to avoid the risk of being kidnapped and sold into slavery. Burns's death from consumption (tuberculosis) at the age of only twenty-eight ended a brief but singularly eventful life that had special significance for Canadians and Americans, black and white, who were increasingly determined to deal with slavery in one way or another.

Academic historians have not forgotten Anthony Burns, although typically they have failed to underscore his agency and determination. They have tended to treat him merely as an object, a victim. However, a number of very able scholars have placed him at center stage in an increasingly divided nation during troubled times. Most of these scholars note that from mid-1854 until the outbreak of the Civil War, even after he had moved to Canada, Burns continued to make headlines in newspapers in both the North and South. They also show that after Burns's untimely death in 1862, his shadow still lingered over the divided nation and influenced public sentiment. But the way these scholars have interpreted Burns's personal drama within the broader context of the republican experiment and the coming of the Civil War gives rise to the other principal objectives of this work.

Broadly speaking, Burns is treated in two ways in the historical literature. First, following in the footsteps of Charles Emery Stevens, a nineteenth-century scholar who witnessed the events in Boston in 1854 and became Burns's first chronicler, several historians have underscored the impact of the Burns drama on abolitionist sentiment in the North. They have suggested that the rendition of Burns into bondage, coming on the heels of the Kansas-Nebraska crisis, gave new impetus to the antislavery movement.[2] For many Northerners, Burns's return to slavery confirmed the horrors they read about in Harriet Beecher Stowe's *Uncle Tom's Cabin,* which was published two years earlier. In an in-depth analysis of the Fugitive Slave Law of 1850 and its enforcement, Stanley W. Campbell argues that Burns's return to bondage boosted antislavery feelings and helped turn public opinion against the federal legislation. Building on Campbell's work, Jane Pease and William Pease examine the Fugitive Slave Law of 1850. Focusing particularly on the law's contribution to sectional strife between the North and South, they portray the Burns drama as one in a long line of controversial cases that heightened Northern resistance to the federal defense of Southerners' rights to own human property. They conclude that the Burns rendition provided evidence of the mounting costs of enforcing legislation that was becoming increasingly unpopular in the North.[3]

In their research on abolitionists, the Peases suggest that the Burns crisis intensified the antislavery impulse in the North. They also argue that the Burns drama spurred the abolitionists' shift to outright "confrontation" from their earlier "disengagement" tactics emphasizing the denunciation of the Constitution and of proslavery churches. The Peases note that abolitionists introduced their new, more aggressive approach at the Fourth of July antislavery picnic in Framingham, Massachusetts, only weeks after Burns was returned to slavery in Virginia. William Lloyd Garrison burned copies of the Constitution, the Fugitive Slave Law, Commissioner Edward Loring's decision in the Burns case, and Colonel Charles Suttle's certified claim to the fugitive slave from Virginia. Jane and William Pease suggest that the Burns case proved to abolitionists that their previous reliance on moral suasion had been woefully inadequate.[4]

Stressing a groundswell in antislavery feeling in response to Burns's return to slavery, Harold Schwartz concludes that "in effect the Fugitive Slave Law was nullified in Boston." Similarly, linking the Burns drama with "Bleeding Kansas," Stanley Shapiro argues that the trial of Burns "fanned into flame resentment that Kansas-Nebraska [had] kindled." According to Shapiro, the crisis fueled Northern fears of slaveholders' power, raised the specter of slavery pushing its way into the free states, and buoyed abolitionist sentiment, thus precipitating the courthouse riot that followed the rally in support of Burns in Faneuil Hall arranged by the Boston Vigilance Committee. The riot led to the death of a guard, a number of injuries, several arrests, and an unprecedented show of force on the part of the Boston police, the state militia, and the U.S. military.[5]

In his research on the Burns affair and the effects of the courthouse riot on Northern sentiment, David Maginnes concurs with Schwartz and Shapiro. Comparing the Burns rendition to earlier fugitive slave cases—notably that of Thomas Sims, returned to Georgia from Boston in 1851—Maginnes stresses the shifts in public opinion sparked by the capture of Burns and his subsequent return to bondage. He argues that the Burns affair boosted anti-slavery feelings and represented a watershed.[6] From Maginnes's perspective, the Burns rendition changed the North; he argues that even industrialists such as Amos Lawrence, who made substantial profits dealing in Southern markets, became converts to the antislavery cause. In a similar vein, James Oliver Horton and Lois E. Horton portray the Burns case as a key event. They label it an antislavery "victory" and suggest that it aroused public outrage against both slavery in the South and federal support of the institution. Likewise, Charles Johnson and Patricia Smith argue that Burns's return to bondage "affected even the most apathetic Northerners" and strengthened their resolve "to defy" the Fugitive Slave Law.[7]

Another group of scholars emphasizes Boston's Revolutionary heritage, founded on a commitment to liberty and equality. In arguments that overlap the views of those discussed above, these historians contend that the Burns drama resulted in the fusion of Bostonians' antislavery leanings with their Revolutionary heritage. These scholars assert that the tragic plight of Anthony Burns forced Bostonians to confront the horrors of slavery on Massachusetts's own free soil. The sight of a shackled slave being returned to bondage thus encouraged Bostonians to lash out against violations of natural rights philosophy, or "higher law." David Herbert Donald's assessment of Charles Sumner's reaction to the Burns drama and Albert Von Frank's work on "Emerson's Boston" are two leading examples of this approach. Donald shows Sumner ratcheting up his antislavery campaign in response to the Burns affair; Von Frank describes the events in 1854 as a "pocket revolution" during which Emerson's Boston took a stand for "equal justice" and "higher law," both of which were deemed essential to a "moral universe."[8]

Although all these scholars provide insight into the Burns drama, the nation, and the times, they tend to read history backward from the Civil War. The arrest of Burns, his trial, the courthouse riot, and the crowd's reactions to his forced departure from Boston are portrayed as critical points on the march toward the Civil War, the Emancipation Proclamation, and the extirpation of slavery from American soil. These historians treat the Burns drama much like other incidents that they suggest fueled antislavery sentiments and sectional strife during the decade before the Civil War—the publication of *Uncle Tom's Cabin,* the Kansas-Nebraska crisis, the caning of Charles Sumner in the Senate, Roger Taney's Dred Scott decision, and John Brown's Harper's

Ferry raid, which was followed quickly by his execution. This scholarship on Burns suggests continuity and almost implies the inevitability of impending violent confrontation in the form of a civil war. There are fundamental weaknesses in such an approach.

First, the scholarship underestimates or masks the confusion and disarray in antebellum America and especially in midcentury Boston, a city fraught with religious, racial, and ethnic tension, and with class antipathy. Although antislavery sentiments certainly existed—notably the pacifist abolitionism of people such as William Lloyd Garrison, the moral high road of Charles Sumner, and the radical philosophies of outspoken activists such as Theodore Parker, men who aimed to sink the Southern "slavocracy" and nullify the Fugitive Slave Law—these were not the only attitudes displayed by antebellum Bostonians and other Americans.[9] At critical moments such as the Burns rendition, antislavery sentiments competed with a wide range of other, much less noble opinions and beliefs. This work aims to expose the conflict and confusion, even chaos, in Anthony Burns's Boston; it suggests that the march toward the Civil War and the extirpation of slavery were not inevitable, nor was there a consensus among Bostonians and other Northern whites that such a march was necessary.

The existing scholarship on Burns is also disconnected from the rich historical literature on African Americans, including recent studies on Northern racism and earlier seminal works such as W. E. B. Du Bois's *Black Reconstruction in America*.[10] Most Burns scholarship focuses on the contest between Southern slaveholders seeking to exercise their rights to human property, supported by federal authorities, and Northern abolitionists, who denounced slavery as a violation of the principles enshrined in the Declaration of Independence, natural rights, and God-given higher law. The way this confrontation unfolded, however, also reflected the patterns of relations between the races in Boston and throughout the North. I endeavor to reveal the very different meanings of the Burns drama for blacks and whites and, in so doing, to demonstrate how prevailing attitudes toward race informed the behavior of key players throughout the crisis. I aim to expose the special message the Burns drama had for Northern blacks and show how it encouraged them to adopt an increasingly militant stance against slavery independent of the white abolitionists with whom they had been accustomed to working closely.

My third objective is to reconsider Anthony Burns and the coming of the Civil War. Not surprisingly, most scholars have emphasized the supposed groundswell of antislavery sentiment in the North during the Burns affair and the resulting trends in emancipation politics and sectional strife after the crisis. Here, too, there are problems. If the Burns rendition ignited a Northern drive for emancipation, it did so in a strange and convoluted way. While Burns languished in solitary confinement in a Richmond slave trader's jail, most Free-Soil advocates, and certainly the Republican Party that emerged in the 1850s, continued to focus their attention on keeping western territories free from slavery rather than on liberating nearly four million enslaved blacks such as Burns.

The Republican Party grew rapidly in the aftermath of the Burns crisis to become the North's leading political organization in the second half of the decade. Yet despite the alleged opposition of Northerners to the Burns rendition, their apparent disaffection with the federal enforcement of the Fugitive Slave Law, and their supposed widespread abhorrence of the peculiar institution, the Republican Party's platform in 1856 did not advocate the repeal of fugitive slave legislation, elimination of slavery in the nation's capital, or the abolition of slavery in the states where it already existed.[11] Nor did this rising Northern party call for the extension of civil rights to African Americans in the free states. As one leading scholar has suggested, most Republican leaders believed that the advocacy of rights for free blacks might prove "politically disastrous." Indeed, in some areas such as the Midwest, Republicans proclaimed that they, not the Democrats, were the "real 'white man's party.'" They "vehemently denied" any inferences that the party intended to extend rights to Northern blacks, rejected allegations that they planned to tamper with slavery in the South, and disavowed charges that they had intentions of "turning the [N]egroes loose among us."[12] Republicans tailored their party's platform to the sentiments of the white Northern electorate, concluding that public opinion had changed little from the time of the Burns crisis to the end of the decade. For Republicans, the Civil War was initially a war for the Union; it became a war against slavery only gradually, in a process cemented by the service of 180,000 black soldiers.[13] Reexamining the link between Anthony Burns and the onset of the Civil War suggests that perhaps one of the most significant impacts of the Burns crisis was on the white South, not the North. For many white Southerners, events in Boston seemed to confirm their suspicions that antislavery sentiments were on the rise in the free states, which fueled their anxiety about the future protection of their interests in a Union marked by the more rapid expansion of the North. The disorder in one of the North's largest cities also accentuated social differences between the sections, and many white Southerners came to view their society, with slavery at its center, as especially good. Against this background, the Pierce administration's unprecedented show of force, which most observers agreed was necessary to ensure Burns's return to the South, also grated against the political culture of limited government embraced by most white Southerners. In this context, many reassessed their commitment to the Union founded by their forefathers.

Walking the Freedom Trail after my encounter at the Visitor Information Center, I could not help but think that the Freedom Trail and the Anthony Burns drama were, however, somehow closely connected—both, after all, revolved around American liberty and rights. Theodore Parker, Wendell Phillips, and the other champions of liberty who spoke at the Faneuil Hall rally talked of extending the Revolution of 1776 to all Americans, including the unfortunate Burns, who was then imprisoned in Boston's courthouse. For decades, black Bostonians, who proved to be Burns's most steadfast allies during and after the crisis, had used similar terms to frame their demands for rights enjoyed by their white brethren. In their struggle against discrimination in all walks of life—religion, education, public transportation, even marriage rights—they typically invoked the principles of 1776. As they did so, many black Bostonians also reminded their white neighbors of the heroic contributions to the Revolution of some of their black forefathers. On the eve of the Civil War, black abolitionists throughout the North appealed to the "first principles of the Declaration of Independence, especially to the right of revolution," and they frequently "invoked Patrick Henry's choice between life and death" as they voiced their demands for immediate abolition.[14]

Yet many who opposed the abolitionist rhetoric heard in Faneuil Hall during the Burns drama likewise invoked the Revolutionary cause. They justified their support of the Pierce administration's enforcement of the Fugitive Slave Law as a means of conserving the Revolution of 1776 and of not jeopardizing the gains they believed the New Nation had already achieved. For many Bostonians, the Revolution and its meaning were thus at issue. For some, black and white, the Revolution was still going on; it was "unfinished."[15] For others, the results of the Revolution were not yet secure; the Revolution needed to be conserved. In both cases, the Revolution and its meaning shaped collective memory—albeit in very different ways. Another of my principal objectives is to elucidate the connection between the Freedom Trail and the torturous path trod by Anthony Burns. In so doing, I show why it was so important to Burns and others close to him that "the work of 1854" not be "in vain." I show too why Anthony Burns must also be considered a Revolutionary.[16]

Finally, like so many of his African American brethren, Burns, during his final years, fought his Revolution from Ontario, a place that became free soil during the first half of the nineteenth century and beckoned fugitive slaves and free blacks who sought not only to build new lives but also to elevate the condition of their race. In the following pages, I emphasize the links between the antislavery challenge in antebellum America and the worldview embraced by many of Canada's early blacks, including Anthony Burns. The fight against slavery transcended national boundaries, and the strategic importance of Canadian communities increased after the British parliament's passage of the Imperial Emancipation Bill in 1833 and, even more so, after President Millard Fillmore's administration began implementing the harsher fugitive slave legislation in 1850. Canadian blacks demonstrated remarkable agency and resolve in making Britain's northern dominion the safe haven it became. The struggle for American liberties stirred many black militants on the northern side of the forty-ninth parallel, and Anthony Burns was among them.

CHAPTER 1

Perceiving the North Star

It is a pity . . . that agreeable to the nature of things Slavery and Tyranny must go together and that there is no such thing as having an obedient and useful Slave without the painful exercise of undue and tyrannical authority.
—*A North Carolina planter*

She [my mother] had been the source of all his wealth; she had peopled his plantation with slaves; she had become a great grandmother in his service. She had rocked him in infancy, attended him in childhood, served him through life, and at his death wiped from his icy brow the cold death-sweat, and closed his eyes forever. She was nevertheless left a slave—a slave for life—a slave in the hands of strangers; and in their hands saw her children, her grandchildren, and her great grandchildren, divided, like so many sheep, without being gratified with the small privilege of a single word, as to their or her own destiny.
—*Frederick Douglass*

I do not think it was intended for any man to be a slave. I never thought so, from a little boy. The slaves are not contented and happy. They can't be: I never knew one to be so where I was.
—*Henry Banks, a fugitive slave from Stafford County, Virginia*

When John Suttle's most valuable female slave gave birth to Anthony Burns, her thirteenth child, on May 31, 1834, while Anthony's father, her third husband, lay dying from the effects of stone dust inhalation, the United States was embarked on yet another period of remarkable economic expansion.[1] The Union had recovered from the Panic of 1819, resolved the Missouri crisis, and survived the Bank War and the Nullification Crisis. President Andrew Jackson, in his own view, at least, had defended the Union from self-interested financial elites and then from South Carolinian advocates of state sovereignty—in both instances, men who failed to recognize the wisdom and virtue of the Founding Fathers. As the market economy expanded westward, Americans looked beyond the Appalachians and across the Great Plains to the Pacific; within a decade, the Democratic editor John O'Sullivan would speak of America's providential mission "from sea to shining sea" and coin the phrase "Manifest Destiny."

Like so many other African Americans who had toiled on plantations, in industry, or in the homes of their masters, Anthony Burns's forefathers and family had been instrumental in building the New Nation. John Suttle of Stafford County, Virginia, operated a large quarry that had supplied much of the stone for America's grand new capital on the Potomac. It was Suttle's slaves who quarried the stone; transported it; and, like Anthony's father, sometimes succumbed to the nefarious effects of its dust. With a slaveholder in the White House in 1834 and a Southern economy dependent on King Cotton, slavery seemed well entrenched, and Anthony Burns would quickly learn that he was a member of a caste that did not have the right to share in the nation's growing riches or even in the fruits of his own labor. His role was to serve the master who owned him. As Burns matured, his growing strength would be a two-edged sword; he could take pride in his prowess but, as a slave, he knew that his increased physical strength and stamina raised his value on the market and that his owner had the right to hire him out or even sell him to the Deep South, where labor was in short supply and sellers received a very good premium for able-bodied slaves.[2]

Even sooner than that, however, Burns learned that a crisis in the "big house," including the death of a master, often precipitated heart-wrenching change in the lives of slaves. When Anthony was just a toddler, John Suttle died and his family came upon hard times, exacerbated by the devastating recession of 1837 and his widow's tendency to live well beyond her means. Burns was about three years old when his mistress lost the quarry and had to sell five of Anthony's siblings to reduce her debts. She then moved to the neighboring village of Aquia. Still unable to pay her bills, Catherine Suttle hired Anthony's mother out to a white family living at a considerable distance from her new home, thus separating the aging female slave from her remaining children. Until he was six years old and Mrs. Suttle suddenly died, Anthony saw his mother only when his mean-spirited mistress permitted him to accompany her on trips to collect his mother's wages from the white folks who had hired her.

After Catherine Suttle's death, her son Charles, a deputy sheriff and a colonel in the militia, took control of the family's affairs, and Anthony confronted more change. Charles Suttle covered his mother's debts by mortgaging the family's remaining slaves and, with the exception of Anthony and his sister's baby, hired them all out to meet the mortgage payments. Anthony went with his sister, who was sent to work for the Hortons, a white family who operated a schoolhouse; he was given the task of babysitting his sister's child while she completed her chores. At the Hortons', he learned that only white children could attend school but, demonstrating youthful curiosity and ingenuity, he ran errands for some white children and secretly obtained a primer, which he used to learn the alphabet.[3]

The following year, when Anthony was only seven years old, Suttle hired him out to live with and do menial chores for three spinsters. The elderly ladies were religious, and their constant reference to the scriptures served as Burns's introduction to the Bible. He had been with the women for twelve months when Suttle hired him out to a schoolteacher's family, where he had more opportunities to advance his learning. Burns found access to books and other educational tools. "His thirst for knowledge thus whetted," he induced some white pupils to teach him to spell by "performing antics and drolleries" for them. He remained with the schoolteacher's family for two years. When they requested to have him for a third year, Anthony boldly refused to stay, indicating to his master that "he had been in some respects shabbily treated." Suttle consented to the ten-year-old slave's demand to go elsewhere and hired him out to William Brent, a friend who later also became the slaveholder's agent.[4]

The youthful Burns spent two formative years at Brent's Falmouth, Virginia, plantation. For the first time in his life, he found himself among a large group of enslaved blacks and became immersed in a very vibrant slave community.[5] In the quarters at night, he heard older slaves telling stories about freedom in the North, which he later said "kindled a fire in his young breast that never went out." By his own account, Burns resolved to continue his learning by whatever means possible and someday escape bondage. He decided to pressure Suttle to hire him out to different employers so that he could gain more knowledge, which he believed would increase his chances of successful flight. At the end of Burns's second year at Falmouth, when Brent asked Suttle to extend the young slave's term for another year, Burns again asserted himself and refused to stay. Perhaps recognizing that escape was the form of resistance that cost slaveholders the most, Burns told his master that if he were forced to stay with Brent, he might make for "the woods." Suttle acquiesced and found another employer during the Christmas hiring season who would pay the twelve-year-old slave wages that he, the master, could pocket.[6]

Suttle struck a deal with a Yankee named Foote who had purchased a sawmill at Culpeper in north-central Virginia. Although Burns took an immediate dislike to the man and protested the arrangement, Suttle sent him off to Culpeper. Foote and his wife proved to be harsh masters who believed in making their slaves "stand in fear."[7] They often beat their bond people with "a board perforated with holes and roughened with tar and sand," designed to "smart without deeply cutting up the flesh and thereby diminishing the market value of the slave";[8] the Footes did not want to inflict the kind of harm that would cause them to have trouble with the masters of the slaves they hired. Foote, however, was a careless man, and one day he started the sawmill without warning Burns. The young slave, who had been performing maintenance on the equipment, caught his hand in a wheel and found himself thrown against the machinery. Burns's hand was mangled so badly that the bone protruded; it remained disfigured for life. His face was also severely cut, and it too remained scarred. Foote returned the injured slave to an unhappy Suttle, who had recently moved to Falmouth.

During Burns's recovery, townspeople in Falmouth experienced the "fervors of the camp-meeting"; the last wave of what would later be called the Second Great Awakening was sweeping the countryside, fueled partly by a scarlet fever epidemic that struck fear in the hearts of many Virginians. The heightened religious feeling took hold of Burns, who requested his master's permission to be baptized. Although Suttle initially refused, he eventually granted his slave's request. Burns was baptized and became a member of the Falmouth Baptist Church. Imbued with this new spirituality, Burns discovered his "gift at exhortation," which awakened in him a desire to preach. In the months that followed, he began slipping away to "hush arbors" under the cover of night in order to preach and worship with fellow slaves away from the watchful eyes of their masters and of slave patrollers. Despite his young age, Burns conducted marriage and funeral services for bond persons.[9]

After Burns's time with Foote, his next employer was a Falmouth townsman, who quickly re-let him to a local merchant. The latter sought to hire Burns directly at the end of the year. Resenting the merchant's treatment of him, Burns, now sixteen years old, insisted again that Suttle make different arrangements, and he was placed in the service of a tavern keeper in Fredericksburg for the next year. He remained in Fredericksburg the following year as well, working in an apothecary. One evening, he met a fortune-teller; she rekindled his dreams of freedom by telling him that he would not be a slave for long.

Burns's yearning for liberty was also fueled after Suttle, having moved to Richmond, sent for him. He wanted to hire his young slave out at the more lucrative rates prevailing in the Virginian capital. Burns spent his first year

in Richmond working at a flour mill where one of his brothers was also employed. Suttle then placed him with a Richmond druggist named Millspaugh,
who did not have work for him but, like the Falmouth townsman, wanted to
make money by re-letting him to others. In fact, Millspaugh told Burns to
hire himself out in the bustling Richmond market at any rate that would allow
the druggist to reap a profit after covering the $125 annual payment agreed to
with Suttle. The young slave found work in the Richmond harbor, where he
met not only free blacks and whites who lived in the city but also "men whose
birthright was in a free land."[10] Although Burns enjoyed his new surroundings,
secretly taught some fellow blacks to read and write at night, and fell in love
with a slave woman, the young man still yearned to be free. In early 1854, he
made his final preparations for flight and shared his dream with a sailor on a
ship that was about to set sail for Boston. Being pious, Burns was concerned
about reconciling his flight with Christian teachings. He studied the scriptures
and concluded that "the Bible set forth only one God for the black and white
races," and that he had an "inalienable right to liberty."[11]

CHAPTER 2

The Elusive North Star over the Cradle of Liberty

When I think of what slavery is . . . its yokes and fetters, its whips and blood-hounds, its thumb-screws and branding-irons—and that this heathenish and frightful system is upheld and defended, in whole or in part, by all the leading religious influences in the land—by Catholics, Episcopalians, Presbyterians, Baptists, Methodists, and other sects—by Whigs, Democrats, and (at least so far as the pro-slavery compromises of the Constitution are concerned) even Free Soilers—I feel how utterly impotent is language to describe the sins of the American people.
  —*William Lloyd Garrison*

Sons of Otis, and Hancock, and the "Brace of Adamses"! See to it that Massachusetts Laws are not outraged with your consent. See to it that no Free Citizen of Massachusetts is dragged into Slavery, WITHOUT A TRIAL BY JURY! '76!
  —*Theodore Parker*

We are united in the glorious sentiment of our Revolutionary fathers—"Resistance to tyrants is obedience to God."
  —*Samuel Gridley Howe*

One night in early February 1854, Anthony Burns gathered a few belongings; donned four layers of clothing, the outer layer being his usual dress for work at the docks; and, before daybreak, made his way to the Richmond harbor to meet the sailor who had agreed to arrange a hiding place on a ship heading north to the free states. Thinking that the vessel would sail that day, he slipped into a coffinlike space, where he would stay for much longer than he expected, nourished only by the bread and water that his friend brought him. After a day's delay, the ship left for Norfolk, where it stopped for two more days. When it finally left port, Burns felt the vessel lurch and sway as it met "contrary winds" on the way from Norfolk to Boston, a voyage that usually took between ten and fourteen days in good weather. Rough seas, however, rocked the vessel, and for about three weeks

Burns endured "pangs of sea-sickness" and felt numbness from the increasing cold as the ship headed northward. Burns said that by the end of the trip, his feet "were frozen stiff in his boots." The ship finally drew into Boston Harbor on either the last day of February or the first of March. Crawling out of his clandestine berth and pretending to be a seaman going ashore, Burns touched free soil for the first time and took in the landscape of a growing city of some 160,000 persons.[1] Although many residents of Boston had arrived recently from Catholic Ireland, Protestants still represented the vast majority. Few Bostonians were black; in 1850, the city's African American residents numbered about 2,000.[2]

Even so, race relations were an overriding concern in Boston. Circulating in the city was a two-hundred-foot-long petition denouncing the Kansas-Nebraska Bill and the westward spread of slavery. Initiated by Harriet Beecher Stowe, the document would be signed by many New England ministers before being presented to Congress by Massachusetts senator Edward Everett.[3] However, the previous decade had witnessed black Bostonians' hard-fought battles for the rights enjoyed by their white neighbors. The city's black leaders assailed Massachusetts legislation against interracial marriage, one of many discriminatory laws that black Bostonians had been forced to endure. It also had not been long since Frederick Douglass had been wrenched from his seat and thrown off an Eastern Railway train leaving Boston after he sat in a regular coach rather than in the dirty car in which blacks were supposed to ride. The continuing fight for school desegregation, a battle in which the famous black Bostonian William Cooper Nell played a major role, was about to reach its climax. As a child, Nell had been forced to attend the segregated Smith School, an institution deprived of the funding and educational resources that went routinely to white schools. Nevertheless, Nell proved to be one of the finest students in the city—yet the Boston School Committee remained firm in its refusal to give him the Franklin Medal awarded to other students of his caliber, simply because he was black.[4]

When Burns arrived in Boston, schooling had become an even more contentious issue for Bostonians in the wake of blacks' renewed demands for desegregation. The city still remembered *Roberts v. City of Boston* (1849), a hard-fought court battle that saw Charles Sumner call for school desegregation on behalf of Sarah Roberts, a five-year-old black girl who "walk[ed] past five white schools" before she reached the less attractive school for blacks that she was obligated to attend.[5] Sumner's challenge to prevailing caste norms reverberated throughout the community. Inventing the notion of "separate but equal," Chief Justice Lemuel Shaw rejected Sumner's motion and ruled that the school commissioners neither "abused [n]or perverted" their authority in segregating public schools.[6] Shaw's opinion satisfied the school board of Boston, which was made up of leading whites who seemed to believe that "the less the colored and white people become intermingled, the better it [would] be for both races."[7] Although this decision would eventually be overturned, when Burns arrived, many respectable white Bostonians and their friends still branded Sumner's demands for equality between the races "old fashioned Jacobinism."[8]

Burns found lodging near the waterfront and mingled with what fashionable Bostonians regarded as the lower sorts around the docks. Many were blacks, who crammed into dilapidated boarding houses or lived in the crowded tenements on the north slope of Beacon Hill, which whites called "Nigger Hill." This landscape contrasted sharply with the "elegant new Federal-style" residences beyond the Common. Many white Bostonians viewed the packed tenements and narrow alleys where the blacks lived as "a breeding ground for vice." Black residents, however, may have told Burns that "these same foul passageways" were perfect for hiding fugitives from bondage when slave catchers and federal marshals converged on the city.[9]

A week or so after his arrival, Burns found a job as a cook on a mud scow operating on Boston's noxious-smelling tidal flats. After a few days, however, he was dismissed because he could not "make [the] bread rise," and once again, he fell to roaming the narrow streets of Boston, looking for employment. He approached a poorly dressed black man named William Jones, who turned out to be a window cleaner. Jones arranged temporary work for Burns washing windows at the Mattapan Iron Works and introduced Burns to some of Boston's black shopkeepers. The Virginian fugitive finally obtained a steady job from Coffin Pitts, a black businessman who ran a secondhand clothing store on Brattle Street. Pitts was a deacon at the Twelfth Baptist Church, where the Reverend Leonard Grimes, one of the bay city's most prominent blacks and a leading antislavery activist, preached. Pitts himself had become a pillar of strength in Boston's tightly knit black community; he offered his new employee room and board. Feeling comfortable in his new environment, Burns wrote to his brother in Virginia, reporting on his flight from slavery, his employment at the Brattle Street clothing store, and his prospects for a much better life in the North.[10]

In late May 1854, thousands converged on Boston for Anniversary Week, the annual gathering of New England clergy that, by midcentury, attracted a host of reformers. Unitarians, Congregationalists, Free-Soilers, and members of the American Antislavery Society shared the city with the

Prison Discipline Society, the American Education Society, the American Peace Society, and other lesser-known organizations.[11] Burns's former master, Colonel Charles F. Suttle, and his agent William Brent also made their way to Boston from Virginia. Suttle had opened the fugitive slave's letter to his brother, in which he stated that he had found work at a clothing store owned by Coffin Pitts. Like many fugitive slaves in Massachusetts, Burns took the precaution of having the envelope postmarked in Canada, but he had addressed his letter from Boston.[12]

On Wednesday, May 24, Burns finished his workday and closed Pitts's shop. He walked toward Court Street at about the same time that Boston Democrats celebrated the passage of the Kansas-Nebraska Act, which opened the possibility of legalizing slavery in the territories, with a 113-gun salute in tribute to the legislators who had voted for the bill. Several men hired by the notorious slave catcher Asa Butman stepped out from the shadows to arrest Burns on contrived charges of petty theft and carried him to the Boston courthouse. Moments later, Suttle and Brent arrived, beginning Boston's last—and most famous—fugitive slave case.[13]

News of Burns's arrest spread quickly in Boston's black community and among leading white abolitionists. After being informed of events by Deacon Pitts the morning following the arrest, Grimes, the pastor, immediately alerted members of his Twelfth Baptist Church and the Boston Vigilance Committee, a group of the city's antislavery activists organized to assist fugitives from bondage.[14] Grimes then hastened to Burns's nine o'clock arraignment before slave commissioner Edward Greely Loring, leaving other members of the Boston Vigilance Committee, including the Reverend Samuel J. May Jr., to continue spreading word of the arrest.[15] May penned a quick note to the radical abolitionist Thomas Wentworth Higginson, then a pastor at a church in Worcester. "Last night a man was arrested here as a fugitive. Vigilance Committee meets this afternoon. Come Strong. In Haste."[16]

At the courthouse, Grimes recognized Seth Thomas, known to abolitionists as "the legal pimp of the slave catchers."[17] He had prosecuted Thomas Sims, the fugitive slave returned to Georgia in 1851; Suttle retained Thomas as his lead attorney as he attempted to return Burns to bondage. At about the same time that Grimes arrived, abolitionist Theodore Parker and the famous Boston attorney Richard Henry Dana Jr. entered the courtroom, where a lonely, discouraged Burns awaited the commencement of proceedings. Dana offered to act in defense of Burns. "It is of no use," responded the fettered fugitive. "[T]hey will swear to me & get me back; and if they do, I shall fare worse if I resist."[18]

Appearing as counsel for Suttle, Thomas and his partner Edward Parker read a transcript from the circuit court in Alexandria, Virginia. They argued that the court records confirmed that Burns, described as "a man of dark complexion, about six feet high, with a scar on one of his cheeks, and also a scar on one of his hands, and about twenty-three or twenty-four years of age," had escaped from Virginia, where he was legally "held to service and labor" by Colonel Charles F. Suttle.[19]

Suttle's lawyers demanded that Burns be returned to his former master in accordance with federal fugitive slave legislation, and they asked for an immediate decision. Before Loring responded, Dana rose, declared that Burns was in a "state of alarm and stupefaction," and requested an adjournment, arguing that the prisoner was "in no condition to determine" his need for counsel. He said that the alleged fugitive did not even know whether or not he should mount a defense. Dana said that no court should "proceed to trial & condemnation under such circumstances." Despite strong opposition from Suttle's attorneys, Commissioner Loring postponed the hearing for two days and called for proceedings to resume on Saturday, May 27. The Boston Vigilance Committee met that afternoon to organize in support of Burns. They scheduled a rally for the following night at Faneuil Hall and arranged for the printing and distribution of handbills to "alert and stir the public."[20]

On Friday morning, handbills and placards appeared throughout the city. One written by Theodore Parker exclaimed, "KIDNAPPING AGAIN!! A Man was Stolen Last Night by the Fugitive Slave Bill Commissioner. He will have His MOCK TRIAL. . . . SHALL BOSTON STEAL ANOTHER MAN?"[21] Another declared, "THE KIDNAPPERS ARE HERE! MEN OF BOSTON! Sons of Otis, and Hancock, and the 'Brace of Adamses'! See to it that Massachusetts Laws are not outraged with your consent. See to it that no Free Citizen of Massachusetts is dragged into Slavery, WITHOUT A TRIAL BY JURY! '76!"[22] That same morning, Wendell Phillips, accompanied by Grimes and Pitts, visited Burns in the courthouse. They convinced the downhearted prisoner to allow them to mount a defense for him. Dana filed a writ of personal replevin with the Massachusetts Supreme Court, which, if accepted by the court, would have enabled Burns to have a trial by jury to determine the legality of his imprisonment. Along with the writ, Dana included a surety bond backed by Wendell Phillips and Samuel Sewall that would have served to guarantee Burns's appearance in court and allowed him to leave custody in the meantime. But Justice Peleg Sprague denied the writ.[23]

Following this setback, a divided Boston Vigilance Committee met again. Theodore Parker was adamant that Burns not be returned to slavery.

Samuel Gridley Howe proposed an immediate attack to rescue the prisoner, arguing that after the rally that evening, Watson Freeman, the United States marshal responsible for guarding Burns in the courthouse, would have his men prepared to defend against an assault. Moderates on the committee insisted, however, on waiting for Commissioner Loring's decision, and they prevailed. Division in the committee's ranks—and indeed among the bay city's antislavery leaders in general—was nothing new; three years earlier when the fugitive slave Thomas Sims was held in chains in the courthouse, Thomas Wentworth Higginson laid much of the blame for the Georgia fugitive's return to bondage on the Boston Vigilance Committee's inability to act, criticizing its indecision and the unwillingness of most committee members to strike out against slaveholders. At about the time the deadlocked committee finished its meeting, members of the Worcester Freedom Club rounded up by Higginson and another radical abolitionist, Martin Stowell, set out by train for the rally in Boston.[24]

That evening, Samuel Sewall, Samuel Gridley Howe, John L. Swift, Dr. Henry Bowditch, George R. Russell, and others spoke to a crowd in Faneuil Hall. Boston's cradle of liberty was packed to capacity and press reports suggest that many "more persons were turned away."[25] Dana was not there; he heard rumors that the meeting would include men who favored rescuing Burns, an act he regarded as treasonous.[26] From the outset, the crowd appeared agitated. Russell declared, "When the foreign slave trade is reestablished, with all the appalling horrors of the Middle Passage, and the Atlantic is again filled with the bodies of dead Africans, then we may think it time to waken our duty!" Swift asserted, "If we allow Marshal Freeman to carry away [Burns], then the word cowards should be stamped on our foreheads."[27] Howe argued that those assembled were "united in the glorious sentiment of our Revolutionary fathers—'Resistance to tyrants is obedience to God.'" This, for some Bostonians, was the meaning of higher law, law based on divine or moral principles, which, some argued, took precedence over statutory laws or the Constitution. To Howe, Southern slaveholders were tyrants "who den[ied] the natural right of a man to his own body—of a father to his own child—of a husband to his wife."[28]

While Howe set the stage, Wendell Phillips and Theodore Parker roused the audience with "powerful rhetorical performances of a revolutionary character" that drew heavily upon Boston's proud heritage of resistance to tyranny.[29] Phillips challenged Bostonians to show that they were "the children of Adams and Hancock," and "not bastards." He admonished them to prove themselves "worthy of liberty." He said that "he wanted [Burns] set free on the streets of Boston." Making reference to the rescue of William "Jerry" Henry in Syracuse in 1851 and the riot that erupted the same year in Christiana, Pennsylvania, when a Maryland slaveholder attempted to snatch his runaway slaves from free blacks who protected them, Phillips asserted that there was "not a state in the Union that would consent" to have a fugitive like Burns taken from it. He called for the crowd to gather again in the morning and to "see to it that tomorrow in the streets of Boston you ratify the verdict of Faneuil Hall that Anthony Burns has no master but his God." Parker seconded the call by sarcastically addressing the crowd as "my fellow subjects of Virginia" and suggesting that the South now extended all the way to Canada. Boston, said Parker, had been reduced to "a suburb of the city of Alexandria," and he declared that the time had come to strike down slavery. Alluding to rescue, he also proposed that the assembled reconvene at Court Square at nine o'clock the next day.[30]

The audience's response to such fiery speeches appeared to exceed the speakers' expectations; intense emotion seemed to prevail. From the back of the hall, voices cried, "[N]o, to-night, let's take him out." Fearing disorder and, like Howe, apparently believing that the courthouse guards expected an attack after the rally, Phillips returned to the podium and urged the listeners to wait until the next morning. Responding to more cries of "[T]onight" and "[T]o the Court House," Phillips once again sought to control the audience by declaring, "[I]f there is a man here who has an arm and a heart ready to sacrifice anything for an oppressed man, let him do it tomorrow. . . . [T]he zeal that won't keep till tomorrow will never free a slave."[31]

As Phillips spoke these words, a man shouted from the back, "A mob of Negroes is in Court Square, attempting to rescue Burns."[32] The crowd began to disperse and pour out of the hall. Some shouted, "Rescue him," and started toward the courthouse, which was precisely what Higginson and Stowell hoped would happen. When they had met that afternoon, Higginson and Stowell both denounced the Boston Vigilance Committee's indecision. An impatient Higginson called for a rescue attempt after the meeting at Faneuil Hall or early the next day, when a sizable crowd would have assembled in the square. Higginson also had in mind the Jerry rescue in Syracuse, which had seen a mob free Jerry and spirit him to Canada. Stowell argued for even prompter action, noting like others that marshals would be expecting an assault after the meeting. He believed that the charge should take place during the meeting. Higginson concurred; they briefed their followers, but they did not have enough time to inform the speakers.[33]

After the cry from the back of the hall, confusion reigned. Apparently leaderless and undirected bands of men headed toward the courthouse, where Higginson, Stowell, and a small group of followers prepared to break down the doors of the building with a battering ram.[34] Some of the crowd collected on the west side of the courthouse; others flocked toward the south side door. But none of the Boston Vigilance Committee members arrived. As Higginson put it, only the "froth and scum of the meeting, the fringe of idlers," appeared in the square.[35] The discouraged Higginson joined the small group of militant blacks led by Lewis Hayden, a fugitive slave and radical abolitionist, assaulting the west side door of the building. They cried, "Rescue him! Bring him out!" When the door finally broke open, Higginson and an unidentified man charged inside, supported by only a handful of followers. Most of Higginson's band did not follow; neither did the crowd. Most onlookers simply continued to mill about, and a few ruffians decided to seize the opportunity to make trouble by throwing stones, "brickbats," and other objects at the courthouse windows. Higginson turned toward the rabble and yelled, "You cowards, will you desert us now?"[36] They did.

An alarm sounded as Marshal Freeman and several of his assistants guarding Burns repulsed the attack. A shot was heard just before a "large deputation of police" arrived in the square. They made several arrests, including that of Stowell and a handful of his coconspirators, before dispersing the crowd. In the commotion, both Higginson and Hayden escaped. Few people knew that a guard, an Irishman named James Batchelder, had been killed.[37] Around ten o'clock, Mayor Jerome V. C. Smith called for reinforcements, and two companies of artillery moved into the square, transforming the courthouse into what Charles Sumner considered a veritable fortress.[38] Shortly after midnight, Boston seemed tranquil. The square was empty except for those charged with the responsibility of securing the courthouse. Around two o'clock in the morning, eighty marines arrived from the Charlestown Navy Yard to strengthen the forces of law and order.[39]

On Saturday, Marshal Freeman telegraphed President Franklin Pierce, saying, "I have availed myself of the resources of the United States. . . . Everything is now quiet." Pierce responded, "Your conduct is approved; the law must be enforced." The president followed up his message with an order instructing Freeman "to incur any expense" that he deemed necessary "to ensure the execution of the law."[40] Around nine o'clock that morning, a heavily guarded Burns appeared before Commissioner Loring. As Dana and his partner Charles Ellis made their way to the hearing, they passed

"2 or 3 companies of volunteer militia" and "a company of U.S. marines from Charlestown & a company of Artillery fr[om] Fort Independence" standing guard outside the courthouse.[41]

When Loring commenced proceedings, Burns's lawyers requested post-ponement until Monday on the grounds that they had been unable to see the prisoner until late the day before and needed more time to prepare their case. Although Suttle's attorneys objected, arguing that postponement might result in a "renewal of the sad scene of the night previous," Commissioner Loring consented to the motion and adjourned proceedings until Monday, May 29.[42] As the courtroom emptied, Grimes, the black minister, approached the slaveholder's cocounsel, Edward Parker, and asked whether Suttle would consider an offer to purchase Burns. He suggested that such an arrangement would circumvent the trauma and cost of the trial. Suttle indicated that he would accept $1,200 for Burns on the condition that the deal be concluded by the end of the day, a deadline that Grimes did not meet.[43]

During the remainder of that Saturday, things seemed to be relatively quiet and most Bostonians apparently went about their business as usual. That evening, however, a mob gathered outside the courthouse and threw stones, bricks, and miscellaneous objects "with a view to breaking windows." After a stone struck one of Marshal Freeman's guards, police moved into action, dispersed the troublemakers, and made a handful of arrests for "riot-ous conduct."[44]

On Sunday, Theodore Parker felt obliged to respond to the events. Speak-ing to a large audience in Boston's Music Hall, he thundered, "I deliberately charge it upon you, Edward Greeley [*sic*] Loring. . . . I charge you deliberately with the murder of a man on Friday night last . . . with putting in peril the lives of nine men who were arrested, [and] charged with [the] murder [of Batchelder], I charge you with filling Boston Court-house with one hun-dred and eighty-four ruffians, and alarming not only our own citizens, but stirring up the whole population of this Commonwealth, and filling them with indignation, the results of which no man has yet seen the end."[45] In mentioning "one hundred and eighty-four ruffians," Parker was alluding to the fact that the only men Marshal Freeman had been able to hire quickly to guard Burns were unemployed Irish laborers, to whom old-time Bostonians imputed heavy drinking, street fighting, and general rowdiness.

Other congregations listened to less fiery sermons that called for judicial interference or "benevolent contributions" to save Burns from being returned to slavery. Some church-goers found in the pews pamphlets and notices requesting prayers for "the escape of Burns" from his oppressors. Others joined in prayers asking God to bestow upon men the strength and wisdom to make laws "in accordance with the peaceful and beneficent precepts of the Christian religion" that would enable them to demonstrate "peace and goodwill" toward all of God's children.[46] Many congregations, however, seemed to be oblivious to the excitement in the city. Some ministers, considering the sentiments of their "solid middle class citizens who had a deep respect for laws and institutions," gave traditional Ascension Day services, ignored the crisis entirely, and certainly avoided any intemperate rhetoric. Not everyone prayed for Burns.[47]

On Monday morning, the hearing commenced in a packed courtroom. The well-known Ohio antislavery politician Joshua R. Giddings joined Theodore Parker and Wendell Phillips in the audience. Seeking to strengthen Suttle's claim to own Burns, which some observers already regarded as "iron clad," Seth Thomas and Edward Parker began questioning witnesses and called Suttle's agent William Brent to the stand.[48] He presented a copy of Virginia's slave codes and identified the six-foot-tall prisoner with a scar on his face and a disfigured hand as Burns. Brent pointed to the man in chains in the courtroom and said he was the "same Anthony Burns whom he had so well known" and hired "in the years 1846, 1847, and 1848."[49] He indicated that the prisoner had recently been hired out to Mr. Millspaugh, a Richmond druggist, and that he had last seen Burns on March 20 in Virginia. Brent said that Burns had disappeared four days later on March 24. Suttle's lawyer Thomas then confirmed statements that Burns had apparently made to Suttle in the courthouse on the night of his arrest, arguing that the prisoner's remarks proved his identity and slave status.

Dana's partner Charles Ellis now rose and objected on two grounds. First, he emphasized that the relationship between master and slave was such that a master's influence could bias evidence, particularly while the "alleged slave [was] in custody." Second, he noted that the Fugitive Slave Law explicitly forbade the use of testimony by the individual alleged to be a fugitive slave. Loring overruled Ellis's objections and stated that "the word testimony in the law must be regarded as referring only to evidence given by a witness, and not, to confessions or admissions." Burns's recognition of Suttle and the statements he made at the time of his arrest could thus be used as evidence against him.[50]

Late that Monday afternoon, Ellis challenged the constitutionality of the Fugitive Slave Law of 1850. He argued that the law did not provide for trial by jury; prohibited important common-law writs, including habeas corpus;

conferred judicial power on a commissioner "who is not a judge"; and contravened "guaranties against unreasonable seizures, and against deprivation of liberty without due process of law." Ellis also argued that Congress did not have the power to legislate on delivering up "persons held to service and labor." Loring listened but did not respond.[51]

Proceedings continued the following day with Dana and Ellis presenting evidence for the defense. They produced witnesses: the window cleaner William Jones and George H. Drew, "the book-keeper at the Mattapan Iron Works." Their testimony confirmed that Brent could not have seen the prisoner on the twentieth of March in Virginia because Burns had been washing windows at the Boston forge that day. They also called James F. Whittemore, a director of the Mattapan Iron Works, to the stand. Whittemore testified that he had seen Burns at work at the facility in March. Dana argued that this testimony confirmed that Burns could not be Suttle's slave—certainly not the slave Brent saw on March 20.

Burns's attorneys also contested Edward Parker's argument that the Virginia Circuit Court transcript provided evidence of escape and service owed. Dana argued that neither the record nor any testimony of witnesses proved that there was an escape at all. He said that even if the alleged fugitive's remarks on the night of his arrest were admitted, Suttle's attorneys had only demonstrated that perhaps the prisoner had fallen asleep on a vessel. They had neither demonstrated premeditated flight nor proved that Burns had "gone off against the will of Millspaugh," to whom he had been hired. At best, they had shown that Burns was missing. Finally, Dana again challenged—albeit indirectly—the constitutionality of the Fugitive Slave Law of 1850 by objecting to the admission of Virginia law codes as evidence for claiming property in Massachusetts.[52]

When the court adjourned to await Loring's decision, scheduled for Friday, June 2, the fate of Burns had become the subject of considerable speculation in Boston. Many observers no longer viewed Suttle's case as iron clad. They had been impressed by the way that Dana and Ellis had handled the question of the prisoner's identity. In particular, they focused on Brent's testimony indicating that he had seen Burns in Virginia in late March when it was clear that the alleged fugitive had then been at work in Boston. Such confusion seemed to undermine Suttle's claim. On the eve of Loring's ruling, Boston journalists had become involved in hairsplitting debates, likely a reflection of the diverse views embraced by their readers. Some reports questioned Suttle's attorneys' reliance on the Virginia court transcript. For example, the *Boston Evening Transcript* stressed that the record only established that Anthony Burns was a "dark complexioned" man having "a scar on his cheek" and "a cut across his hand." The newspaper noted that the record did not indicate that "he is a Negro at all—and it is only of that race that slaves are manufactured."[53]

Sharing the view of Dana and Ellis, the *Evening Transcript* also questioned whether flight had been proved, citing the lack of evidence that Burns "escaped from Virginia." The newspaper reported that Burns might "still be at sea, in Europe, or anywhere but here." The *Evening Transcript* also noted that, if the Virginia Court record "were good for anything, any dark complexioned man, having a scar and cut like those mentioned, was liable for arrest as Col. Suttle's slave."[54] Evidence also indicates that, at least privately, the attorneys, especially Dana, were drawn into the speculation on how Loring might rule. Despite the favorable review of his arguments in the city's press and a consensus among his friends that his defense had been outstanding, in his diary Dana worried that "Judge Loring paid great attention to all that related to identity, but took no notes of my points as to the record, the escape & the title" to Burns as property. Dana admitted that this greatly "pussled" him.[55]

Perhaps Loring's behavior was not so puzzling. The commissioner had close ties to the Cotton Whigs, the strongest supporters of the champion of the Fugitive Slave Law of 1850, Daniel Webster. That group included Boston's wealthy and powerful Curtis clan, to whom Loring was related.[56] Perhaps Loring's conservatism and links to the Cotton Whigs help to explain his decision and why, at daybreak on Friday, "a company of United States Infantry and a detachment of Artillery" positioned a cannon in front of the courthouse—long before the scheduled time for the ruling, and before thousands began to mill about the square, waiting to hear what the commissioner would decide about Burns's fate. Around seven o'clock in the morning, militiamen and regular troops "assemble[d] at their respective armories" and then paraded to Court Square. A detachment of U.S. marines also moved to the courthouse and guarded the cannon. They loaded their muskets and fixed their bayonets. "Streets resounded" with the sounds of marching soldiers and "strains of martial music." By the time Loring rendered his decision, police had already "cleared all persons in the Square."[57]

In his opinion, Loring affirmed the constitutionality of the Fugitive Slave Law, dismissing the arguments presented by Ellis and Dana. He said that the arrest of a fugitive was a "ministerial, not a judicial act"—that is, simply an act to be carried out by an official having executive authority. Loring stated that "there is no provision in the Constitution requiring the identity of a person to be arrested to be determined by a jury." He disagreed with Ellis's contention that the federal legislation was unconstitutional because it gave "the record of the Court of Virginia an effect beyond its constitutional effect"—in other words, beyond its state boundaries. Finally, Loring cited Massachusetts chief justice Lemuel Shaw's ruling in the Sims case confirming the constitutionality of the Fugitive Slave Law. He declared that it was "the duty of all judges and magistrates to expound and apply" the Fugitive Slave Law, adding that "it behooves all persons, bound to obey the laws of the United States, to consider and regard them." Loring concluded that the only points to be clarified in the case before him were whether the prisoner was Anthony Burns and, if so, whether he owed service to the claimant Suttle.[58]

On the question of service, Loring considered that Suttle's attorneys had provided "conclusive evidence" of the labor owed to their client by Burns and of his "escape." According to the commissioner, this left the identity of the prisoner as the only outstanding issue. On this matter, Loring recognized Brent's testimony, noting that the witness's knowledge of Burns was "personal" and "direct"; he believed that it permitted Brent to "testify confidently." Loring suggested that the evidence of Dana's witnesses was "less full and complete than that of Mr. Brent." With a view to allaying all doubts, however, Loring decided to base his decision on Burns's remarks on the night of his arrest. "In every case of disputed identity," declared Loring, "there is one person whose knowledge is perfect and positive, and whose evidence is not within the reach of error; and that is the person whose identity is questioned." He reasoned that the statements Burns had made on the evening of his arrest proved his identity. Even though the Fugitive Slave Law prohibited the use of an alleged fugitive's testimony, that morning Loring recognized Suttle's ownership of Burns on the basis of the fugitive's own words.[59] He immediately signed a certificate stating that the Virginian slaveholder was "authorized to remove him, the said Burns, from the State of Massachusetts back to the State of Virginia." Burns's departure from Boston was then scheduled for two o'clock that afternoon, only a few hours after Loring's ruling.[60]

If the stage had already been set for "a spectacle" never before seen in Boston, Loring's decision ensured that the show would go on. Between ten and eleven o'clock that morning, the members of the U.S. artillery manning the cannon outside the courthouse demonstrated their proficiency by "practicing leading and firing (without discharging)," sending a message of military preparedness to onlookers. After these maneuvers, authorities began what some reporters called the "grand official movement." In accordance with Marshal Freeman's orders, which were supported by President Pierce, the military took measures to clear all streets and sidewalks between the courthouse and the wharf along which Burns would be escorted on his way to the harbor. Troops marched down Court and State streets "in solid column" while police and firemen attempted to push back the throngs. These security measures were also deemed to be consistent with a proclamation by Mayor Smith, which "urgently requested" that "all well-disposed citizens and other persons" remove themselves from streets that police considered necessary to "clear temporarily." The mayor emphasized that nobody was "to obstruct or molest any officer, civil or military, in the lawful discharge of his duty." No one did, although some curiosity seekers and others grumbled. The sweep took more than one hour. After it was completed, the troops were ordered to form columns on either side of Court and State streets to check the pushing and shoving of the steadily increasing "multitudes."[61]

A sideshow developed at the corner of State and Washington streets. Several men appeared with a coffin upon which they had written the word "Liberty." They intended to display the coffin when the Burns procession passed. A fight soon erupted, however, between the pallbearers of Liberty and the crowd in the immediate vicinity. The former were only able to retain their hold on the coffin by escaping into the Commonwealth Building via its State Street entrance. Moments later, they lowered the coffin from a window but kept it out of the reach of the group that had sought to wrest it from them. By noon, most buildings along the route over which Burns would pass were packed—indeed, overflowing. Onlookers jammed virtually all the "windows and passageways" of the Old State House, which provided a bird's-eye view of the route that the Burns procession would follow as it turned down State Street.[62]

Many businesses in the vicinity, notably stores and offices belonging to abolitionists, were closed. Some of their doors, windows, and awnings were "festooned with black," symbolizing, like the Liberty coffin, the death of liberty.[63] Someone had also draped three American flags in mourning across State Street. One newspaper reporter suggested that, as the scheduled hour for Burns's departure approached, the forces of law and order held in check "thousands upon thousands of people."[64] By no means, however, were all those assembled in sympathy with Burns and his supporters. When some onlookers near Court Square sighted Wendell Phillips and Theodore Parker leaving the courthouse, a cry of "There go the murderers of Batchelder," a reference to the guard killed during the courthouse riot, went up.[65]

Along State Street, a reporter from the *Boston Evening Transcript* found himself buffeted by a crowd larger than any other he had ever seen before in Boston. The multitudes had come to catch a "parting glimpse" of the now-famous fugitive slave. Near the docks, "an immense concourse gathered . . . at every possible point where the slightest view could be had" of Burns boarding the *John Taylor*, already waiting at T Wharf. The *John Taylor* would take Burns to a U.S. revenue cutter, the *Morris*, stationed offshore, which in turn would carry Burns to Norfolk, Virginia. In the words of one observer, "Thousands upon thousands of people gazed upon this *strange spectacle* at high noon on a brilliant day; some estimated that around 50,000 onlookers had congregated by the time that Burns emerged from the courthouse."[66] They were not going to be disappointed.

Just before two o'clock, Burns's escort formed in Courthouse Square. Out front in full military dress was a detachment of the crack cavalry known as the Boston Lancers. Behind them, a company of U.S. infantry and a detachment of U.S. marines fell in with great precision. More marines guarded the flanks and more still protected the members of the U.S. artillery who manned the fieldpiece at the rear. The cannon was loaded, and a constantly "burning match" signaled to everyone that it could be used on a moment's notice.[67] At the center of the imposing military formation, some sixty men armed with swords and pistols who had volunteered from the Bay Street Club, an association made up mostly of Irish tradesmen and laborers, formed a square into which Burns was led by Marshal Freeman and his deputies. Reports suggest that members of Burns's escort "had loaded rifles and fixed bayonets" and had "orders to fire" upon any would-be rescuers. The young free black Charlotte Forten, who was in Massachusetts at the time, recorded in her diary that the soldiers and deputies were ready "to shoot down" anyone who resisted Burns's return. The military were "without mercy."[68] As this scene unfolded in front of the courthouse, bells began to toll in Boston's black churches. When Burns appeared in the square, some of the crowd groaned and hissed at his escort. But others cheered Burns's captors as they dutifully went about their business of taking him to the docks and returning him to bondage. Press reports indicated that there were all sorts of "manifestations of approval or detestation."[69]

When Burns emerged from the courthouse, he was wearing a new set of coattails similar to the outfits that slaves being sold as house servants were often forced to wear at auctions in Southern slave pens. Apparently Burns's guards had decided that he should be suitably dressed to parade before the multitudes on his way to board the *John Taylor*. When the procession left the courthouse, more marines and troops from Fort Independence moved toward the waterfront. Marines also patrolled the harbor in a steamer.[70]

The military power brought to bear was impressive, but the crowd, with Virginia's now-famous slave in its midst, became boisterous and difficult to control. Nobody attempted a rescue, but there were several incidents and arrests for disorderly conduct, including that of Burns's friend the window cleaner William Jones. When the procession reached the corner of Court Street, tensions escalated as onlookers demonstrated all kinds of emotions. Press reports indicate that the crowd became "loud and uproarious," and some people shouted "Shame! Shame!" Others cried or hissed. But still others cheered the forces of law and order, for whom there was much applause. Some of the troops began to sing, "Carry Me Back to Old Virginny."[71]

At the Commonwealth Building, someone threw a bottle containing a liquid, "believed to be vitriol" (sulfuric acid), toward the procession as it passed. It shattered on the ground, but no one was injured. Shortly thereafter, another member of the crowd threw cayenne pepper or some "other noxious substance" as Burns and his escort went by.[72] On State Street, Captain Wright's regiment of Light Dragoons drew their sabers to keep the growing crowd from entering the street. As they brandished their swords, cutting left and right, they struck a man from Vermont in the head. He was taken to the police station nearby, where he received treatment for his injury. Near the customhouse, a "truckman" tried to drive his team of horses through the line of troops guarding the route.[73] A soldier thrust his sword through one of the animals, killing it instantly. A nervous captain then ordered his troops to open fire, but fortunately a senior officer immediately "countermanded" the order.[74] Also near the customhouse, a man returning to his office attempted to cross the line of troops, and a soldier "thrust his bayonet" at him, slicing the man's shirt collar and slightly injuring his neck.[75] Police converged on the scene and eventually ushered the man through the lines. On Commercial Street, a horse belonging to a member of the Lancer corps was stabbed by someone who quickly disappeared into the crowd. The horse died, adding to the confusion.

When the procession turned toward T Wharf, thousands converged on the harbor. U.S. marines and troops from Fort Independence had to move quickly to ensure order at the docks. Some unruly members of the mob began to throw various objects at the marines, and an officer issued an order for his men to "aim," which had the effect of "scattering the assemblage."[76] When Burns arrived at the *John Taylor,* Marshal Freeman and his deputies whisked him onboard and took him to an inside cabin, where he remained heavily guarded and out of the sight of the crowd. The troops loaded the cannon onto the vessel before it pulled out to meet the *Morris*. Late in the day, somebody sighted the revenue cutter around "ten miles east of Nantucket Beach," confirming the end of the spectacle.[77]

Some ten days later, Burns arrived in Norfolk, shackled and tightly guarded. From Norfolk, he was taken to Richmond and placed in solitary confinement in Robert Lumpkin's slave jail, where—as Frederick Douglass reported—he was kept in an empty room, without even a cot or a stool; fettered; and poorly fed, receiving water only "every two days." He faced a reality far different from his expectations some two months earlier when he wrote to his brother of his prospects for a better life in a land of liberty.[78] He could take no solace from having been the center of attention in a degrading spectacle that represented, at the time, America's largest show of military force in peacetime. The deployment of the military and the gathering of multitudes upon the quaint cobblestone streets of old Boston was a spectacle never before seen in the city—and it would not be seen again.

CHAPTER 3

The Background to the Spectacle

Slavery has a guaranty . . . in the prejudices of caste and color, which induce
even large majorities in all the free States to regard sympathy with the slave as
an act of unmanly humiliation and self-abasement.
—Senator William Dayton, New Jersey

And why is it that the old spirit has left us—the spirit of '76? It is not merely
the Commissioners, and the Marshals, and the Mayors, who have disgraced us.
They are but the creatures of public sentiment.
—Rev. James Freeman Clarke

The position of the colored citizens of Boston is in many features a peculiar
one. . . . [T]hey enjoy certain facilities denied to their [black] brethren . . . yet
the extremes of equality and proscription [meet] in their case.
—William Cooper Nell

What really happened during Anthony Burns's travail in Boston? In
the days that followed Burns's embarkation, strong antislavery sentiments, genuine admiration for the Virginian fugitive, and disaffection with
the Pierce administration motivated Charles Emery Stevens to write the
first history of the Burns affair. Although he deplored the outcome of the
trial, Stevens sought to portray the drama in a positive light, suggesting that
the crisis had fueled a groundswell of antislavery sentiment in Boston and
throughout much of the North. Later historians, often drawing extensively
on Stevens's work, picked up where he left off. They depicted the Burns rendition as a critical step on the path toward the Civil War and the elimination
of slavery. For many, the Burns affair constituted a watershed.

But what about the cheers and the applause for Burns's captors, the clashes
between crowd members and abolitionists, the branding of Theodore Parker
and Wendell Phillips as murderers, the inconsistent or lackluster support
for the rescue of Burns even among antislavery advocates, and the predominance of indifferent spectators in the multitudes? Many of the thousands
who gathered seemed to be curious rather than incensed.[1] They appeared

determined to see the now-famous Burns as he was escorted to Boston's T Wharf, the *John Taylor*, and slavery in the South. That indifferent and curious spectators were not exceptions but represented the majority belies the usual interpretation of the Burns drama as an important antislavery groundswell. The situation was more complex. We need to take a new look at the historical context in which the Burns drama unfolded, particularly the genesis of the federal government's new fugitive slave legislation and the landscape of race relations in the antebellum North.

The new Fugitive Slave Law represented what many white Southerners considered the only major "concession made to the South" in the Compromise of 1850, a grab bag of measures designed to resolve the sectional conflict over the expansion of slavery into the Mexican cession. Other components of the Compromise included the admission of California into the Union as a free state, the organization of the remaining portions of the Mexican cession as territories with no a priori restrictions on slavery, settlement of the boundary dispute between Texas and New Mexico in favor of the latter, federal assumption of Texas's pre-annexation debt, and abolition of the slave trade in the District of Columbia, coupled with a guarantee that no measures to abolish slavery in the nation's capital would be adopted without the consent of both its citizens and those of neighboring Maryland. Senator Henry Clay initially combined these measures into a single piece of legislation dubbed the Omnibus Bill. When the unified package failed to pass Congress, Senator Stephen Douglas steered the individual measures through both chambers as distinct pieces of legislation. The process sparked debates on each measure that revealed the attitudes of Northerners and Southerners.[2]

The debates on the bill that became the Fugitive Slave Law of 1850 shed critical light on the context in which the Burns drama unfolded. In particular, the exchanges between politicians underscored the prevalence of Northern racism and the recognition of it by both Northern and Southern leaders. Indeed, some white Southerners viewed the racist attitudes of Northern whites as the best assurance that slave owners' rights to their human property would be respected and that fugitive slave legislation would be enforced.[3] Jefferson Davis put forth his view that the enforcement of the Fugitive Slave Law ultimately depended on public opinion and racial attitudes, not on bureaucratic regulation. His principal concern was whether or not the appeal to higher law by some white Northerners who regarded slavery as inconsistent with God's will would outweigh the racist attitudes of many of their neighbors. Davis thought that if the appeal to higher law proved stronger, fugitive slave legislation would be "a dead letter"; if Northern whites' resentment of blacks living and working among them held sway, enforcement would not be an issue.[4]

The remarks of Senator William Dayton of New Jersey during the debates in 1850 indicated that the latter scenario was more likely. Dayton regarded fugitive slaves as "pests and an annoyance." He suggested that "slavery [had] a guaranty . . . in the prejudices of caste and color, which induce even large majorities in all the free States to regard sympathy with the slave as an act of unmanly humiliation and self-abasement." Simply put, although "mad abolitionists" might protest, neither free-state authorities nor the white general public in the North would obstruct the capture and return of slaves.[5] Dayton's pronouncements lent weight to Davis's conclusion that "the non-slaveholding states' object[ions] to the presence of Negroes among them" was unquestionably "the best check we have upon the popular feeling in favor of runaway slaves."[6]

The assessment of Senator Jeremiah Clemens of Alabama was even more remarkable. He too counted on the presence of unbridled racism in the North. Clemens actually questioned the need for any elaborate enforcement apparatus whatsoever. He argued that it was not federal legislation that best protected the South's property rights but the legislation excluding blacks enacted by most free states. Referring to racist laws in the Old Northwest, Clemens suggested that Northerners had done "precisely what we wanted done" to restrict blacks from fleeing northward. Clemens concluded that Northern attitudes and racist legislation in most free states made the Fugitive Slave Law almost "superfluous." In short, he said that Northern whites' racism was the best assurance that fugitives would "not come among them."[7]

Dayton was not the only Northerner who shared Jefferson Davis's opinions about the impact of flourishing racism in the free states. Two of slavery's most outspoken foes, Theodore Parker and Frederick Douglass, seconded these assessments. Underscoring the "fierce antagonism" toward blacks in southern Ohio and Illinois, Parker lashed out against racism, arguing that the attitudes of whites in these areas were a barrier that prevented blacks, fugitive or free, from leaving Virginia and Kentucky.[8] Frederick Douglass agreed that racism was without question "the greatest of all obstacles in the way of the antislavery cause." After the passage of the Fugitive Slave Law of 1850, he noted that the new legislation and the racist codes enacted in several Northern states complemented each other. The Black Laws in the free states were "in harmony" with the "malignant spirit evinced by the national government towards the free colored inhabitants of the country."[9]

Douglass condemned the proslavery stance of the Pierce and Buchanan administrations, notably their rigid enforcement of the Fugitive Slave Law, which he said "put thorns under feet already bleeding—to crush a people already bowed down."[10]

Racist attitudes, however, were not confined to proslavery Northerners. Free-Soilers and many of their supporters shared such sentiments. The antislavery stance of many Free-Soilers was rooted in demands that free white laborers in the territories not suffer the supposed degradation of competing with blacks, free or enslaved. Leading Free-Soil advocates voiced these concerns both before and after the Burns drama. For example, in 1846, the Democratic Pennsylvania congressman David Wilmot, author of the Wilmot Proviso, which would have outlawed slavery in the territories acquired from Mexico, declared that he wanted to "preserve to free white labor a fair country, a rich inheritance, where the sons of toil, of [my] own race and own color, can live without the disgrace, which association with [N]egro slavery brings upon free labor." The Republican senator William H. Seward expressed similar sentiments as late as 1860, arguing that "the great fact is now fully realized that the African race here is a foreign and feeble element, like the Indians incapable of assimilation . . . and it is a pitiful exotic unnecessarily transplanted into our fields, and which it is unprofitable to cultivate at the cost of the desolation of the native vineyard."[11]

The views of these Northern politicians meshed with the attitudes and aspirations of many white laborers in the North, who exercised increased political clout after the extension of the franchise to most white males. In the late antebellum period, attitudes of this rapidly growing constituency were often tinged with race hatred sparked by fears of job competition from blacks. Frederick Douglass observed that "the wrath of [white] laborers is stirred up" against blacks, and they learned "to hate and despise the Negro." They became convinced that the black worker "eats the bread that belongs to them."[12] In 1851, labor leader John Campbell embraced these sentiments when he said, "Will the white race ever agree that blacks shall stand beside us on election day, upon the rostrum, in the ranks of the army, in our places of public worship, ride in the same coaches, railway cars, or steamships?" He answered his own query, declaring, "Never! Never . . . God never intended it; had he so willed it, he would have made all one color."[13] Many white laborers, the fastest-growing segment of the Northern electorate, simply saw no place for either free or fugitive blacks. Some journalists, including Samuel Medary, the editor of a newspaper called the *Crisis* in Columbus, Ohio, tapped these racist attitudes. Responding to his white working-class readers' concerns about job competition from blacks if slavery were abolished, he fueled fears by asking whether liberated blacks "would take the places" of white workers and perhaps "drive out the white laborers of the North."[14]

At the time Burns made his way northward in 1854, blacks seeking to make new lives on free soil often faced formidable barriers. As Senator Clemens of Alabama and Frederick Douglass noted, a number of Northern states had passed statutes designed to restrict blacks or even bar them from settling within their boundaries. Some states introduced additional stringent provisions in the 1850s. In 1853, the Illinois legislature passed its infamous Black Law, which fined both individuals who aided blacks settling in the state and newly arrived blacks seeking to remain permanently. The Black Law also stated that if a black could not pay a fine levied against him or her, he or she was subject to arrest and could be hired out for a forced term of service to anyone willing to cover the fine—a penalty that differed little from slavery. Most of Illinois became "enemy territory" for blacks, free or fugitive. Although sometimes less restrictive than that of Illinois, racist legislation in other Northern states also guaranteed that blacks confronted institutionalized discrimination in everyday life.[15] "They were either excluded from railway cars, omnibuses, stage coaches, and steamboats or assigned to special 'Jim Crow' sections," notes historian Leon Litwack. "They sat, when permitted, in secluded or remote corners of theatres and lecture halls; they could not enter most hotels, restaurants, and resorts, except as servants; they prayed in 'Negro pews' in white churches." If taking communion, "they waited until the whites had been served the bread and wine."[16]

Overt racism pervaded other areas of social and political interaction between the races in the North. Like little Sarah Roberts in Boston, who could not attend a school close to her home simply because of her color, most blacks faced segregation in schools. Some Northern whites asserted that allowing blacks into white schools "would result in violence and prove fatal to public education."[17] Others argued that their black neighbors were intellectually inferior and "incapable of being cultured beyond a particular point."[18] Many Northern whites refused to share space in hospitals, prisons, and cemeteries with blacks. Some states provided no poor relief to blacks, and laws against interracial marriage and black participation in the militia and on juries were common. Many free states prohibited blacks from testifying in the trials of whites. In the late antebellum period, some 94 percent of Northern blacks resided in states that did not allow them to vote, and many others were "disenfranchised by ruse."[19] When Burns headed to Boston, Northern blacks lived in a world of restrictions. Perhaps H. Ford Douglass, a fugitive from slavery in Virginia who made a new life in Cleveland, Ohio, and became a great antislavery orator, said it best. "From Maine to Georgia, from the Atlantic waves to the Pacific shore, I am an alien and an outcast, unprotected by law, proscribed and persecuted by cruel prejudice." He also suggested that regardless of any efforts blacks made to show their worth as upstanding citizens, their white neighbors in the free states would resent their presence. In fact, he argued that "every achievement, contribution, or significant act performed by blacks" would be regarded with "contempt." He was convinced that "prejudice mounted almost in direct proportion to [black] accomplishments."[20]

Cultural and demographic factors, including the emergence of pseudo-scientific racism, legitimated and accentuated trends toward antebellum segregation. The 1830s witnessed the birth of a new American school of ethnology suggesting that blacks were a separate, inferior species. Foreshadowing late nineteenth-century social Darwinism, these theories fit neatly with the less noble strands of Free-Soil thought and became widely accepted among Northern whites in the 1840s and 1850s. These pseudo-scientific doctrines became the basis for the Negrophobic theories of writers such as Dr. John H. Van Evrie of New York. In pamphlets and other writings, Van Evrie popularized "biological arguments for permanent Negro inferiority" among a growing audience in the North.[21] Although such racist ideologies seemingly justified the South's peculiar institution, they also responded to the anxieties of lower-class whites in the North, where markets made the exchange of goods and services impersonal and the distribution of wealth became highly skewed. George Fredrickson has pointed out that these ideologies reassured working-class whites that they "were better than somebody and not at the rock bottom of society."[22] Pseudoscientific racism not only reinforced Negrophobic fears of competition for jobs from Southern blacks flooding the North but also complemented minstrel shows, which caricatured blacks and had become the rage among whites in the antebellum North by the 1850s.[23] To rationalize their racism, many whites argued that segregation simply reflected "the working out of natural laws, the inevitable consequence of the racial inferiority of the Negro. God and Nature had condemned the blacks to perpetual subordination."[24]

Most Northern whites' lack of close contact with blacks helped make pseudoscientific racism attractive, even compelling. In the antebellum South, blacks and whites lived close together, and relations between them, particularly in rural communities, were characterized by oppression but also by "a measure of racial fluidity." In the North, by contrast, the races usually lived

very much apart. Their separateness precluded intimacy and the development of what Melvin Patrick Ely refers to as "kindred cultures," which could
mitigate racial tensions and result in less rigid enforcement of racist legislation. Unlike the occasional white Southerner, white Northerners had little
incentive to stray "from the path their social ideology prescribed."[25] Despite
the growth in the number of blacks in Northern cities during the antebellum period, blacks still accounted for a small percentage of the population
in the major urban centers, and typically they were relegated to segregated
areas. Such measures both reflected and fueled the racial antipathy evident
in specific fugitive slave crises, which often escalated into major disturbances
or race riots.[26]

The most famous mid-nineteenth-century race riot, the New York
draft riot of 1863, effectively capped about three decades of racist violence
precipitated in part by white fears that the North would be inundated by
fugitive or emancipated slaves. These concerns made even a small black
population seem like "an imposition."[27] For example, in 1829, Cincinnati
experienced the first of four major outbreaks of racial violence, a three-day
riot during which whites relentlessly attacked free blacks and fugitive slaves.
Some three hundred whites descended on the area where blacks resided;
they killed and wounded several blacks, forcing others to flee to Canada.
In 1843, a white mob of about 1,500 carried out a similar attack. Racial hatred sparked a series of similar riots in Philadelphia in 1829, 1834, 1842, and
1849. In 1834, a "pitched battle" continued for three days. Not long after, a
white Philadelphia mob "sacked some thirty houses occupied by colored
inhabitants, many of whom were driven into the woods like wild beasts to
hide themselves from the fury of merciless assailants."[28] In 1842, the City of
Brotherly Love experienced another outburst of racial hatred that lasted two
days. In 1849, a bloody race riot left three persons dead and many injured.[29]
After such disturbances, one Philadelphia newspaper, the *Spirit of the Times,*
reached new heights of Negrophobia, calling blacks "the Thick-Lipped,
Wooley-Headed, Skunk-Smelling, combination of the MONKEY AND THE
DEVIL."[30] During the antebellum period, white hostility helped produce a
migration that eventually brought some 40,000 blacks to Canada, where
they established settlements near the Ontario towns of Windsor, Chatham,
London (Wilberforce), and St. Catharines, the community where Anthony
Burns lived out his final years. Despite this exodus, racism continued to
flourish in the United States.[31]

The presence of fugitive slaves in the North contributed to much of this
antebellum racial violence. Slaveholders' efforts to reclaim their human

property often ignited violence that pitted racist white mobs against blacks and their abolitionist allies. One of the most notorious incidents was the so-called *Pearl* affair, which occurred in the nation's capital in 1848. In early April, seventy-seven fugitive slaves, mostly from northern Virginia, boarded a schooner named the *Pearl* near the mouth of the Potomac. Daniel Drayton, William L. Chaplin, Gerrit Smith, and other abolitionists had secretly chartered the vessel to take the fugitive slaves to the North. Because of high winds and bad weather, the *Pearl* put in at Point Lookout, a short distance from the capital. A free black hack driver who had been jilted by a fugitive slave woman onboard the *Pearl* betrayed the scheme, and the ship was overtaken by a posse. An angry mob of whites, many from northern Virginia, tried to lynch the ship's captain, Edward Sayres, and Drayton and vowed to vent their fury on the fugitives. Authorities averted widespread bloodshed by jailing Sayres, Drayton, and the fugitives "for safekeeping," but they were unable to stop the unruly whites from going on a rampage that involved the destruction of the offices of the *National Era,* Washington's leading abolitionist newspaper.[32]

The explosiveness of fugitive slave crises became especially apparent in the town of Christiana in southeastern Pennsylvania in the autumn of 1851, the scene of one of the hardest-fought battles between Southern slaveholders and their allies and fugitive slaves supported by abolitionists. Four fugitive bondsmen owned by Edward Gorsuch of Maryland escaped to Christiana, where they hid in the home of William Parker, himself a fugitive slave. Gorsuch and several whites pursued his slaves to Parker's home, triggering a fierce gun battle in which Gorsuch was killed and both his son, Dickinson, and his nephew, Dr. Thomas Pearce, were badly wounded. President Millard Fillmore responded to the crisis by dispatching fifty U.S. marines to Christiana, where they joined a citizens' posse of about equal size and effectively terrorized the black community. They rounded up forty-one men, including some antislavery whites, who they alleged had been involved with Parker. Authorities charged thirty-six of them with treason and tried one of them, Castner Hanway, as a test case. William Parker and three of his black allies fled to upstate New York, where Frederick Douglass helped them cross the Genesee River and escape into Canada. Instructing Hanway's jurors, Judge Robert C. Grier described the Christiana incident as "a most horrible outrage" upon the Fugitive Slave Law and a "flagrant outrage on the peace and dignity" of the state of Pennsylvania and the United States.[33] In reporting on the incident, the Northern press tended to agree with Grier and emphasized the need to uphold the supremacy of law, alleging that Gorsuch had been murdered by abolitionist agitators, and that "there was no room for blacks in the free states."[34] These themes resurfaced in most fugitive slave cases, indicating that racism and white fears never lay far beneath the surface in the antebellum North.

Fugitive slave rescues sent shock waves through other communities as well. In the daring Jerry rescue in Syracuse in 1851, emotions ran particularly high after a mob assaulted the Syracuse courthouse, "broke doors and windows, overpowered the officers, and at last bore Jerry away in triumph."[35] Although white abolitionists and blacks rejoiced, the rescue heightened fears of lawlessness and social disorder among many white citizens who believed that the Fugitive Slave Law was a compromise necessary to preserve the Union.[36]

Through sensational reporting, rescues often had an impact reaching far beyond the communities in which they took place, providing encouragement to antislavery forces throughout the North but provoking among others resentment against blacks, distrust of abolitionists, and sentiments favoring the maintenance of law and order, which underpinned demands for the firm enforcement of the Fugitive Slave Act. After the Jerry rescue, the *New York Herald* published a letter denouncing the triumphant abolitionists and suggesting that more such rescues "would be good for a general *stampede* by the slaves of the South, under false representations of the Abolitionists, and their general flight to the North; good for the speedy alienation and secession of the Southern States from the Union; and good for the revival, on a larger field [including the North], of the bloody and horrible atrocities of Santo Domingo." The message was that "good citizens' allegiance to the laws" was imperative to avert disorder, if not disaster.[37]

These reactions further alienated—and imperiled—abolitionists, who had long been the target of criticism and even violent attacks. In 1835, Garrison had narrowly escaped a white mob intent on using him as an example to teach abolitionists a lesson. Two years later, the abolitionist editor Elijah Lovejoy was less fortunate, meeting death at the hands of an angry mob in Alton, Illinois.[38] Some Northerners believed that these abolitionists got what they deserved. Such criticism of abolitionists resurfaced in the 1850s, especially after they adopted strategies of confrontation and overt defiance of United States laws, notably the Fugitive Slave Law. The *New York Daily Times* portrayed abolitionists as "reckless and desperate men" and "enemies of the peace of the land."[39] In the minds of many whites, militant abolitionism put the Union at risk. America's fitful recovery from the economic crisis of 1837, followed by the social and political unrest that swept across Europe beginning in 1848, increased the desire for stability among a growing population of middle-class Americans and capitalists who believed that their fortunes and status were dependent on the maintenance of the social and political order. Industrial workers, concerned about the security of their jobs and fearing the black migration that any undermining of slavery might precipitate, began to deplore abolitionism.

Not long before he died, Samuel May recalled that a Northern merchant had written to him in the early 1850s, stating, "We cannot afford, sir, to let you and your associates endeavor to overthrow slavery. It is not a matter of principles with us. It is a matter of business necessity."[40] Moved by such concerns, Northern business leaders convened a mass meeting in New York in the fall of 1850, during which they adopted resolutions stating that respect for the Compromise of 1850, including enforcement of fugitive slave legislation, was "the only means of safeguarding the Union." They formed a Union Safety Committee and a Correspondence Committee to inform the public "that further agitation of the slavery question was fraught with incalculable danger to our Union and should be halted at all costs." A similar meeting of business leaders took place in Boston at Faneuil Hall not long after; the participants concluded that the Compromise of 1850 "ought to be carried out in good faith and that every form of resistance to the execution of a law, except legal process, is subversive and tends to anarchy." Antebellum Northerners who harbored law-and-order sentiments and a strong commitment to the Union felt threatened by the tumult and apparent lawlessness of fugitive slave crises.[41]

In the early 1850s, politicians, judges, clergymen, and other white Northerners in positions of authority joined the chorus against abolitionists, legitimating views of them as socially disruptive—even anarchic. After the Compromise of 1850, the New Jersey legislature issued a statement declaring that "every patriot, in every part of our widely extended country, has cause to rejoice in the adoption of said measures, as a triumph of constitutional rights over a spirit of wild and disorganized fanaticism."[42] Judge Grier, who presided over the Hanway treason trial following the Gorsuch affair in Christiana, branded abolitionists "infuriated fanatics and unprincipled demagogues" who counseled "bloody resistance" to the laws of the land.[43] Judge John McLean voiced similar views in ruling on the well-publicized case of George Washington McQuerry, a fugitive slave from Kentucky claimed in Ohio by his master. McLean declared, "Sooner or later a disregard for the law could bring chaos, anarchy, and widespread ruin; the law must be enforced."[44] The Reverend George F. Kettell considered resistance to the Fugitive Slave Law "wicked and abominable, answering no end but to exhibit the ferocity and madness of those who make it, and exposing them to the just indignation of all good citizens."[45] John T. Brady, a leading New York merchant, suggested that abolitionists' flagrant disregard for and sabotage of federal legislation threatened law and order, made a mockery of the Constitution, and jeopardized the Union.[46]

During fugitive slave crises, sentiments of "loyalty to the Constitution" and concerns about national security sometimes approached hysteria.[47] Some Northern whites believed that "all the powers of the Federal Government" needed to be exercised to guard against "the daring outrages of [the abolitionists'] Higher lawism."[48] Frederick Douglass noted that many whites in the North regarded returning fugitive slaves as a "duty" and treated individuals who quashed fugitive slave crises as "heroic warriors."[49] In the early 1850s, the future president James Buchanan spoke for many Northern whites when he called for an end to bickering over fugitive slave legislation and declared that it would be best "to put down agitation at the North on the slave question, by the force of enlightened opinion, and faithfully execute the provisions of the Fugitive Slave Law."[50] He cast abolitionists as irresponsible outsiders, not warriors for liberty in the tradition of their Revolutionary forefathers, and he asserted that support of the Fugitive Slave Law was not merely "a remedy for the South's chronic runaway problem" but rather an essential step to ensure the survival of the Union.[51]

The heart of the problem for Northern blacks and abolitionists was that although they sought to extend the gains of the Revolution of 1776 to blacks, turmoil associated with fugitive slave crises convinced many of their neighbors that they needed to *conserve* what the Revolution of 1776 had achieved by upholding the Fugitive Slave Law—in other words, by preserving order and the Union as it was, not by extending the fruits of the Revolution to a subordinated race. These were the Northern whites whom President Fillmore congratulated in his second annual message for their "general acquiescence" and their "spirit of conciliation" in supporting the Compromise of 1850. Their response, said Fillmore, gave him "renewed assurance that our liberty and our Union may subsist together for the benefit of this and all succeeding generations."[52]

Even in areas traditionally regarded as antislavery bastions, politicians defending the Fugitive Slave Law as a means of saving the Union received hearty welcomes—sometimes not only from racists or proslavery advocates but from ordinary Americans who considered slavery morally wrong but felt the Union was threatened by controversy over the slavery issue. In Syracuse, where the Jerry rescue took place, whites embracing the Union and its laws applauded Daniel Webster on his swing through upstate New York in 1851.

From the podium at Syracuse's Frazee Hall, Webster proclaimed, "If men get together and declare a law of Congress shall not be executed in any case and assemble in numbers to prevent the execution of such a law—they are traitors and guilty of treason and bring themselves the penalty of law." The champion of the Fugitive Slave Law went on to say that it was "time to put an end to this imposition upon good citizens." As the audience cheered, he thundered against resistance to the Fugitive Slave Law—"It is treason! treason! TREASON! and nothing else"—and he received even more enthusiastic cheers when he announced that "the law will be executed in its spirit and to its letter." He finished by taking direct aim at abolitionists and Northern blacks who supported fugitives from bondage, saying that the Fugitive Slave Law "will be executed in all the great cities" and "here in Syracuse—in the midst of the next antislavery convention, if the occasion shall arise." For this, Webster received "tremendous applause."[53]

At midcentury, the divisions between Americans who supported the Fugitive Slave Law, or at least advocated compliance with it, and abolitionists were sharper in Boston than in any other place in the Union. Bostonians felt that from the time of the first settlements on the shores of Massachusetts Bay through the Revolutionary era, their home had always occupied a special place in the American drama. For many, it was still the "city on a hill," and they were the proud custodians of Boston Harbor, Lexington and Concord, Bunker Hill, Faneuil Hall, and the various haunts of John and Samuel Adams, Paul Revere, and their compatriots. Many Bostonians viewed their city, not only Faneuil Hall, as the cradle of liberty. That heritage magnified differences between those who sought to extend the principles of the Revolution of 1776 to all Americans and others who proposed to save the Union that the Revolution had produced by respecting the compromises of the Constitution.[54]

Boston's fugitive slave crises threw these differences into sharp relief. On one hand, the city was a hotbed of abolitionism. Men such as William Lloyd Garrison, Wendell Phillips, Theodore Parker, and the Reverend Leonard Grimes sought to extend the Revolution of 1776. On the other hand, men such as Daniel Webster wanted to conserve the Revolution's legacy—the American Union as it was. Boston was the bastion of the Cotton Whigs— men such as Amos Lawrence, who commanded financial and industrial empires closely tied to the interests of Southern slaveholders. Midcentury Boston was also home to a growing middle class of salaried employees and professionals who saw their well-being linked to the stability of the Cotton Whig empires. On the eve of Burns's arrival, they too were sensitive to concerns of law and order, particularly in the wake of the two major fugitive slave crises that already had recently rocked Boston—the cases of Frederic Wilkins, best known as Shadrach (and sometimes as Shadrach Minkins), and Thomas Sims.

Shadrach escaped from Norfolk, Virginia, in the early summer of 1850 and arrived in Boston, where he worked as a waiter at Taft's Cornhill Coffee House before his arrest by slave catchers to whom he unsuspectingly served breakfast. On February 15, 1851, a group of about fifty militant blacks led by Lewis Hayden overpowered courthouse guards in broad daylight and spirited Shadrach to Canada, alarming white Southerners, Fillmore's administration, Cotton Whigs, and many Bostonians who accepted the Compromise of 1850. Mayor John P. Bigelow complained that the Commonwealth's "dignity had been criminally assaulted." Webster thought the rescue was a "case of treason," and some press reports suggested that Boston had become the cradle of "mad Abolitionism." The *Savannah Republican* referred to Boston as "a black speck on the map—disgraced by the lowest, the meanest, the BLACK-EST kind of NULLIFICATION."[55] Speaking for many Cotton Whigs, Robert C. Winthrop declared that it was "lamentable to have such triumph given to Nullification and Rebellion," and Amos Lawrence asked, "Shall we stand by the laws or shall we nullify them? Shall we uphold the Union or shall we break it up?" Some extreme Cotton Whigs wanted to lynch Shadrach's rescuers.[56] Meanwhile, abolitionists took great pride in their liberation of Shadrach. Dr. Henry Bowditch thought that the rescuers had honored a "holy" cause. Theodore Parker deemed it "the noblest deed" in Boston since "the destruction of the tea in 1773."[57]

If the Shadrach rescue rocked Boston, so too did the Sims crisis some two months later. "A mulatto about twenty-two years of age," Thomas Sims escaped from Savannah on May 21, 1850, aboard a vessel named the *M. & J. C. Gilmore*. Discovered shortly before the ship arrived in Boston, he eluded his captors by "unscrewing the lock on the door of the state-room" where he had been confined, and he made it ashore. He was arrested on April 3, 1851.[58]

Determined to avoid further national embarrassment, Boston's mayor allowed the city's police to be deputized as federal marshals so that they could participate legally in the arrest of Sims under the Fugitive Slave Law.[59] Boston's constabulary thus became part of what abolitionists derogatorily called the "Sims Brigade." After Sims's arrest, authorities cordoned off the courthouse with heavy iron chains, increased the police presence throughout the city, called out two companies of militia, and guarded Sims at all times in order to avoid a repeat of the Shadrach affair. Richard Henry Dana Jr.

and Charles Sumner helped mount a defense for Sims. They attempted a number of legal maneuvers, including demanding a writ of habeas corpus and challenging the constitutionality of the Fugitive Slave Law. Chief Justice Lemuel Shaw denied the writ and upheld the federal statute.

Infuriated abolitionists attempted to organize public meetings in the State House yard and at Faneuil Hall, but the state legislature refused them the use of either location. Increasingly militant, they met at Tremont Temple and frightened many Bostonians with rhetoric that Daniel Webster and his supporters considered "treasonably violent." The mayor bolstered the forces of law and order by calling out the state militia, further antagonizing abolitionists, and prompting Wendell Phillips to declare, "[T]his is the first time hostile soldiers have been seen in our streets since the red-coats marched up Long Wharf." The disposition of Sims came as no surprise: slave law commissioner George Ticknor Curtis declared him chattel "to all intents, uses, and purposes whatsoever." Before dawn on April 12, 1851, some one hundred troops backed by about "the same number of volunteers" escorted Sims to Boston's Long Wharf, where he was put aboard the *Acorn,* the vessel that would carry him back to slavery in Georgia. On his return to Savannah, Sims received "thirty-nine lashes in the public square."[60]

In Boston, press reports asserted that "most of the respectable citizenry were relieved." Boston had proved its "attachment to the Union" and redeemed its reputation. The mayor proclaimed himself pleased that support among the white citizenry for the actions of the civic authorities had been widespread, and that many of the city's "most wealthy and respectable citizens" had offered their services to assist in maintaining order and ensuring Sims's return to Georgia.[61] President Fillmore thought Bostonians had "done nobly"; the Sims affair, the president said, represented the "triumph of law in Boston." In contrast, antislavery Bostonians despaired at the behavior of their fellow citizens who supported the Fugitive Slave Law as a necessary compromise with the South and denounced abolitionists.[62] Josiah Quincy summed up the discouragement of many antislavery activists. He said, "I find my fellow citizens are not only *submissive* to, but that they are earnestly active for [the Fugitive Slave Law's] enforcement. . . . The Boston of 1851 is not the Boston of 1775. Boston has now become a mere shop—a place for buying and selling goods; and I suppose, also, of *buying and selling men.*"[63]

Quincy was not alone in lamenting that Boston had changed for the worse. A mood of gloom permeated the ranks of abolitionists as they recognized their increased alienation from most of white Boston. Austin Bearse, the famed doorkeeper of the Boston Vigilance Committee and captain of the

Moby Dick, a vessel that carried many fugitive slaves to their freedom, complained that public resentment of abolitionists was widespread, making it difficult for them to win "the fair fame of our city." Bearse suffered personally when many wealthy Bostonians decided that it was no longer appropriate to make reservations for his bay cruises after it became widely known that he had used the *Moby Dick* to spirit fugitive slaves to Canada.[64] Wendell Phillips, too, recognized the powerful stigma attached to abolitionism. On the first anniversary of Sims's return to Georgia, Phillips shifted his criticism from the deputized officials who had executed Judge Curtis's order to the general public and the business community. "I find but little fault, comparatively, with the City Marshal of Boston," said Phillips. "The fault that I rather choose to note is, that the owner of the brig 'Acorn' can walk up State Street, and be as honored a man as he was before." He complained that "no merchant shrinks" from recognizing the *Acorn*'s captain or supporting fugitive slave legislation; such men, he said, were responsible for the city's fall into disgrace and owed him, Phillips, "full atonement for the foul dishonor they have brought on the city of my birth."[65] Thomas Wentworth Higginson concluded, "There is neither organization, resolution, plan nor popular sentiment—the Negroes are cowed & the abolitionists irresolute & hopeless, with nothing better to do on Saturday than to send off circulars to clergymen."[66] He was not far off the mark—except in the case of the black Bostonians.

If the Sims rendition exposed divisions among white Bostonians, it also had a wrenching impact on Boston's blacks and shaped their stance during the Burns drama. The euphoria after the successful rescue of Shadrach temporarily masked black Bostonians' disillusionment with the federal government after the passage of the new fugitive slave legislation. But the strict enforcement of the Fugitive Slave Law and the cooperation of state and local officials with federal authorities in the Sims case sparked increasing bitterness and fear among the city's blacks, particularly those who were fugitives from bondage.

In the wake of the Sims affair, Boston's blacks adopted a more radical course, distancing themselves even from white abolitionists such as Garrison who remained committed to political nonintervention and pacifism. Boston's black clergymen played an instrumental role in this process—and they were well positioned to do so. They headed churches that had been established in the preceding decades largely in response to black disaffection with discrimination in white churches, where blacks had been confined to Negro pews and ridiculed for their "more demonstrative style" of worship. With their newfound independence, Boston's black clergymen transformed their churches into institutions that responded to their community's broader concerns and focused on the here and now as well as the afterlife. After the passage of the Fugitive Slave Law and especially after the Sims rendition, these black leaders made their churches "institutional centers for the antislavery movement" that reflected their own views, which sometimes differed from those of white abolitionists. This transformation stemmed from their belief in the need to increase political involvement and expand the antislavery arsenal—including forcible resistance to slave catchers—to protect the interests of blacks. The Reverend Jehiel C. Beman of the First African Methodist Episcopal Zion Church became one of the strongest early proponents of political action. The Reverend Leonard Grimes joined militants such as Lewis Hayden in the congregation at Boston's Twelfth Baptist Church in efforts to protect and free fugitives, using force if necessary.[67]

As Boston's blacks became more militant, they showed less patience with the prejudice of white abolitionists—some of whom, like white Northerners in general, viewed blacks as inferior. Blacks recognized that even some members of the Boston Vigilance Committee "harbored a belief in the inferiority of the black race."[68] Wendell Phillips, for example, had "confessed to feeling uncomfortable sharing hotel rooms with fellow abolitionists who were black on lecture tours."[69] Other white opponents of slavery sometimes exhibited astonishment "at the impudence of the colored people" when they chose to sit anywhere they wished at antislavery meetings. Stressing the need for unity among members of their race, black Bostonians increasingly asserted racial pride. In the mid-1850s, they petitioned the state legislature for a monument to Crispus Attucks and lobbied for black participation in the militia. They were strongly supported by blacks in the areas surrounding Boston, but they were refused on both issues. Schooling also remained a contentious issue throughout the early 1850s. Despite the ruling against integrated schooling in *Roberts v. City of Boston* (1849), the city's blacks persevered and renewed their efforts for school desegregation by petitioning the state legislature. White Bostonians, who feared that state legislation to integrate public education would primarily affect Boston's white schools, initially succeeded in blocking these proposals.[70]

These controversies confirmed the existence of persistent racial intolerance among white Bostonians and reinforced feelings of insecurity within the black community. Many blacks, mostly fugitive slaves and their families, opted to leave Boston and the surrounding area during the early 1850s; many went to Canada. Theodore Parker estimated that about "400 persons of color" fled to that country from the Boston vicinity within a year of the enactment of the Fugitive Slave Law—this out of a total black population of about 2,000.[71] Such an outflow weakened the tightly knit black community and jeopardized its institutions. It especially hurt the churches and further promoted militancy among black clergymen. On the eve of the Burns crisis, the "African Methodist Episcopal Church lost eighty-five members, the African Methodist Episcopal Zion Church lost ten members from a small congregation, and the Twelfth Baptist Church lost more than one third of its members."[72] The last, often called "the fugitive slave church," also saw two deacons depart. These dislocations, coupled with continuing discrimination in a job market made more competitive by an influx of Irish immigrants, convinced many blacks who remained that the community's only alternative was increased solidarity and militancy—especially given white Boston's ambivalence about their lot.[73]

A glance at Boston during the early 1850s confirms not only that the small black community faced serious problems but also that white Bostonians did little to alleviate the conditions confronting their black neighbors. High rates of infant mortality among poor blacks, combined with rising Irish immigration, steadily undermined the welfare and relative strength of Boston's black community. Job competition between blacks, who were relegated to low-paying, often seasonal, occupations, and unskilled Irish laborers fueled racial animosity, which constantly threatened to erupt in violence—as it had in the previous decade when Irish sailors attacked four blacks in Boston's North Square, precipitating a riot involving several hundred people. "Some gentlemen of property and standing" had joined in that assault against the blacks.[74] The rallying cry of the whites had been "Kill the Niggers."[75]

On the eve of Anthony Burns's arrival in Boston, then, racial tensions constantly reminded black Bostonians that the conditions that provoked the North Square riot in 1843 and the earlier attack on Garrison still existed. Blacks continued to confront groups of hard-drinking white laborers, who enjoyed hurling racial epithets at them. Going to and from their jobs, many Boston blacks felt insecure. Furthermore, recently arrived white Irish laborers often displaced them in the workplace. Irish domestics also took jobs from black women, whose incomes from cooking and cleaning were crucial to their households, given their husbands' low—and often seasonal—wages. In the male-dominated seafaring trades, new restrictions on free black seamen in Southern ports gave Irish labor an edge in competing for employment in Boston's maritime trades.[76]

In sum, although the issues black Bostonians faced on the eve of Burns's arrival were similar to those confronted by their black brethren throughout the North, the city's unique heritage and development exacerbated both their problems and their frustration with their plight. Midcentury Boston represented a complex, even confused, environment in which relations between blacks and whites were informed by an array of political, social, and intellectual beliefs as well as by the varied, often conflicting, aspirations of peoples with different allegiances and interests. The fugitive slave crises revolving around Shadrach and Sims sharpened divisions and set the stage for the Burns drama to further test relations and prove that midcentury Boston was not necessarily fertile ground for antislavery sentiment. Widening rifts between pacific, apolitical abolitionists and black Bostonians, who saw their families, communities, and livelihoods at risk, occurred alongside divisions between antislavery Bostonians and their neighbors, who embraced law-and-order sentiments and valued the stability of the Union above all else. In this environment, the Burns drama provoked local responses far more varied than the emphasis of earlier historians on abolitionist rhetoric and antislavery feeling allows for.

CHAPTER 4

The Meaning of the Spectacle
"No More Tumults" and the Black Bostonian Response

If Boston were unanimous on the side of Freedom and Justice . . . the Commissioners would easily discover the legality of setting free the slave; the Marshals and their followers would soon be of the same mind, and no more slaves could be carried from Boston.
—*Rev. James Freeman Clarke*

We have, as a people, depended upon the abolitionists to do that for us, which we must do for ourselves. . . . We must disapprove the allegation of our innate inferiority. This cannot be done by proxy.
—*James Watkins*

A review of events in Boston in late May and early June 1854 shows that divisions within the abolitionist movement, differing commitments to law and order, and diverse ideologies of race produced varied reactions among Bostonians to the Anthony Burns drama. As many scholars have ably demonstrated, there was significant antislavery sentiment, but such feelings had to compete with other concerns. It is also far from clear that antislavery sentiments were on the rise in Boston as the drama unfolded or even after Burns had been returned to Virginia. Uncertainty bordering on chaos reigned throughout the affair, accentuating the confusion, hesitation, and anxiety of many white and black Bostonians.

Whites usually portrayed as kindly neighbors to Boston's blacks, friends of the antislavery movement, and sympathizers with fugitives from bondage felt these crosscurrents. Many who listened to the likes of Samuel Gridley Howe, Wendell Phillips, and Theodore Parker at Faneuil Hall shared in the confusion. Parker knew this. A close reading of his words on the night of the courthouse riot suggests that he was especially concerned about divisions in the abolitionist movement, and particularly about the strong commitments of some of his listeners to law and order, which he saw as a major obstacle to saving Burns from being returned to slavery. "Men and brothers, I am not a young man," Parker shouted. "I have heard hurrahs and cheers for liberty many times; I have not seen a great many deeds done for liberty. I ask you, are we to have deeds as well as words?" Parker spoke not only to the crowd but also to several of his colleagues on the platform who had participated in the deadlocked meeting of the Boston Vigilance Committee the day before. Parker knew that although they cherished the heritage of their forefathers' resistance to tyranny and acknowledged contradictions between America's founding principles or higher law and Burns's imprisonment, they had difficulty straying from the law-abiding ways expected of upstanding citizens in Boston.[1]

Parker was not alone in recognizing the deep-rooted dilemma of many Bostonians. The Boston press dealt with it head-on, often recommending actions consistent with the maintenance of law and order. The day after the courthouse riot, the editor of the *Boston Morning Journal,* a newspaper that appealed to the sentiments of many Cotton Whigs, surmised that while Bostonians might "smart under the blow inflicted by the Nebraska bill" and have "no especial love for the fugitive slave law," they would sanction "only *lawful* means" to resist Burns's return to slavery. He concluded that there was "nothing in the antecedents of the metropolis of Massachusetts" to suggest that "citizens will now deliberately trample upon any law, however obnoxious it may be." Referring to the rhetoric of Parker, Phillips, and others at Faneuil Hall the previous evening, the editor guessed that efforts of "fanatical agitators to get up an excitement and a riot in our city will signally fail." His comments about abolitionists echoed those of law-abiding citizens during other fugitive slave crises and are remarkably similar to the sentiments expressed by the likes of businessman John T. Brady and justices Robert Grier and John McLean. The editor of the *Morning Journal* also refused requests to print abolitionists' denunciations of the Fugitive Slave Law as well as their demands for the state legislature to ban federal officials and slave catchers from using the Boston courthouse. The editor said that he did not want to "publish anything which would tend to produce excitement."[2]

The Democratic *Boston Post,* not surprisingly, also adopted an unequivocal law-and-order stance. Reacting to the courthouse riot, the *Post's* editor reprinted a letter from the deceased champion of the Fugitive Slave Law, Daniel Webster, and called for the good citizens of Boston to faithfully observe "law and order in opposition to the riot and treason which reckless and desperate men who denunciate the Union of the States and the Constitution which binds them together as a 'covenant with death and an agreement with hell' [call for]." The paper expressed confidence that the forces of law and order would triumph over the agitation of irresponsible men who "attempt to arrest the due course of the law." The latter, warned the *Post*, would be "properly dealt with."[3] A few days later the *Post*'s editor also invoked the legacy of the Founding Fathers to justify a law-and-order stance in support of the Fugitive Slave Law. "To deliver up these fugitive slaves is a *constitutional obligation*, assented to by the foremost men in the revolution from New England and their companions in arms and in council," he declared. Referring to the fugitive slave legislation passed in 1793, he reminded his readers that "the first law enacted to carry out this constitutional obligation . . . was rendered complete by receiving the signatures of George Washington and John Adams." He stressed that the most outspoken opponents of the Fugitive Slave Law—men such as Theodore Parker, Wendell Phillips, and William Lloyd Garrison— paled in comparison to these legendary figures, "whose patriotism, wisdom, purity, and love of country" were beyond question.[4]

Similarly, the *Boston Daily Courier* appealed to Bostonians' concerns about law and order, portraying antislavery activists as "enemies of the peace of the land." The editor suggested that their intentions were "to make this city, if possible, again a scene of disorder and violence," and he emphasized that such resistance to the law could once again "bring discredit upon Boston." He railed against the abolitionists' "inflammatory rhetoric," suggesting that it threatened to "kindle a mob spirit." He hoped that "apostles of sedition" would meet with a sharp rebuke, and that there would be "no more mobs—no more violation of laws—no more tumults to disgrace our city and State." In short, the *Daily Courier* did not want to countenance a repeat of the Shadrach affair.[5]

These newspapers were not the only ones that proved sensitive to concerns about maintaining law and order. As the day of reckoning for Burns's fate drew near, the *Boston Evening Transcript*, a Whig paper, published an article titled "Conflict of Laws" underscoring the manner in which the Fugitive Slave Law negated traditional liberties such as habeas corpus. The paper, however, also published letters counseling respect for the law and emphasizing the importance of avoiding violence at all costs. A message from the well-known poet John Greenleaf Whittier noted that "nothing good" could be expected from "any demonstration of violence" and averred that "a blind mob is not the tribunal for settlement of this awful question." Despite his antislavery leanings, Whittier concluded that "it becomes all then to avoid all unlawful and rash expedients."[6] The paper also printed the reflections of Judge George Ticknor Curtis on the causes and consequences of the courthouse riot. Curtis reminded antislavery Bostonians not to act like South Carolina nullifiers. Drawing a parallel between the "extradition of fugitives" and respect for tariff laws, Curtis argued that "one cannot fail to see that the government would cease to exist if it should yield obedience to these local influences." He concluded that "while government stands, all these laws must be executed, or it becomes the merest tool of faction, and mob law would become an acknowledged authority, ready to be turned against any man or measure, and bloodshed and ruin would ensue."[7]

The *Evening Transcript*'s editors walked a fine line on the question of whether it was appropriate for the city of Boston to furnish the courthouse to United States marshals for the execution of the Fugitive Slave Law, an issue raised when some antislavery aldermen presented a motion to have the "officers of the United States" evicted from the courthouse. Although the proposal failed to pass, the editors felt obliged to comment. Their reflections came down on the side of the law, but in a particularly striking way. "While we would not countenance the movement in the Board of Aldermen yesterday," said the *Evening Transcript*'s editors, "we would insist that if Negro catching is to be a common practice here, the slave pens, as at the South, should be in some back lane, where what are legally known as 'offensive trades' are carried on."[8] The editors faced a momentous quandary. The Fugitive Slave Law clashed with traditional liberties that they and their readers embraced. It was morally and aesthetically offensive, and it tainted Massachusetts's free soil. Law and order, however, simply had to be maintained to prevent anarchy and save the Union. Ironically, the solution the editors proposed drew on the practices of Southern slaveholders, whose tyranny, they argued, created the problem to begin with.

Many Bostonians demonstrated their law-and-order sentiments through action. Recently arrived Irish accounted for most of the "fifteen hundred members of the Bay Street Club" who volunteered their services to Mayor J. V. C. Smith and Marshal Watson Freeman to maintain order and ensure Burns's return. The Irish also constituted the bulk of a group called the Columbian Artillery, which further boosted the forces of law and order. But the Irish were not the only Bostonians to offer their services. After the attack on the courthouse, newspapers reported that "a number of our most respectable citizens," people concerned about the riotous behavior of Higginson, his followers, and the ruffians breaking windows, "tendered their services to assist in maintaining peace and order." Press reports also congratulated the police and the militia for reestablishing peace. "Chief of Police Taylor manifested the greatest intrepidity and daring," wrote one reporter for the *Boston Evening Transcript*, a paper that traditionally told its readers about the importance of protecting individual liberties. Supporting the law-and-order stance taken by the authorities, it also informed radical abolitionists and their sympathizers that "there may be blows to take as well as blows to give, and that if one mob can break into a court house, another one can destroy a private dwelling. If officers are killed, private citizens may also suffer violence. Who can say to an infuriated mob thus far thou go and no further?"[9]

What is particularly interesting is the press's reading of public sentiment during the crisis. The day before Commissioner Loring rendered his decision on Burns's fate, as the presence of the military in the city burgeoned, the *Evening Transcript* published an assessment of the general public's reaction to the heightened law enforcement. Its reading casts doubt on scholarly arguments suggesting that Bostonians disapproved of Mayor Smith's request for reinforcements, that citizens generally abhorred the Pierce administration's show of force, and that the crisis fueled antislavery sentiment and sympathy for Burns. "Our military friends have responded with great promptness to the numerous calls which have been made upon them during the exciting times of the past few weeks," asserted the *Evening Transcript*'s editors. "The public, we believe, duly appreciate their loyalty to the law, and many persons who in former times have questioned the expediency of their organization, now feel that their own persons and property are secure against mob violence by reason of the large military force we have to support the supremacy of law in every emergency which may arise."[10] The *Evening Transcript* thus saw the forces of order as guarantors of economic, social, and political stability and believed that most Bostonians supported the actions that the authorities had taken. Some of Boston's most outspoken abolitionists read public sentiment in much the same way, emphasizing that Bostonians valued stability and order above all else. Referring to the impotence of the antislavery movement during the Burns crisis, Samuel Gridley Howe wrote, "[T]he fear of the law—the fetish of the law, disarmed and emasculated us."[11]

Such assessments were consistent with President Fillmore's earlier view of Northerners' continuing "general acquiescence" to federal fugitive slave legislation—and William Lloyd Garrison and several other abolitionists also agreed. In the first issue of the *Liberator* published after Burns's return, Garrison lamented that "no voice came from the public at large, none from the Governor of the insulted Commonwealth, none from the Mayor of the disgraced city. They did not care to take the trouble; they did not see that the enslavement of this poor man was *their* own enslavement, their own *infamy*."[12] The antislavery pastor the Reverend Edmund B. Willson was of like mind. He admonished his West Roxbury congregation for not having taken a stand. He too invoked the Revolutionary legacy of the Bay State's forefathers—but in a way that differed from that of the editors of the *Boston Post*. Willson said that he was "saddened and ashamed" by the return of Burns. Calling June 2, 1854, "Bad Friday," he scolded his listeners, saying that "your grandsires and mine, not a long time back, broke away from what they called tyranny, though it was freedom, justice and indulgence . . . as compared with the tyranny from which this man [Burns] fled."[13] Another antislavery man, E. H. Gray, also blamed law-abiding citizens for their inaction. They were at fault for Burns's return to bondage; they had strayed from the Revolutionary fathers' example. "Just reflect," exclaimed Gray. "Our Fathers not only would not obey, but actually resisted the 'Stamp Act and Tea Tax;' and these were *virtues,* compared with this kidnapping, heaven defying Slave Bill." He told Bostonians that they should have followed the example of the Sons of Liberty. They "caught the Commissioner who issued stamps and made him take a solemn oath that he would not execute his commission," Gray recalled, adding, "Would that the Commissioners of the Slave Bill were served in the same manner."[14]

Abolitionists such as Garrison, Willson, and Gray felt justified in criticizing their neighbors; many white Bostonians had shown striking indifference to Burns's fate and steadfastly supported Mayor Smith. Three days after Burns's departure, some prominent Bostonians gathered to congratulate the military and Mayor Smith for their defense of the law. Although a Whig governor—indeed, the last Whig governor of Massachusetts—Governor Emory Washburn shared in praising those who had ensured Burns's return, underscoring how the militia in particular had "promptly met" the demands made on it. In accepting these accolades, Mayor Smith likened himself to a captain at the helm: he said that he had asked himself, "[S]hall I trust to the moral character of the sharks, or shall I be master of my own ship?" He believed he had acted to ensure that Bostonians reached a safe haven and that "the honor of Boston [was] saved."[15]

What happened in the Massachusetts political arena following Burns's return to Virginia is even more remarkable and casts more doubt on scholarly interpretations suggesting that the Burns rendition fueled an antislavery groundswell. As the campaign for the fall elections got underway, Washburn did an about-face and sought to distance himself from Mayor Smith and his American Party cohorts. Sounding suddenly like a Conscience Whig, Washburn vehemently attacked the Fugitive Slave Law and the Pierce administration's commitment to it, which he said had "aroused the indignation of the freemen of the North." He accused Pierce of "having stooped from his high position and prostituted the influence of his office."[16] It was, however, Mayor Smith—not Governor Washburn—who apparently gauged public opinion accurately: Smith was reelected by a significant majority in the fall of 1854, one of the victorious members of the American Party who won office in the so-called Know-Nothing Revolution in Massachusetts. In fact, Smith "received the largest vote ever cast for a mayor in Boston."[17] From the steps of city hall, he once again thanked Bostonians for their support. To resounding applause, Smith said, "Under all circumstances, fellow citizens, I have had an eye to the law; and whatever the law may be, if I am called upon to administer it . . . I shall maintain the law at all hazards." Having trounced his opponents, he had good reason to believe that most citizens heartily approved of the law-and-order stance he had adhered to throughout the Burns affair. Thoroughly revolted by Smith's victory, William Lloyd Garrison concluded that the election of this man who had "disgraced" the city by his "unlawful and wicked complicity in the kidnapping of Anthony Burns" undoubtedly marked "the last phase of Free Soilism, of political antislavery in the Old Bay State."[18]

Henry Gardner also shared in the benefits of the Know-Nothing Revolution; he trounced Washburn and registered the biggest win in the history of Massachusetts gubernatorial elections.[19] What is particularly striking, however, is that Gardner had been a longtime supporter of Daniel Webster, who, of course, thought resistance to the Fugitive Slave Law was treason. Gardner was of like opinion, and during the fall campaign, Washburn, thinking his own recent conversion to the antislavery cause would please Massachusetts voters, constantly harped on Gardner's proslavery beliefs. On the eve of the election, Washburn even had the *Evening Transcript* publish a letter that Gardner wrote during the Shadrach crisis defending the Fugitive Slave Law and claiming that Bostonians were committed "to support the majesty and supremacy of the laws" of the land.[20] Washburn also unveiled a militant antislavery platform. He assailed the Kansas-Nebraska Act, declared that he wanted the Missouri Compromise prohibiting slavery in the territories north of 36° 30' to be restored, and demanded the immediate repeal of the Fugitive Slave Law. The antislavery *Boston Daily Atlas* printed an article absolving Washburn of any association with Mayor Smith and the latter's calling out of the militia to deliver Burns to bondage. The governor, said the paper, had been "guilty of no sin." But Washburn's antislavery campaign fell on deaf ears; as the *Daily Atlas* put it, Gardner "swept the entire state like a tornado." In commenting on Washburn's defeat, the *Boston Post* concluded that the "Seward Whigs of Massachusetts had bid [too] high for abolition votes. Their state convention platform was of the very worst sort. It took with some freesoilers, but seems not . . . to have helped them."[21]

Other contemporary assessments also suggest that Gardner's victory and Washburn's loss should not be viewed as surprising. In the weeks after Burns's return, the Bay State's antislavery activists were discouraged by their neighbors' sentiments. The political trends leading up to the fall elections seemed only to underscore the weakness of the antislavery forces—even in the wake of the Burns drama. When the pragmatic Henry Wilson jumped to the Know-Nothings and sought to fill the party's ranks with other Free-Soilers, Charles Francis Adams complained that most antislavery militants had left the Free-Soil cause for the people's movement that was sweeping the Bay State. That populist movement demanded political reform and measures to check the alleged threats associated with the rising tide of immigration and Catholicism—not measures to check the advance of slave power. Northampton Free-Soiler C. P. Huntingdon concluded that neither the Kansas-Nebraska crisis nor the kidnapping of Anthony Burns had deeply stirred antislavery sentiment. When the Free-Soilers who had not taken the Know-Nothing pledge met in Worcester about one month after the Burns drama to create a fusion antislavery party under the Republican banner, they found little support among Bay Staters. They decided, nevertheless, to take a strong antislavery stance. They demanded the repeal of the Fugitive Slave Law and the Kansas-Nebraska Act, which they saw as evidence of the encroachment of slave power. They also called for the abolition of slavery in the nation's capital. In the weeks that followed, they made no headway with voters and, like Washburn, fell victim to Gardner's Know-Nothing machine on election day.[22]

When he assumed office, Gardner obviously felt that he had accurately sensed the pulse of the people; in his inaugural address, he did not touch on the slavery issue. Rather, he stressed his "progressive nativism programme," which, according to the *Evening Transcript,* consisted of five major promises—strong measures to ensure the separation of church and state to protect against a rising Catholic population using "the School Fund" to advance their sectarian interests, lengthening residency requirements for naturalization, deporting "all foreign paupers and criminals," prohibiting the charter of "militia companies composed of persons of foreign birth," and excluding immigrants from holding public offices in a stance consistent with the principle that "Americans should rule America."[23] During 1855, Gardner strayed little from this platform, but he also showed that he still had a bias toward compromising with Southerners. He allayed any doubts about this when he vetoed the new personal liberty law proposed by Free-Soil members of his party and stood firmly behind Commissioner Loring's decision to return Burns to bondage, refusing to dismiss the Harvard lecturer from his position of judge of probate. And Gardner was not alone in seeking to remove slavery from the Bay State's public agenda. Within a year, "fifteen hundred of the most prominent citizens of Boston appended their names to a call for a public meeting in Faneuil Hall, to denounce the agitation of the question of Slavery, as putting in peril the existence of the Union." Little had changed after the Burns drama.[24]

Editorial commentary in the days after Burns's departure contained echoes of earlier fugitive slave crises and again underscored Bostonians' commitment to the Union and their strong inclination toward law and order. Some Boston papers actually printed letters from Southerners thanking Bostonians for "the firm and patriotic manner in which they had acted" during the Burns crisis. One letter to the editor of the *Boston Post* noted that the city's "order-loving" and "law-abiding" citizens had "respected and firmly maintained" Southern rights. The writer let Bostonians know that now the North and the South were "connected by every tie of blood, of friendship, and of interest." "Cursed be the hand that shall ever break them apart," he railed, and he asked, "Shall a few misguided men make [Boston] odious?" In light of Burns's return, he said that he could answer, "No, never."[25]

Even the Boston Vigilance Committee proved to be remarkably ambivalent. As previously noted, the committee's inaction reflected the influence of moderates motivated by law-abiding instincts. They dominated the committee's deliberations and quashed plans for a rescue. Most committee members were "completely unwilling" to challenge even institutions that they openly admitted were "corrupted."[26] Most, including keynote speakers at the Faneuil Hall rally in support of Burns, proved it on the night of the courthouse riot. Like others in the audience, they did not participate in the attempt to rescue Burns. In fact, some did not even go to Courthouse Square. Despite his statement that "nothing so well as the most determined resistance becomes Faneuil Hall" and his rallying cry of "Resistance to tyrants is obedience to God," Samuel Gridley Howe did not join Higginson and the others in the attempted rescue after he went to the square.[27] Instead, he paused and then returned home because his wife was not well. Perhaps feeling guilty as a result of his inaction that night, he reported that he "wept for sorrow and shame" when Burns was returned; he said that Boston was a "disgraced community."[28]

John L. Swift also did not follow the advice that he gave to the Faneuil Hall audience. He proclaimed, "If we allow Marshal Freeman to carry away [Burns], then the word cowards should be stamped on our foreheads. When we go from this cradle of liberty, let us go to the tomb of liberty, the Court House."[29] He never went to the square. He limited his participation in the rescue attempt to telling others, including Dr. Henry Bowditch, to proceed to the courthouse. And even though Bowditch headed "up the hill," he confessed to having believed at the time that those who wanted to free Burns were "foolhardy"; he thought Higginson and his mostly black followers "too ardent," and he "pass[ed] from the square." Later, however, Bowditch admitted to feeling unworthy because of his inaction. Of the militants, he wrote, "Would to God we had been more like them!"[30]

Equally remarkable was the behavior of Wendell Phillips, Samuel Sewall, and Bronson Alcott, the famous social reformer and transcendentalist. Phillips apparently spent his entire fury when he shouted that "Anthony Burns had no master but his God"; he had guests at home, his wife was not well, and so off he went. Sewall, too, left Faneuil Hall and returned straight home to report that the audience had been "enthusiastic" and unanimously disapproved of Burns's being returned to slavery; he did not bother to go to the courthouse. Alcott proved only slightly more assertive. He went to the square, gazed at the scene, and asked Higginson, "Why are we not within?" Higginson responded that the crowd would "not stand by us." Alcott calmly watched the rabble throwing bricks and stones through windows, and then he too moved on. He would later admit to feeling "ashamed of the Union, of New England, of Boston, almost of myself, too," for the lack of effort to rescue Burns.[31]

If the ambivalence, or at least inaction, of the Boston Vigilance Committee was remarkable, so was the relatively weak support of women, a sharp contrast from the Jerry rescue in Syracuse, where women had joined the crowd and played an instrumental role. On the night of the courthouse riot, women were conspicuous by their absence. Indeed, few descendants of the Boston women renowned for their participation in 1776 and earlier boycotts turned out for the speeches at Faneuil Hall that night. Harriet Beecher Stowe, who was in Boston, did not attend.[32] Describing the drama, one journalist also later remarked that relatively "few ladies were seen among the multitude."[33]

The absence of women perhaps explains the disillusionment and anger of Sarah Pellet, a prominent female antislavery activist. At an antislavery meeting that Lucy Stone called to order shortly after Burns's departure, Pellet reprimanded Boston women. "Had the ladies acted up to the dignity of true women," she said, "they might have saved Anthony Burns. Had the women of Boston turned out *en masse,* and placed themselves before the cannon's mouth, would any man have dared to fire at them?" In her view, the women of Boston had to shoulder much blame for Burns's return. She was "ashamed of her native state" and also of Boston.[34]

Some white clergy also fostered ambivalence toward the plight of Burns, thus helping to boost the number of indifferent or even hostile spectators who wanted "to get a parting glimpse of the fugitive."[35] Their posture had special relevance because many in the crowd on the day of Burns's departure had been participating in the activities of Anniversary Week, the annual gathering of New England's clergy. They too behaved very differently from participants at the antislavery meeting in Syracuse that coincided with the rescue of Jerry a few years earlier. The latter boosted the mob that converged on the police station where Jerry was confined, helped rescuers break into the building, and then assisted in spiriting him to Canada. In contrast, the behavior of most Anniversary Week attendees mirrored that of supposedly respectable Bostonians. They showed curiosity but went about their business in an orderly manner. Harriet Beecher Stowe maintained such a "low profile" that some people wondered why she "was saying nothing."[36] One antislavery Anniversary Week participant criticized the clergy for their "pious temporizing" while Burns remained in chains in the courthouse.[37] Some Protestant clergymen showed more concern about the supposed threat posed by Catholicism in America than about the fate of Burns. They joined the ranks of "solid middle class citizens," whose law-and-order leanings prevented their active participation in antislavery activities.[38]

Other members of the Boston clergy who observed events closely that week refused, however, to remain among the unengaged. Having witnessed his coreligionists' ambivalence throughout the crisis, the Reverend James Freeman Clarke, one of the city's most outspoken antislavery ministers, lashed out on July 4 in much the same way as Sarah Pellet had done two days earlier. He was aghast at the apathy that Bostonians had demonstrated. Speaking in Williams Hall, Clarke said that "the eyes of the whole North" had turned toward Boston. Americans, he continued, had wanted to know whether "the tocsin of liberty was to sound out again from Faneuil Hall and State Street." He lamented that Bostonians had disappointed their fellow countrymen and declared, "Oh! What an opportunity has been lost by Boston! . . . [T]he old spirit has left us—the spirit of '76."[39]

The Unitarian minister wanted Bostonians to accept guilt for Burns's return to slavery. "It is not the Commissioners, and the Marshals, and the

Mayors, who have disgraced us. They are but creatures of public sentiment," asserted the minister. "If Boston were unanimous on the side of Freedom and Justice . . . the Commissioners would easily discover the legality of setting free the slave; the Marshals and their followers would soon be of the same mind [and] no more slaves could be carried from Boston."[40]

Clarke directed much of his fire at the "Churches and Clergy of Boston"— clearly meaning the city's white churches and their leaders. "If they had been faithful to their Master," he said, Burns never would have been returned to bondage. He pointed a finger at Unitarians, who "had fallen away" from the "teaching and example" of the famous Dr. William Ellery Channing, but he argued that the blame extended to all Christian churches in Boston and the North. He concluded that "rich churches in commercial cities, whether calling themselves Episcopalians, Presbyterians, or Unitarians, will always have much the same faith, a faith in the Dollar, rather than a faith in God." He surmised that these churches undoubtedly contained some good men and women, but that their "ruling spirit" had become "hard, cold, worldly, and selfish." "We have grown too rich in Boston," Clarke complained. "The rich Boston of 1854 . . . has not the same energy and patriotism as the poor Boston of 1776." Unrestrained materialism had displaced virtue as the governing principle in the city, and Burns's freedom had been sacrificed as a result.[41] Clarke must have felt his criticism vindicated a couple of months later when the Congregationalist churches of New England held an assembly in Connecticut and invited a Virginian clergyman named Dr. William S. Plumer to preach the sermon. Plumer was renowned for hiring out his church's slaves "on every Christmas to the highest bidder" to support himself and the church.[42]

Clarke did not mention, though he may have had in mind, the Reverend Leonard Grimes's inability to collect from wealthy white Bostonians the funds needed to purchase Burns's freedom. Perhaps nothing better demonstrates the apathy of many white Bostonians toward Burns's fate. The black pastor initiated two major attempts to buy Burns's freedom from Suttle before he successfully clinched a deal in the autumn of 1854 with David McDaniel of Rocky Mount, North Carolina, who had purchased Burns from Suttle.

Grimes's first attempt occurred on Saturday, May 27, the day after the courthouse riot, when Suttle agreed to sell Burns for $1,200 on the condition that the deal be closed that day. Although in the end U.S. district attorney Benjamin Hallett made sure that the deal was not completed before midnight by delaying the closing, Grimes, who earnestly tried to raise the funds demanded, had enormous difficulty finding Bostonians who were willing to contribute financially to freeing Burns. The black pastor had much experience in fundraising, and his contacts in the city included some two hundred persons on the Boston Vigilance Committee, who were presumably strongly committed to freeing Burns. Moreover, the wealthy Bostonian Hamilton B. Willis offered to advance the cash to purchase Burns once Grimes obtained sufficient pledges, and Grimes had all Saturday to solicit donors. Even so, the pastor failed to meet the midnight deadline and come up with the $1,200 demanded by Suttle—this in Boston, the thriving financial center of the Northeast.[43]

A deal to buy Burns's liberty might have averted further disturbances in the city. A contribution of less than $6 from each member of the Boston Vigilance Committee would have freed Burns that day; a contribution of $60 from each officer of the Boston Vigilance Committee likewise would have emancipated the Virginian fugitive.[44] Although Boston's merchants, businessmen, and professionals supposedly had been moved by antislavery sentiment, Grimes had little success. The wealthy Amos Lawrence, reputedly converted to abolitionism, refused to contribute. By late Saturday afternoon, in utter desperation, Grimes even solicited a contribution from Benjamin Hallett, President Pierce's main official in Boston. By evening, Grimes had collected only $700, so he set up a meeting with Dana, presumably to solicit funds from the attorney or to ask for his assistance in contacting potential subscribers. Later, having still not collected the necessary pledges, Grimes even turned to the opposing lawyers for aid: as Suttle's midnight deadline passed, it was Suttle's own attorney, Edward Parker, who actually agreed to cover the difference between the pledges that Grimes had obtained and Suttle's purchase price. Presumably the claimant's lawyer, a longtime resident of Boston, recognized the chaos and divisiveness that Burns's trial would cause if it continued. But the slaveholder's deadline had not been met, and Massachusetts law made it illegal to transact business on the Sabbath. After all his efforts in New England's richest metropolis, Grimes had raised only $800 in pledges, and that included contributions from the members of the Twelfth Baptist Church, where he preached.[45]

White Boston's lack of support for Grimes's second major purchase attempt in late June 1854, after Hamilton Willis received a letter from Suttle indicating that he would sell Burns north for $1,500, is even more striking. There was no Benjamin Hallett, Watson Freeman, or Franklin Pierce to interfere with negotiations or block a deal. Sympathy for Burns, if it existed, should have been at its height, given the spectacle of his return and knowledge, widespread at that point, of his confinement in Lumpkin's jail. Again, Grimes asked for pledges, but he was unable to raise the necessary funds from Bostonians—including even small donations from the reputedly ardent antislavery activists on the Boston Vigilance Committee and some Cotton Whigs who supposedly were swept up by antislavery sentiment and sympathy for Burns. In Virginia, Suttle waited for a response from Boston, thinking—as he said in his letter—that the purchase of Burns's freedom could now be supported by "those who struggled to maintain law and order," since the rendition had "fully vindicated" the Fugitive Slave Law.[46] Suttle probably also thought that Burns's confinement in Lumpkin's jail would have increased Bostonian support for a deal. Such was not the case. Suttle received no word from Boston, even after Anthony Burns succeeded in getting a letter to Richard Henry Dana with the help of slaves who worked at Lumpkin's. Burns's letter stated, "I am for Sale" and "if you all [sic] my friends please help your friend."[47] In November, an impatient Suttle sold Burns at auction in Richmond. Burns stood before a taunting crowd for about an hour before David McDaniel purchased him for $905.

The failure of white Bostonians to support Burns's liberation cannot be rationalized by the argument that they opposed dealing with Southern slaveholders on moral grounds. This was true only of a few pacifist abolitionists such as Garrison and moral crusaders like Sumner, who were adamant in refusing to deal with slaveholders. Most white Bostonians showed little hesitation about doing business with those Sumner called the "lords of the lash."[48] Wealthy Cotton Whigs transacted business daily with the slave South. Boston shipbuilders and shipping magnates, iron makers, and manufacturers of wood products constantly dealt in Southern markets. Boston lawyers, accountants, public notaries, and even doctors earned their livelihoods serving individuals and firms carrying on business with the South. Laborers in textile mills and seafarers transformed and transported materials purchased from slaveholders. Finally, educators at colleges such as Harvard sought out the sons and daughters of leading slave owners to bolster enrollments.[49] The notion that moral arguments underlay white Boston's lack of participation in purchasing Burns's freedom simply does not hold for the lion's share of Bostonians. Most city residents identified with the sentiments of the merchant who wrote to Samuel May: "We cannot afford, sir, to let you and your associates endeavor to overthrow slavery. It is not a matter of principles with us. It is a matter of business necessity."[50]

If white Bostonians' apathy about slavery and bias against blacks bothered Sarah Pellet, James Freeman Clarke, and like-minded antislavery activists, it particularly irked black Bostonians, who saw the Burns drama as evidence of continuing white prejudice. Indeed, the city's blacks were convinced that racism remained just as strong an influence on whites as law-and-order sentiments or economic interests. Little had changed in Boston's race relations; white ambivalence about the needs and problems of Boston's black community persisted. While Burns was being held in the courthouse, the black orator Charles Lenox Remond articulated these concerns. Emphasizing that he could not start his speech "by saying 'Fellow Citizens,' because that would be an unwarranted assumption," he spoke explicitly about racism to a largely white Boston audience. His listeners included many members of the New England Antislavery Society. Remond's message must have disturbed the supposedly well-intentioned New Englanders: he told them that racism was the principal reason that the "liberation of Anthony Burns" could not be expected as a "moral certainty."[51]

Remond said that he regretted that it was "necessary for a black man or a red man ever to refer to his complexion on an antislavery platform," but he said that he had little choice. His involvement in antislavery activities for more than eighteen years and his observations of the current drama in Boston proved to him that "every thing hinges on [the] circumstance" of a person's color. Remond told his audience that they needed to ask themselves: "Do we not need to have the complexion of the slave population changed, at least in imagination, to have the [antislavery] work done?" He added that "it is the North that practically keeps [blacks] in slavery," and he suggested to his listeners that if they could "only be black for eight and forty hours," they would understand exactly what he meant.[52]

Remond asserted that whites "do not understand [the] character" of blacks or know the "constant pressure, from our nation's history, which has been exerted on their manhood, their morality, upon all that is noble, magnanimous, and generous in their characters." "God," he stressed, "has made us men." He was certain that if whites recognized blacks as human beings, blacks would conduct themselves in a noble fashion. But Remond said that history and the current crisis in Boston proved that whites were incapable of acknowledging the humanity of blacks. "It has become not only a part of [white education], but almost a part of [white] nature, to look upon the colored man in this country as born to the vile inheritance of slavery, from his cradle to his grave; to have the word *slave* written on his brow." This reality, Remond believed, underpinned a "spirit of negro hate" much in evidence on the streets of Anthony Burns's Boston. Walking the streets of the city, Remond said, he heard men say, "Kick the niggers, drive them out of the country," and "Hustle the niggers out of Court Square." He also heard some white Bostonians complaining about fellow whites who supported the antislavery cause; they called them "the d----d *white niggers.*" He noted that some of the people expressing these sentiments were of Irish origin.[53]

But racism was not confined to Boston's Irish. White Bostonians' persistent resistance to the demands of the city's blacks proved their unwillingness to recognize their neighbors on the poor side of Beacon Hill. Touching on American history, Remond stressed widespread racial prejudice in the North, saying that white racism prevented blacks from sharing in the glory of Bunker Hill, in the "noble deeds" at Lexington, and more generally "in the memory of men who fought and bled for liberty." Blacks, said Remond, were told that a sacred place such as Bunker Hill was "no place for niggers."[54] Theodore Parker shared Remond's concerns. Parker disdained "attempts to erase the memory of black participation" in the American Revolution. He said that "he remembered engravings of the Battle of Bunker Hill in his youth that had shown the black soldier Peter Salem in the act of shooting Major Pitcairn, but noted with disgust that . . . reproductions on banknotes" had replaced Salem with a white soldier.[55]

As Remond suggested, racism pervaded most aspects of white Boston society—sometimes in subtle ways. Even men closely identified with the city's antislavery movement revealed racist attitudes. Visiting the courthouse the morning after Burns's arrest, Dana portrayed the Virginian fugitive as "a piteous object, weak in mind and body." Dana considered him "cowed" and wondered how such an "obscure" figure had captured the nation's attention.[56] Although he defended Burns, Dana later strongly supported Commissioner Loring's decision and federal fugitive slave legislation in the interest of maintaining law and order. Wendell Phillips suggested that Burns had "cowered" and that he was a "helpless object."[57] Other whites identified with the antislavery cause in Boston described Burns as "hapless," "feeble," "miserable," or "wretched."[58] Samuel Gridley Howe even mused that Burns could have elevated himself to martyrdom by committing suicide before the multitudes on the day he was escorted to T Wharf. Treating Burns's fate as a *spectacle,* perhaps a romantic tragedy with an unfortunate black as the central figure, Howe wrote that "had he, then and there, struck a knife into his own heart, he would have killed outright the fugitive slave law in New England & the North."[59]

Such reflections, of course, also implicitly transferred white guilt associated with inaction to a member of the oppressed race who supposedly did not do what he should have—even if it meant taking his own life—to oppose the Fugitive Slave Law. Howe, Dana, and several other leading whites never acknowledged Burns's intellect, literacy, courage, and perseverance—the qualities that had allowed him to survive his ordeal with dignity and later enabled him to fashion a new, albeit short, life as a beloved pastor in Canada. As Remond stressed, white Bostonians kept blacks at arm's length in different ways. Even to an individual like Howe, a key player in the drama, Burns's ordeal remained a spectacle. Boston's most famous white abolitionist, William Lloyd Garrison, even thought Burns should have continued his spectacle before the nation after he became free by accepting P. T. Barnum's offer to go on display at a salary of $100 a week for a minimum of five weeks. Garrison said that it was a pity Burns refused the promoter's offer. Burns, however, was no piteous object; he demonstrated his strength and pride. Insulted by the entrepreneur's offer, he flatly refused it, saying that Barnum "wants to show me like a monkey."[60]

Many ordinary Bostonians as well, some of whom demonstrated support for the antislavery cause, were also often unable to escape or in fact even recognize their racist ways. After the Burns affair, Josiah Quincy, the disillusioned former mayor of Boston, spoke at several meetings with a view to reinvigorating the Free-Soil cause. His worries, however, were not about Burns or his enslaved brethren—not at all—and he said so. In the town of Quincy, he told his audience, "My heart has always been much more affected by the slavery to which the Free States have been subjected, than with that of the [N]egro."[61] His real concern was with the political power exercised by Southern slaveholders, something that became apparent in an address that he delivered in Boston's Music Hall only ten weeks after Burns's return to bondage. During that speaking engagement, Quincy never even mentioned Burns's name but railed against Southern power and revealed disdain for members of Burns's race. "The free states agreed, in 1789, to be field-drivers and pound-keepers for the black cattle of the slaveholding states, within the limits and according to the fences of the old United States," declared the aging Free-Soiler. He complained that the Southern slaveholders "have multiplied their black cattle by millions . . . every day extending their black cattle field into the wilderness." Then he too returned to Boston's legacy of 1776, asking, "[A]re we bound to be their field-drivers and pound-keepers any longer? . . . people of Massachusetts. Are you the sons of the men of 1776? or do you 'lack gall to make oppression bitter?'"[62] The workers at the Mattapan Iron Works, where Burns washed windows in cold, damp March weather, were another example of whites unable to shed their racist ways. They simply "could not imagine a black man [working with them] as a fellow tradesman." For most white Bostonians, irrespective of their occupation or political stripes, Burns remained a member of a caste apart.[63]

While white Bostonians acted out their parts in the Burns drama in a variety of conflicting ways that reflected different commitments to law and order, economic interests, and racial ideologies, black Bostonians drew a special message from the Burns crisis: they had to take care of their own interests. Some, such as William Cooper Nell, who had special ties to white antislavery activists, evinced some hesitancy, but others, including the Reverend Leonard Grimes, quickly embarked on a course independent of their white allies. In fact, despite his cooperation with whites on the Boston Vigilance Committee, Grimes had begun moving in this direction even before the Burns drama, aligning himself with the more militant members of his black congregation, many of whom were fugitive slaves. From 1850 on, working with the likes of Lewis Hayden, the architect of the Shadrach rescue, Grimes stepped up his involvement in hiding fugitives, spiriting them to Canada, and rescuing those who were captured by forcible means, which most law-abiding Boston Vigilance Committee members frowned upon. He sought to tap the financial resources of the city's five black congregations independently of his efforts to raise funds from wealthy white allies. In 1850, he arranged for funding from the black community to purchase the freedom of four members of his congregation, including two deacons who had fled the city after the passage of the new Fugitive Slave Law. Although unable to close a deal, Grimes raised $1,800 to purchase the freedom of Thomas Sims after he was returned to bondage.[64]

The behavior of Grimes's white neighbors during the Burns drama almost certainly reinforced his increasing radicalism and commitment to independent action. Despite their rhetoric and alleged disaffection with the Pierce administration's enforcement of the Fugitive Slave Law, on the night of the courthouse riot, only a handful of Boston whites had demonstrated that they were ready to resist federal authorities intent on upholding fugitive slave legislation.[65] Most of the small group of men who supported Higginson and Stowell were black militants like Hayden, who recognized the weak commitment and ambivalent attitudes of white antislavery Bostonians—people who talked equal rights, invoked higher law, and supposedly embraced the legacy of their forbearers, but who could not be counted on to take a meaningful stand for their black neighbors' rights. Recognizing this, Grimes and other black leaders held several meetings on their own during the Burns crisis and began taking their own initiative, including the printing of handbills and the distribution of messages throughout the community to mobilize support. For example, on Sunday, May 28, Grimes and Deacon Pitts circulated a prayer to the congregations of all Boston churches calling for Burns to be "delivered from his peril" and asked for their support.[66] Grimes's observation of the crowds in Courthouse Square during Burns's confinement undoubtedly confirmed his suspicions about his white neighbors. After the testimony of witnesses ended on May 30, and after Commissioner Loring announced that he would render his decision on June 2, newspaper reports suggested that the "excitement in the vicinity of the Court House was very visibly abated." Interest in Burns's fate diminished; only "200 or 300 persons" lingered in Courthouse Square. Most Bostonians and Anniversary Week participants went about their own business, awaiting the next act in the spectacle.[67]

When the crowds reassembled on June 2, Grimes would have seen little to alter his suspicions. Many crowd members were not "well-disposed" to Burns, nor did they "clamor for his release."[68] According to press reports, most people who mingled about Courthouse Square or gathered along the streets between the courthouse and Boston Harbor were there "from no other motive than that of curiosity."[69] The majority, according to observers, were "respectable citizens, indifferent spectators."[70] Many people willingly and quickly heeded requests from city authorities to "leave those streets" that the mayor declared "necessary to clear temporarily." He ordered Bostonians not "to obstruct or molest any officer, civil or military, in the lawful discharge of his duty."[71] Grimes probably heard or noticed the applause for Mayor Smith when he announced from the courthouse steps "that the laws of the city, the laws of the State, and the laws of the United States SHALL be maintained."[72]

More disconcerting still would have been the many members of the crowd demonstrating proslavery sympathies, along with the *"fifteen hundred men"* of Boston's Bay Street Club and the Columbian Artillery who offered their services to help control the throngs and ensure Burns's return to bondage.[73] When General Edmands's troops formed in the square, they were both applauded and hissed at, but the "cheers predominated."[74] When Phillips and Parker left the courthouse after their final conversations with Burns, some members of the crowd shouted, "[T]here go the murderers of Batchelder."[75] These onlookers included those of the same political stripe as the Bostonians who threatened demonstrations against the abolitionists, including protests outside the homes of Theodore Parker and Wendell Phillips, and others who wrote letters to newspapers demanding the incarceration of antislavery activists, and still others who supported the assault on Dana in front of Allen's Oyster Saloon on the corner of Court and Stoddard streets for his having acted as counsel for Burns. Some people even thought the outspoken Free-Soil senator Charles Sumner should be held "responsible" for the courthouse riot.[76]

If Grimes followed the crowd to the docks to watch Burns step aboard the *John Taylor,* he must have experienced mixed emotions when the troops struck up the tune of "Carry Me Back to Old Virginny," and many onlookers cheered or applauded as they caught a "parting glimpse" of a now-famous slave.[77] It was a spectacle, and they were there. The Burns rendition was not a minstrel show, but white Bostonians, like most nineteenth-century Americans, loved entertainment. The spectacle, however, came at the expense of Burns and the interests of Grimes's black community in Boston. Black Bostonians had no choice but to strike out on their own and look after their interests.[78]

Rather than reflecting a groundswell of abolitionist sentiment that spurred the march toward civil war and the extirpation of slavery, the Burns drama represented a spectacle that exposed and even confirmed the racism of many white Bostonians; the ambivalence, indifference, and even cowardice of many antislavery whites; and the embrace of law-and-order sentiments by Bostonians of different political stripes. The message for black Bostonians was that they had to take care of their own interests—something that they already had begun to do. To borrow Albert Von Frank's words, if there was a "pocket revolution," this evidence suggests that it was not in Emerson's Boston; rather, it was centered in what white Bostonians derogatorily referred to as Nigger Hill, and it had the support of only a few white radicals such as Theodore Parker, Thomas Wentworth Higginson, and Martin Stowell. Other shows of white support were limited to rowdiness in Court Square, including window smashing by misfits who enjoyed throwing rocks, bricks, and other objects, and speeches, which often were not backed up by action. After the enactment of the Fugitive Slave Law of 1850, black Boston's pocket revolution gained momentum with the Shadrach rescue before encountering public criticism and opposition from the forces of law and order during the Sims crisis. The Burns drama thrust black Boston's pocket revolution into the national spotlight, but it also proved to black Bostonians that they could not count on their white neighbors.[79]

In the months following Burns's return to bondage, Grimes took this message to heart. When he learned of Burns's whereabouts in the autumn of 1854 from the Reverend G. S. Stockwell of Amherst, who had a parishioner with relatives in Rocky Mount, North Carolina, Grimes did not take to the streets of white Boston to raise the $1,300 required to purchase Burns's freedom, as he had done before. Rather, Grimes closed the deal in great measure with small contributions from poor black Bostonians, including members of his Twelfth Baptist Church. These contributions were probably supplemented by blacks from the surrounding countryside, some of the "400 from New Bedford" about the courthouse that week and those who came from Worcester with Stowell.[80]

In addition to sending a message to black Boston, the Burns drama served as a call for independent, unified action by black communities throughout the North. Because of their color and shared oppression, many Northern blacks felt their fate was closely tied to that of Burns. They cringed at a spectacle to which most of their white neighbors were at best indifferent. They could take away but one message from the drama—the same one that Grimes had taken away. Always in the shadow of the South's peculiar institution, Northern blacks were caught in the "labyrinth" of federal fugitive slave legislation and many white Northerners' embrace of law and order, proslavery economic interests, and racism. Burns's fate showed them that they simply had to unite, build their own institutions, and look out for themselves. Several black leaders quickly articulated this challenge.[81] Speaking in Columbus, Ohio, the black orator James Watkins discussed the Burns drama and concluded, "We have, as a people, depended upon the abolitionists to do that for us, which we *must* do for ourselves. . . . We must disapprove the allegation of our innate inferiority. This cannot be done by *proxy.*"[82]

Frederick Douglass declared that African Americans had "a special mission to perform in the United States—a mission which none but themselves could perform." The Boston of Anthony Burns had just proved it: justice and liberty had been silenced—at least for persons of color. After what he had seen, Douglass concluded that "slavery has a right to go any where in this Republic and Liberty no where, except where Slavery will let it." Embittered by the Pierce administration's policies, Douglass reserved harsh words for those supposedly sympathetic white Bostonians who had demonstrated their ambivalence, their law-and-order leanings, and their ties to the interests of the slaveholding South. They had permitted Burns's return to slavery; they had acted to preserve the fruits they had reaped from the Revolution of 1776, not to extend that revolution for the benefit of African Americans.[83]

"Now let all true patriotic Christian Republicans rejoice and be glad," Douglass wrote with bitter sarcasm. "The example of the model republic still shines refulgently, to the confusion of tyrants and oppressors in Europe.

After a mighty struggle . . . the arms of the Republic have gloriously succeeded in capturing Anthony Burns. . . . Under the Star Spangled Banner, on the deck of our gallant war ship Morris, the said Burns, whose liberation would have perhaps sent asunder our Model republic, has been safely conveyed to slavery and chains."[84] In the turbulent 1850s, the Burns drama had different meanings for different people. For black Bostonians, it was a call to action—their own action.

CHAPTER 5

A Call to Action in Virginia

There can be no confidence between the two sections of the country as long
as it shall be required to call on the armed forces of the General Government
to enforce a reluctant and constrained obedience to the laws which have been
passed for our protection.
—Richmond Enquirer, *June 2, 1854*

The greatest strength of the South arises from the harmony of her political and
social institutions. This harmony gives her a frame of society, the best in the
world . . . such as no other people ever enjoyed upon the face of the earth.
—*James Hammond*

If the Anthony Burns drama aroused and united blacks throughout the
North, it also served as a call to action for many slaveholding Virginians
and other whites in the South. Undoubtedly President Franklin Pierce
thought that decisive action in support of the Fugitive Slave Law, particularly
the commitment of U.S. troops and financial resources to return Burns to his
master, would set white Southerners at ease and make them feel secure in the
Union.[1] He probably remembered that a few years earlier, during the debates
surrounding the Compromise of 1850, many Southerners had embraced the
series of resolutions that became known as the Georgia Platform, which
declared that the Union could only be preserved by "a faithful execution of
the *Fugitive Slave Law.*"[2] John Reuben Thompson, the renowned editor of
the *Southern Literary Messenger,* supported this position and argued that it
was consistent with that taken by the Founding Fathers in Philadelphia in
1787. "No man of sound mind can read the Debates of the Convention that
framed the Constitution," wrote Thompson, "and not be convinced that
without the clause for the rendition of fugitive slaves, no compact could
have been formed between our ancestors. And surely when that compact is
set at naught—when we can no longer safely repose under its over-arching
canopy—when bad, base men, with the lie upon their lips, withhold from
us what it clearly prescribes, it will be time to dissever the bonds that unite
us as the fetters of an ignominious thralldom."[3] The *Lynchburg Republican,* a Whig paper, concluded, "Should the compromise of 1850, carrying

with it the constitutional provision for the restoration of fugitive slaves be 'swept away' that will be sufficient cause for the withdrawal of the Southern States."[4] North Carolina's legendary editor William W. Holden also pushed the Georgia Platform. Like many North Carolinians, he had supported the Compromise of 1850 as "a final settlement of sectional differences." In his *North Carolina Standard,* he sent a message to Northerners, saying, "Let the question of slavery alone; take it out and keep it out of Congress; and respect and enforce the Fugitive Slave Law as it stands. If not, *we leave you!* Before God and man . . . if you fail in this simple act of justice the bonds shall be dissolved."[5]

But Pierce was only partially right in believing that faithful execution of the Fugitive Slave Law would appease the South; he soon found out that his intervention in the Burns affair would strike many below the Mason-Dixon line as necessary but not sufficient. Some white Southerners did breathe a sigh of relief after hearing about Commissioner Loring's decision to certify Suttle's claim and return Burns to bondage. In North Carolina, the *Fayette-ville Observer* published a celebratory article and congratulated the forces of law and order. "We rejoice to find that the law has triumphed," declared the *Observer.* "All honor to the Mayor of Boston, the U.S. Marshal and Commissioner, and the militia of the city, who have nobly done their duty, in defiance of popular clamor."[6] In a similar vein, H. W. Allen of Louisiana, a friend of both Charles Suttle and William Brent, sent a letter of thanks commending the Pierce administration and praising the U.S. military and Boston police for having tightly guarded Burns in the courthouse.[7] Some of Richmond's leading citizens gave an elaborate banquet for the marshals who escorted Burns from Boston to Lumpkin's jail.[8] But surprisingly few Virginians and their white neighbors in other Southern states really celebrated; those who did, did not rejoice for long. Despite their approval of the firm stance of President Pierce and Boston's Mayor Smith, many Southerners were very perturbed.

The first thing that bothered many of them was the substantial amount of resources that federal and civic authorities had needed to muster in order to ensure Burns's return to bondage. For them, the show of force and the exorbitant costs required to overcome Northern abolitionists' resistance to the Fugitive Slave Law represented a direct affront to slavery and clashed with their embrace of Jeffersonian ideals of limited government. Charles C. Jones Jr., a young Southerner who was studying law at Harvard and attended the Burns trial, wrote to his father at Maybank Plantation in Georgia that the courthouse was "filled with armed men." Jones said that "even the counsel at bar have their revolvers and bowie knives." He described the area surrounding the courthouse, saying that "the passages are strictly guarded night and day by the military, of whom over one hundred marines from the navy yard are garrisoned in the courthouse proper, besides two other companies, while the city hall contains four volunteer companies ordered out by the mayor." Jones added, "Hourly are the streets opened around the courthouse and cleared of the mob by companies marching in solid columns for that purpose. . . . The halls of justice are literally thronged with armed men. [A] singular and I may say [an] awful sight!"[9]

The situation in Boston reminded many white Southerners of John C. Calhoun's famous warning to slaveholders. In his last Senate speech on March 4, 1850, which had been read to that body by Virginia's own James Mason because of the South Carolinian's failing health, Calhoun declared that the Union was "endangered." Emphasizing the need for the federal government to protect Southern interests in the face of the rapid growth of the antislavery North, which he said undermined the previous "equilibrium between the two sections," Calhoun predicted that agitation against slavery would "snap every cord" in the Union. He concluded that force alone could not hold the states together and questioned whether the Union could "be called a Union, when the only means by which the weaker [South] is held connected with the stronger portion is *force*."[10]

Four years after Calhoun's speech, white Virginians and their neighbors throughout the South read with dismay about the Burns crisis and Northern abolitionists' denunciations of slaveholders, which Southern newspapers, including influential Democratic papers such as the *Richmond Enquirer,* founded and edited by Thomas Ritchie, frequently published.[11] The reports grated against Southerners' pride and political culture, making some more determined than ever to defend what they believed to be their constitutional right to enjoy the fruits of the labor of their human property and to assert the superiority of the Southern way of life. Coming on the heels of the Kansas-Nebraska crisis, the disorder in Boston and the abolitionist tirades seemed to foreshadow the demise of what remained of the Compromise of 1850 and alienated Virginians as well as other Southern whites from Northerners. Following the Burns drama, B. J. Barbour of Orange County, Virginia, delivered a lengthy address to the Literary Societies of the Virginia Military Institute attacking Northerners and their "morbid philanthropy and calculating humanity, which takes a fugitive slave for its hero, drapes a city in mourning when the constitution is obeyed, appeals to a higher law for revenge, and flies with cowardly terror . . . with blood on its hands and scripture on its lips, to lift the assassin's knife and light the incendiary's torch"—a reference to the death of the guard James Batchelder during the courthouse riot.[12] Published in the widely read *Southern Literary Messenger,* Barbour's address reached an audience throughout the South.

Southerners' tendencies to overestimate the strength of Northern abolitionism, often fueled by outspoken politicians such as James Mason and Robert M. T. Hunter, who embraced the cause of Southern rights in Virginia, exacerbated the impact of threatening assessments such as Barbour's.[13] Furthermore, after the Burns drama in Boston, many Southern newspapers printed articles describing what some Southerners came to believe was a veritable groundswell of antislavery sentiment and activity in the North. In North Carolina, for example, the *Daily Register* spoke of the "fantastic follies" of Burns's sympathizers and how Marshal Watson Freeman had narrowly escaped "through showers of brick bats" from an abolitionist mob. The paper said that this assault was more evidence of the "riotous and disgraceful proceedings of the Boston Abolitionists," lawless men who earlier had "deliberately stained their hands in the blood of one of the deputy Marshals."[14] In Savannah, the *Daily Morning News* denounced the "bloody demonstration of abolitionism" and the "mob spirit in Boston." The paper indicated that "inflammatory circulars" that Burns's sympathizers sent throughout New England had stirred "large delegations of abolitionists."[15]

Elsewhere, the *Charleston Mercury* culled antislavery rhetoric from columns of the *National Era,* convincing South Carolinians of the "rapid growth and development of the Abolitionism feeling at the North."[16] In Columbia, the *Daily South Carolinian* described the abolitionist mob during the drama in Boston as "formidable" and emphasized their "hisses and cries of shame" on the day of Burns's return to bondage. A week later, the paper's editor said that reports from Massachusetts indicated no "abatement in the anti-Southern feeling in Boston since the rendition of Burns," and he criticized the "solid men of Boston" who continued to display antislavery sympathies. The editor also suggested that some "nine-tenths" of the soldiers, militia, and citizen volunteers who had maintained order and escorted Burns to the docks actually harbored antislavery sympathies.[17] From the Burns crisis onward, the Southern press fueled the specter of rising abolitionism in the North. On the eve of the Civil War, Edmund Ruffin attached a clipping of an article that he wrote for the *Charleston Mercury* to his diary. It stated, "Every year the anti-slavery majority is increased, and every year there is, and will be, one or more new non-slaveholding, and therefore, future abolition States, added to the Union."[18]

Even the *Richmond Whig*, which was typically much more restrained than its Democratic counterparts, the *Richmond Enquirer* and the *Charleston Mercury*, joined in the chorus. In the wake of the Burns affair, the *Richmond Whig* struck out against the supposedly growing number of antislavery Conscience Whigs in the free states, who, it argued, "mislead the Whig masses of the North . . . into the support of Free Soil doctrine." Conscience Whigs and their Northern presses, asserted the *Whig*, had fanned the flames of fanaticism as well as the "more filibusterish spirit and movements of a huge part of the North."[19] Similarly, the *Lynchburg Virginian* assailed Northern abolitionists—and suggested that their ranks were growing. "It is not enough for them to have exhibited their demented and demonic hostility to the South by every species of villainy in action and falsehood in argument—by every imaginable trick to circumvent, defraud and debase her—by introducing anarchy and revolution into the halls of Congress and practicing rebellion and treason in the streets of Boston," proclaimed the paper's editor, "but they must keep alive the vile passions upon which they have so long played by renewed appeals to sectional prejudice and animosity." The events in Burns's Boston had convinced him that it was now the "time for those who occupy the posts of sentinels in the South to sound the alarm." Indeed, only two weeks later, he concluded that "the whole history of the slavery question has been a prolonged insult to the South." Despite Southerners' respect of the Union's "glorious past," they now had to acknowledge that on the slavery issue, they "have appealed in vain."[20]

Letters from friends and relatives of Southerners visiting or temporarily residing in the North sometimes augmented the anxiety and fears such newspaper editorials and reports produced. For example, Charles Jones Jr. wrote his anxious father in Georgia saying that "for [the] two days I have been present in the courthouse attending this trial . . . mob law, *perjury, free-soilism*, and *abolitionism* . . . [have been] *running riot*." Such letters again sounded alarms. Jones warned of the effects of the "war of words"; in his opinion, words had become "incendiary in their character, bitter against the South, Southern men, Southern institutions, and particularly vehement upon topics of 'Chains and Slavery,' [the] Nebraska Bill, [and the] Fugitive Slave Law."[21] In this context, the Burns crisis had a two-sided message for many white Southerners: although they could take solace in Pierce's decisiveness in supporting the Fugitive Slave Law in 1854, with the South's political influence on the wane, they certainly could not count on future presidents to defend their rights with the same determination.

Like the debates over Senator Stephen Douglas's proposal to repeal the Missouri Compromise and adopt the principle of popular sovereignty to resolve the sectional deadlock on bondage in the territories, the Burns crisis revolved around slavery. But this time the controversy involved slavery in the South, not hypothetical slavery in an undeveloped West.[22] Simply put, the Burns affair turned the gaze of antebellum Americans on the South, bringing Southern society and its peculiar institution more sharply into focus. Both Southerners and Northerners saw the South as a distinct society at the center of which, of course, was slavery; the issue was no longer only about whether the institution of slavery should be allowed to extend westward. What is especially important, however, is that in their introspection many white Southerners became increasingly proud of their distinct society and saw it as distinctly good; this, as we shall see, encouraged their embrace of slavery as a "positive good."[23] The Burns crisis played an instrumental role in this process.

The Burns affair also prompted many white Virginians to rethink their commitment to the Union, something that many had hesitated to do even during the tension-filled days leading up to the Compromise of 1850, when some Southern leaders advocated disunion.[24] Astonishingly, within weeks of the Burns drama, a large number of Virginians, like many white Southerners in neighboring states, appeared to have completely changed the way they viewed the Union. Regardless of whether they had previously interpreted the Compromise of 1850 as the Union's salvation, a call for peace, or simply an "armistice," they viewed the Burns crisis as a signal that things had changed—and not for the better.[25] For many Virginians, now it was time to think about the South.

On May 26, 1854, two days after Burns's arrest and only twenty-four hours after the Boston Vigilance Committee began posting handbills declaring that kidnappers had taken another fugitive slave, the *Richmond Enquirer* assailed Northern abolitionists and the *New York Tribune*. The latter had evinced a strong antislavery bent in reporting on the Kansas-Nebraska crisis. Not only did the *Enquirer* brand the New York paper as nothing more than an abolitionist mouthpiece; ominously, the Richmond paper now revived the option of Southern independence that had been put aside after the Compromise of 1850. It ran a hard-hitting editorial underscoring the economic advantages that the North allegedly enjoyed within the Union, which the editor now denounced as an "instrument of Northern aggrandizement." He argued that Northern development had come at the expense of the South. Moreover, the continuing agitation in the free states proved that abolitionism had gone too far. "Yankee shopkeepers" who benefited from the Union even while waging a "relentless war against slavery" would have only themselves to blame if the nation splintered along the Mason-Dixon line. By allowing abolitionists to continue their agitation, Northern industrialists were about to "kill the goose that lays the golden egg."[26] The *Enquirer* conveyed a message that was also put out by the *Daily South Carolinian*—the Burns drama in Boston had made it clear that disunion was now being "forced upon us."[27]

Surveying the turmoil in the North, the *Enquirer* told its readers not to fear disunion and assured them that the South was "fully competent to the protection of its own interests and to the development of its own great destinies without the cooperation of Northern abolitionists." The editor also observed that "recent developments have diffused and strengthened the conviction [for disunion], with the mass of the Southern people. Men of timid and conservative disposition stand now where stood the most ultra in 1850."[28] Continuing agitation in the North—radicals breaking down the doors of the Boston courthouse while Anthony Burns's sympathizers and indifferent spectators looked on and abolitionist preachers thundered from their pulpits in the name of higher law—proved that Southern nationalists, men who had questioned the viability of the Union, had been right all along.[29] The South should not shrink from a violent or desperate struggle but rather accept the "challenge to mortal combat without dismay." Issuing a veritable call to arms, the editor declared that men of the South "know the desperate designs of the enemy, and they witness the formidable preparations for the execution of his vengeance. If they still hesitate and parley, they are not dupes but traitors."[30]

The *Enquirer* interpreted abolitionist rhetoric and agitation not merely as a challenge to Southern interests and rights but as ridicule and defamation. In the midst of the Burns hearing, it reported that "such an execution of the Fugitive Slave Law, as that which we witness in Boston, is a mockery and an insult." It also argued that "denunciations of slavery and pathetic pictures" of the mistreatment of bond persons in Northern papers had irresponsibly inflamed the passions of the mob and "incited the rabble to riot." Southern property rights were not any better protected under the Fugitive Slave Law of 1850 than they had been before. Boston had proved itself to be a city where a master had "to plead like a culprit before a jury of abolitionists."[31] After Burns's trial, many Southerners shared this view. Indeed, Charles Jones Jr. expressed anger at seeing Charles Suttle become the target of "vile epithets" simply because he claimed his property. Writing from Boston to his father at Maybank Plantation, he exclaimed, "You have no idea what he [Charles

Suttle] endured and what indignities he is still forced to suffer at the hands of the thousand miserable monomaniacs by whom he is surrounded." Jones also pointed out that he felt "an attachment as only a Southerner can know for his brother Southerner when he finds him in a land of abolitionists, conspiring not only against his property but his *life*."[32]

Only days later, while the vessel carrying Burns was still in Northern waters and abolitionists continued to rail against Commissioner Loring's decision, the *Enquirer* reiterated its secessionist stance in a lengthy article titled "The Boston Riot—Southern Rights." A stinging attack not only on abolitionists but also on "the better portion of the people of Boston," the piece called on white Southerners to take stock, draw the only conclusion possible, and prepare to leave the Union. The *Enquirer* emphasized that most of Boston's supposedly law-abiding citizens had shown that they were ready to stand by and watch Southerners be robbed of their rights.[33] As the *Weekly Raleigh Register* put it, Boston's supposedly better sorts had been witness to the "trampling [of] the laws [protecting a Southerner's property rights] under foot in the most outrageous and violent manner." Furthermore, many newspapers noted that this was not the first time that reckless abolitionists had abused a Southerner's rights; such scenes, they said, had been "acted over and over again" and were often "winked at" by law-abiding citizens and authorities in the North.[34] In these circumstances, any self-respecting Southerner had to take a stand. "Our connection with the North cannot be maintained," proclaimed the editor of the *Enquirer*. "There can be no confidence between the two sections of the country as long as it shall be required to call on the armed forces of the *General Government* to enforce a reluctant and constrained obedience to the laws which have been passed for our protection." Events in Boston proved that patience was no longer a virtue; patriotism and self-interest required that Southerners "sever a connexion which is maintained only for their oppression and their degradation."[35]

Slaveholders throughout Virginia revealed growing concern about the abolitionists' attacks on the Fugitive Slave Law and Northerners' apparent lack of respect for Southern interests, which they also saw as contributing to the need to use the military to enforce the Fugitive Slave Law. The Burns drama had proved this. In Elizabeth City County, residents convened a special public meeting during the week of June 16, 1854, and criticized Northerners for the apathy and indifference that they had shown throughout the Burns crisis. These citizens also commended President Pierce and Mayor Smith for their decisiveness. They clearly agreed with Charles Jones's conclusion that "the powerful military force on the ground and the efficient disposition of the soldiers is all that prevented Boston from becoming one miserable arena of riot, blood, and lawlessness."[36] But the Elizabeth City County residents were deeply troubled by what they believed had gone on in Boston, and they expressed disappointment that the enforcement of the Fugitive Slave Law had necessitated calling out the troops. At the close of their meeting, they issued a "solemn warning" suggesting that "the enforcement of law by the bayonet cannot long continue."[37]

Accentuating such concerns were growing suspicions among many white Virginians that Northern and Southern societies were simply too different to be reconciled within the Union. The Kansas-Nebraska debates had proved that sectional differences transcended constitutional issues; disagreements between Northerners and Southerners on Stephen Douglas's popular sovereignty proposal reflected very different visions of the societies to be created in the territories. The Burns case reminded Southerners of the clash between the Fugitive Slave Law and personal liberty laws enacted by free states, but because the drama unfolded in one of the North's wealthiest and most heavily populated cities, it also seemed to magnify the societal differences between the sections, which a new generation of proslavery thinkers had already begun to stress. Preoccupied with disparities between the Northern and Southern systems, a new and diverse group of Southern spokesmen that included George Fitzhugh, Josiah Nott, and Edmund Ruffin stepped forward to influence white Southerners as they weighed their options. With the passing of John C. Calhoun, other leading politicians such as James Hammond, Alexander Stephens, and Jefferson Davis helped disseminate these men's ideas across the South.[38] In Virginia, politicians such as James Mason, Robert M. T. Hunter, and Henry A. Wise convincingly extolled the virtues of the South.[39] The Burns crisis served as a critical test of the ideology of slavery as a positive good.

The focus of white Southerners on the distinctive features of their biracial society and the differences between the North and the South was not in itself new. In his *Notes on the State of Virginia,* Thomas Jefferson had wrestled with the question of whether the black and white races could live together after emancipation, underscoring his fears of "deep-rooted prejudices entertained by whites" and "ten thousand recollections, by the blacks, of the injuries they have sustained."[40] At the time of the Missouri Compromise of 1820, Thomas R. Dew, president of the College of William and Mary, argued that the differences between the races and the rapid growth of the slave population in the South made slavery a "necessary evil."[41] Suggesting that blacks were backward and inferior, he contended that because it would not be possible to colonize the entire population of blacks if slavery were to be abolished, there was a vital social role for slavery—the black slave had to be civilized and readied for freedom.[42] Dew argued that "liberty [had] been the heaviest curse to the slave, when given too soon." Believing that Virginia's enslaved blacks were not ready for emancipation, he contended that freedom "would check at once that progress of improvement which is now so manifest among them."[43]

In the wake of the black abolitionist David Walker's militant denunciation of slavery in his *Appeal to the Coloured Citizens of the World* and Nat Turner's Revolt in Virginia in 1831, which reminded white Virginians of their vulnerability to insurrections, social concerns again underpinned Southerners' defense of slavery.[44] Apologists for slavery portrayed Northern abolitionists as irresponsible "fanatics." Men such as William Lloyd Garrison, white Southerners insisted, did not understand the South; their doctrines threatened the stability of the social order and endangered the lives of whites.[45]

As Northern cities grew and crime rates, disease, intemperance, urban riots, and other social problems increased, Southern spokesmen continued to stress the differences between the North and the predominantly rural South, which they saw as much more stable and wholesome. In the 1830s, some, including Richard Colfax, sought to insulate the South from developments in the North and raised the specter of what they considered to be Northern degeneracy spilling over the Mason-Dixon line.[46] Colfax argued that the goal of preserving an appropriate social order was central to the South's well-being. He advanced pseudoscientific theories suggesting that blacks were inherently inferior and needed to be controlled for their own benefit as well as that of society. He believed the Old South had found the appropriate social order and needed to guard it carefully.[47] After Parliament abolished slavery throughout the British Empire in 1833, white Southerners who feared strong ties between abolitionists in the North and those in Britain increasingly shared this view. They warned of impending social disorder, blamed abolitionists for social strife in the North, and argued that the threat to Southern stability justified clamping down on the distribution of antislavery literature by mail and the gag rule adopted in 1836 to silence antislavery petitions sent to Congress.[48]

From the Burns crisis until the outbreak of the Civil War, the defense of slavery as a positive good, born in the 1830s, became widespread in the South, and its exponents took pains to expose the alleged flaws in Northern society. No longer was slavery merely a necessary evil; as a contributor to the

Southern Literary Messenger boldly stated one month after the Burns crisis, "the doctrine . . . that moral evil is inherent in slavery is altogether fanciful and untenable."[49] Indeed, like many white Virginians, he now argued that slavery made the South a better society. This defense evolved into a "coherent philosophy" that spoke to white Southerners' desires to protect their social order and strike a balance between tradition and progress.[50] In an era of increased literacy, a flourishing print culture, and an active partisan press, reviews such as the *Southern Literary Messenger* and newspapers such as the *Richmond Enquirer* and the *Richmond Whig* became vehicles for Virginians of all political allegiances to put forth their views and strengthen the defense of slavery as a positive good, making it a movement that united people through common beliefs, shared fears, and a growing alienation from the North. In the post-Burns period, Southern newspapers often borrowed from each other, reprinting articles advocating slavery as a positive good. The *Charleston Mercury,* for example, reprinted a *New Orleans Delta* editorial stating that "black slavery is a blessing—indeed, an institution indispensable to the South." It was a positive good; as the paper claimed in another editorial, a better institution "more promotive, in the long run, of human happiness had yet [to be] discovered."[51] The Burns crisis catalyzed this process.[52]

As the movement gained momentum, the leading defenders of slavery did not always agree with each other. Some of Fitzhugh's contemporaries regarded him as too extreme and initially hesitated to support his views.[53] Despite their differences, however, the new generation of white Southern spokesmen remained united by their embrace of slavery as a positive good and, in this regard, they spoke, through their diversity, with one voice. Their differences often helped to fuel debate, promoted correspondence between them, and inspired public discussion about the merits of the Southern order with slavery at its center.

Fitzhugh's comprehensive theories of society made him an especially key player. Hurriedly completed and published in the same year as the Burns drama, his *Sociology for the South, or The Failure of Free Society* was timely, particularly as he juxtaposed turmoil in the North against an ordered South.[54] Fitzhugh rejected the theories of John Locke, free trade, and the democratic agrarianism that underpinned Jefferson's vision for the South, to which many Virginians still clung. He argued that slavery lent stability to Southern society by providing a hierarchical, almost organic, order that assigned everyone an appropriate station in life but ensured that even the weakest members of society—slaves and poor whites—would be cared for by enlightened planters who looked out for their extended families and blessed their dependents with the familial affection that radiated from the big house.[55] Such beneficence contrasted sharply with what Fitzhugh saw in the free states, where, he argued, "crime and pauperism had increased," and "riots, trade unions, strikes for higher wages, discontent breaking out into revolution are things of daily occurrence."[56] Newspaper accounts constantly emphasized such themes and carefully reminded Southerners of the uniqueness of their social order. Drawing on Fitzhugh's theories, the *Charleston Mercury* asserted that "all the riots, incendarism, and revolutions of Europe, for seventy years, have been the direct and immediate consequences of the privations and famine of the poor. The history of the English Poor Laws, if investigated alone, will show that free society in Europe has been from the first, and throughout, to this day, a cruel, awful, and appalling failure."[57]

Interest in *Sociology for the South* positioned Fitzhugh to make his views known throughout the South. Between 1854 and the publication of his most famous work, *Cannibals All!* in 1857, his fame grew as he contributed articles to the *Richmond Examiner,* the *Richmond Enquirer,* and *DeBow's Review.* Fitzhugh's denunciation of Adam Smith became central to his critique of the North and his defense of the Southern way of life. He assailed laissez-faire economics and wage labor, arguing that free society was anything but free for most people, that capitalism was inherently unstable, and that Northern financiers and industrialists, whom Fitzhugh accused in *Cannibals All!* of living in "ten times the luxury" of Southern masters burdened with the care of their slaves, particularly the children, the aged, and the infirm, were the worst kinds of masters. He said that factory workers in the North were "slaves without a master" and declared that "the free laborer must work or starve. He is more of a slave than the Negro."[58] Some commentators, of course, drew on Fitzhugh's observations to emphasize the condition of the many free blacks in the North who were impoverished and thus had been "*injured*" by emancipation and the defective order in the free states.[59]

Fitzhugh was perhaps influenced by the Virginian agrarian reformer Edmund Ruffin, who had published *The Political Economy of Slavery.* According to Ruffin, one of the many benefits of the institution of slavery was its capacity to cushion bonded workers from the effects of economic, political, and natural crises. "When temporary evils, great loss, and distress, fall upon slaveholding countries, it is not the laboring class (as in free society) that feels the first and heaviest infliction, but the masters and employers," wrote Ruffin. "If a slaveholding country is visited by dearth, ravaged by war, or by pestilence—or suffers under any other causes of widespread calamity—every domestic slave is as much as before assured of his customary food and other allowances, and of the master's care in sickness and infirmity, even though the master class, and the country at large, have but half the previously existing profits, or value of capital."[60] Fitzhugh borrowed little from contemporary racists such as Josiah Nott, who expanded on Colfax's doctrines, which rooted the defense of slavery in the alleged inferiority of blacks. In fact, Fitzhugh argued that slavery did not need the excuse of racial difference to make it the optimal form of labor and, indeed, that enslavement need not be confined to blacks.

In defending slavery as a positive good, leading politicians typically drew on several strands of thought, including Fitzhugh's. In his infamous "Mud-Sill Speech," James Hammond, one of the most outspoken defenders of the South's peculiar institution, took from both Fitzhugh and Nott. "In all social systems," said the senator from South Carolina, "there must be a class to do the menial duties, to perform the drudgery of life. That is, a class requiring but a low order of intellect and but little skill. Its requisites are vigor, docility, fidelity. Such a class you must have, or you would not have that other class which leads progress, civilization, and refinement." The latter was Fitzhugh's benevolent planter class. Hammond, however, also shared some of Nott's most distasteful ideas. "Fortunately for the South," he said, "she found a race adapted to that purpose. . . . A race inferior to her own, but eminently qualified in temper, in vigor, in docility, in capacity to stand the climate, to answer all her purposes. We use them for our purpose, and call them slaves. We found them slaves by the common 'consent of mankind,' which, according to Cicero, *lex naturae est* [is the law of nature]."[61]

As the Burns drama made the social differences between North and South loom large for influential white Southerners, newspapers such as the *Enquirer* made the defense of slavery as a positive good a staple of popular discourse among white Virginians, fueled readers' concerns about whether sectional differences could be reconciled within the existing political framework, advocated Southern rights, and reignited the secessionist impulse. On June 7, 1854, the *Richmond Enquirer* published an editorial arguing that the Boston riot revealed the "disease and corruption inherent in the social system of the Northern States," which led to disorder, generalized discontent, and even anarchy. It suggested that the social development of the North fostered "vicious principles . . . at the expense of the deeper and more solid virtues," and that Northerners now reaped the consequences of a defective order that promoted urbanization and wage labor, which both contributed to fanaticism and social chaos. The paper stressed that "in a city, the growth of the vices is stimulated with unnatural rapidity, and the social diseases which they engender are propagated by contagion." Such arguments appealed to many property-owning Virginians and seemed to be consistent with sectional disparities in demography and the rising incidence of urban crime in the North. On the eve of the Burns crisis, cities accounted for about 40 percent of the Northern population but less than 5 percent in some Southern states, and ordinary Americans everywhere worried about the astounding number of deaths in urban riots, which they believed reflected more than "random crime or growing pockets of poverty in northern cities."[62]

Addressing the system of wage labor in the North, the *Enquirer* noted that "the laboring population, instead of constituting an element of social stability and strength, are themselves the most active agents of discontent and disorganization." Invariably, Northern workers fell under the influence of irresponsible leaders: "[T]he *prolétaire* and the demagogue burn with an equal desire for change, excitement and agitation."[63] Virginia's less extreme newspapers shared many of these sentiments. The *Lynchburg Republican*, for example, spoke of the "ravings of the North," "anarchy," and "vile passions"— all allegedly seen on the "streets of Boston."[64] On June 7, 1854, before Burns had even arrived back in Virginia, the *Enquirer* seized upon such images of disorder in the North to drive home its message. The state of affairs in Boston, said the paper, contrasted with the situation in the slaveholding South, where "the impulse of labor combines with the discerning instinct of intellect and education in maintaining the supremacy of order."[65] In short, the wisdom and intimacy of the benevolent master at the head of his extended plantation family lent stability and made the Southern order more attractive.

Against this background, the *Enquirer* took the position that "not only is the South a loser in a commercial point of view, from its connexion with the North, but it is exposed to the evil influence of Northern fanaticism and vice" that had loomed so large in the Burns affair. Clearly, if the Union's status quo were maintained, social intercourse and political relations between the sections would corrupt Southern society. "A rigid quarantine," the paper stated, "can alone save us from infection."[66] Secession was the answer—and it was a position that even the *Lynchburg Republican*, a paper that claimed to be "tolerant and patient" and previously "never had one pulsation or feeling in common with Southern incendiaries and disunionists," was also ready to embrace on June 7, 1854.[67]

By no means were all the Virginians who were disturbed by the events in Boston in 1854 ready to call for Southern independence, but even avowed conservatives demanded change and called at least for preparedness. A few days after recommending a cultural and political quarantine between the sections, the *Enquirer* printed a lengthy letter from a Virginia farmer under the heading "The Boston Riot—the Duty of Virginians." Following in the celebrated Revolutionary tradition of John Dickinson, the Virginia farmer sketched the course that he believed was necessary in the wake of the Burns drama.[68] Declaring that Virginians would never unlawfully seize Northern property, he denounced the attempted rescue of Burns by Northern abolitionists and by "the people of Boston [who were ready] to rob a Virginian of his slave."[69] He repeated the conclusions arrived at in other newspaper editorials that even the better sorts in Boston had stood aside to watch abolitionists thwart a Virginian in his "prosecution of his lawful rights."[70] The Virginia farmer also argued that Northerners invariably revealed their true values when they became slaveholders. Never, he said, did native Virginians treat their slaves as harshly as Yankees did when they moved to the South and acquired slaves. He said he knew of a Yankee "who will sell or buy a negro to make twenty dollars" and believed in locking up slaves at night, actions that he said were "revolting to a Virginian."[71]

Despite his avowal of past allegiance to the Union, the Virginia farmer concluded that the agitation in Boston proved drastic measures had to be taken. He believed that it was now the duty of Virginians to apprise Northerners, whom he referred to as "our enemies," of Southern rights. In the wake of the Burns crisis, he proposed far-reaching changes aimed at distancing the South from the North, especially lessening its economic dependence. Appealing to Southern pride, he said that "when we are maltreated and abused, our property taken from us by violence, our feelings outraged, and our characters traduced and vilified, it is not in the disposition of the Virginian to submit tamely to such outrages and wrongs."[72] Simply put, the time for self-respecting Southerners to talk with Northern abolitionists was over; it was now time to act, a position that Charles Jones also adopted during the Burns drama when he told his father, "I have recently from observation formed an estimate of the elements of fanaticism more vivid and real than ever before, and willingly subscribe to the old rule: 'Never dispute or argue with fools or bigots either in religion or politics.'"[73]

By analogy with Virginia's actions toward Britain during the Revolution, the farmer's first recommendation was to boycott Northern manufactures; he said the South should expand its manufacturing capacity to further process cotton, wood, and iron, and he proposed the taxation of merchants and businessmen who sold cheap raw materials or semifinished goods to Yankees. He argued that the latter typically processed such products and reaped huge profits shipping the finished goods back to the South. The Virginian singled out shipbuilding as an industry to be developed in locations such as Norfolk and Portsmouth in his own state, to replace the practice of shipping Southern timber to the North at very low profits.[74] Three days later, the *Lynchburg Virginian,* now recommending Southern economic independence and self-sufficiency, echoed his thoughts. The paper printed an article that also appeared in the *Savannah Georgian,* declaring, "[T]his is the true line of policy for the South to pursue, not only as the best means of developing her strength, but as the surest corrective of Northern abuse and imposition." It then concluded with a strong appeal to sectional sentiments, reminding its readers that "all Southern men should regard it a patriotic duty to give preference in their purchases to products of Southern labor" and that it was time for them to "discontinue their trips of pleasure, their summer tours, and winter sojourns, and all unnecessary expenditures of money in the North."[75] The Virginia farmer also looked at strengthening the South's trade balance with the rest of the world; he advocated affirming the South's independence in international markets, notably by expanding direct trade with Europe and diverting Southerners' expenditures away from the purchase of luxury goods from the North.[76]

The farmer's remarks on the education of Virginia's sons and daughters showed that he thought the Commonwealth's future generations were its most valuable asset. He built on criticism that surfaced during the Burns affair of wealthy Virginians "heedlessly sending our sons and sometimes our daughters" to "Yankee colleges," which had become "the hotbed of abolitionism." Virginians who continued this practice ran the risk of their children joining the ranks of Charles Sumner's admirers and becoming "antagonistic to Southern institutions." He believed that subjecting young Southerners to such instruction constituted the "political prostitution" of Virginia's youth. He sought also to check the influence of Yankee women hired to teach in primary schools in the South and recommended instead the hiring of Southern women educated at improved Southern colleges.[77] In the days following the Burns affair, this Virginia farmer was not alone in demanding a new independence in education for the South. Arguing that Northern professors abused their positions by advocating fanatical abolitionist doctrines, the *Richmond Whig* told its readers not to send their children to Northern colleges, the *Lynchburg Republican* called for the South to develop "its own agricultural schools," and the *Southern Literary Messenger* proclaimed that "our professors, our teachers, should all be Virginians," and that Virginia needed to "lay a solid foundation for Southern literature."[78]

North Carolina's William Holden, who was traveling in the North at the time of the crisis, also took a firm stand. In the *Standard,* he congratulated a young Southern student who withdrew from Harvard and declared that "it is time all Southern students should seek knowledge outside of Harvard."[79] The young student was not the only Southerner who was quick to take action. Following the Burns drama, South Carolina College's Francis Lieber, reputedly the leading American political scientist at the time, was denied the college's presidency because of his unwillingness to embrace proslavery views. "He that is not for us is against us, and should be so treated" was apparently the justification used by the college's board of trustees.[80] Lieber quickly left for the North.

At the same time that he focused on education, the Virginia farmer sought to promote Virginia manufacturing and improve the "Mechanic Arts" or skilled trades in order to make Virginia a vibrant industrial center capable of serving the entire South. In the *Southern Literary Messenger,* Barbour also touched upon this issue and stressed the importance of diversifying Virginia's economy.[81] The Virginia farmer noted that young men who wanted to learn skills were often forced to go to the free states, and that they seldom came back. He denounced what he saw as Virginians' traditional preference for commercial occupations over skilled crafts, arguing that it impeded manufacturing and left Virginia dependent on the North. He pointed out that in Virginia, commercial occupations had traditionally been regarded as having higher status such that the Commonwealth's sons aspired to be merchants, not mechanics.[82] He believed that attitudes toward the "Mechanic Arts" had to be changed for the South to succeed in diversifying its employment base and displacing Northern manufactures.

The farmer considered Richmond and Fredericksburg particularly well suited for medium-sized manufacturing facilities and called for factories to be set up to produce items such as shoes, textiles, brooms, clocks, water buckets, and pianos.[83] Focusing especially on footwear, he noted that Virginians imported some 90 percent of their shoes—mostly from the North. He also had a recommendation for traditionally music-loving Virginians. "Let a manufactory of pianos be opened in Richmond, that will employ the best workmen," he proclaimed, "and there is no reason in the world, why as good toned pianos cannot be made there as in Boston or New York."[84] After the Burns crisis, Virginians had a duty to defend their society, and the memory of great music-loving Virginians could inspire them to make the necessary change.

If the Faneuil Hall rally, the courthouse riot, Northern indifference to Southern rights in human property, and the spectacle of marshals escorting

Burns to T-Wharf before thousands of onlookers encouraged a new white Southern defense of slavery and underscored the merits of economic independence and secession, several incidents immediately following the Burns crisis sounded more alarms. The first was the return to the podium of some of the most outspoken critics of the South, including some of the men who had "started the monster mob into life and power"—the *Savannah Daily Morning News*'s vivid description of Boston's courthouse rioters.[85] The resurgence of the abolitionists' tirade against slave power in the South ensured that the shock waves emanating from Boston would not subside; if anything, they would continue to grow.[86] The Burns drama saw Charles Sumner's oratory reach new heights as the Free-Soil senator initiated a relentless campaign against Southern slave power that continued unabated until Congressman Preston Brooks temporarily silenced him in the Senate with his cane for insulting Senator Andrew Butler of South Carolina. Shortly after the Burns drama, Sumner told a Worcester audience that the "tyranny of the slave power has become unmistakably manifest" and demanded, "No slave hunt in our borders; no pirates on our strand: no fetters on the Bay State; no slave upon the land."[87]

The Burns rendition stoked the fury of Theodore Parker as well as more moderate advocates of higher law such as the Reverend John Weiss, who argued that in cases such as that of Burns, "obedience to temporal authority [was] sinful." The law had been corrupted, said Weiss, and the Fugitive Slave Act turned "its shining blade against the breast of justice."[88] Ohio's John P. Hale joined these Massachusetts Free-Soilers in proclaiming that the "Fugitive Slave Law is destitute of every attribute of justice or humanity; is at war with the spirit of liberty, with the principles of law, with the purposes of the Constitution, with the best feelings of mankind, and ought to be at once and forever repealed."[89] Such rhetoric seemed to corroborate Southerners' suspicions that antislavery sentiments among Northern whites were on the rise. The Southern press also treated their readers to Northern derision and challenges—not just from the likes of Theodore Parker, Garrison, and Sumner but from practical politicians such as Henry Wilson. The *Richmond Whig* reprinted one of his most critical and cynical speeches in its entirety. "If the South should go out of the Union—if the North should allow her to go out—not a State would remain out for twenty-four hours," asserted Wilson. "They would not dare to do so . . . the Slaves of the South would rise up en masse, and carry fire, blood and death into every dwelling tomorrow." Sardonically, he concluded, "Why, sir, you can't kick a Southern State out of the Union."[90] Southerners also disdained the new militancy of

Northern blacks, including Frederick Douglass, who, after the Burns crisis, vehemently rejected Garrison's pacifism and championed aggressive resistance against the Fugitive Slave Law.[91]

Also disturbing to Southern whites was the fact that Northern abolitionists were joined by a growing number of antislavery activists abroad, who seized upon Burns's misfortune. Given their usual suspicions of a conspiracy between Northern and London abolitionists, white Southerners undoubtedly expected a reaction from England. The reaction from Ireland, however, was astonishing and revealed an important rift between the Irish in America and their brethren in the homeland. In Dublin's *Freeman's Journal,* antislavery spokesmen denounced Boston's Irish for having participated in Burns's return to bondage, expressing dismay that "a corps of Irish volunteers with deadly weapons in their hands, lined the streets of Boston, while poor Burns was being delivered to his tormentors." They accused Boston's Irish of being "the bitterest enemies" of liberty; they renounced ties with men who engaged in the "work of darkness and of demons." For white Southerners, these attacks suggested mounting abolitionist sentiments overseas, and when Garrison published such criticism, it reminded Southerners that their Northern brethren were teamed up with foreigners—a circumstance that chafed at the nerves of many Southerners as long as they remained in the Union.[92]

Fourth of July celebrations less than five weeks after U.S. marshals escorted Burns to the South delivered more messages that fueled Southern whites' fears of what they perceived to be a rising tide of abolitionism. The famous Fourth of July picnic at Framingham, where Garrison burned copies of the Constitution, the Fugitive Slave Law, Commissioner Loring's decision, and Suttle's certified claim to Burns, grabbed the attention of Virginians and especially irked slaveholding Southerners. But there were other incidents as well that caused angst. For example, the *Virginia Gazette* published the demands of the selectmen of the town of Marblehead, Massachusetts, who called on "the cities and towns of the commonwealth to imitate the example of Providence [Rhode Island], and omit the usual celebration of the 4th of July next, and to mark, by tolling of bells, and other appropriate means, the fresh insult offered to the commonwealth by kidnapping Anthony Burns in the city of Hancock and Adams."[93]

More disturbing to Southerners, however, was an opinion on the constitutionality of the Fugitive Slave Law rendered by Abram Smith, a justice of the Supreme Court of Wisconsin and a virtual unknown in the South before June 1854. Only days after Loring validated Suttle's claim on Burns, Smith ruled on a habeas corpus motion filed by Sherman Booth, a flamboyant abolitionist editor who had been charged under the Fugitive Slave Law with having aided and abetted a fugitive slave named Joshua Glover in his escape to Canada in March 1854. Judge Smith denied the constitutionality of the Fugitive Slave Law, shocking slaveholders throughout the South, who were already reeling from the events in Boston. Headlines and dispatches in Southern newspapers announced, "Fugitive Slave Law Declared Unconstitutional."[94] Smith's ruling quashed any satisfaction Southern whites felt after Loring's decision, and they were reminded of their earlier commitment to the Georgia Platform, which demanded the faithful execution of the Fugitive Slave Law. Southerners were also upset because the Glover rescue bore similarities to both the Jerry rescue in Syracuse and that of Shadrach in Boston. Glover had lived in obscurity for a couple of years near the town of Racine on the Wisconsin frontier, where he was discovered by his master, Benjamin Garland. Garland hired slave catchers, seized Glover, and took him to Milwaukee for a hearing before a federal slave commissioner. As he awaited the commencement of proceedings, a boisterous crowd, supposedly aroused by Booth shouting, "Freemen to the Rescue," converged on the jail and freed Glover after a blacksmith battered down his cell door with a wooden beam.[95] Foreshadowing the Pierce administration's stringent enforcement of the Fugitive Slave Law in Burns's case, the United States district attorney indicted Booth for having sparked the agitation that freed Glover. The editor's detention prompted his filing of a habeas corpus suit in May 1854.

On June 7, 1854, only five days after Burns boarded the *John Taylor*, Smith delivered his opinion, contradicting earlier rulings by U.S. Supreme Court associate justice Joseph Story, New York Supreme Court judge Samuel Nelson, and Massachusetts chief justice Lemuel Shaw. Pronouncing the Fugitive Slave Law unconstitutional, he declared null the main concession Southern whites believed they had received in the Compromise of 1850 and undermined the federal apparatus that had allowed for Burns's return days earlier, thus increasing angst in an already restless South. The *Enquirer* reported that by rejecting Congress's authority to legislate on the rendition of fugitive slaves and declaring that the Fugitive Slave Law's denial of a jury trial contravened the Constitution, Smith had revealed his "abolition *animus*" and basked in the "glory of having rendered the first judicial decision against the constitutionality and validity of the statute for the recapture of fugitive slaves."[96]

The *Enquirer* drew a couple of far-reaching conclusions. First, it suggested that Smith's decision showed that abolitionism in the North had become so strong that "even the Bench is infected by its spirit and submits to its treasonable purposes."[97] Second, stressing that Southerners' right to recover their human property had been central to the formation of the Union, the *Enquirer* proclaimed that "it devolves upon the South to enforce its rights, or to annul the constitutional compact by secession from the Union." Noting also that Southern rights could not be indefinitely upheld by force, the paper again concluded that secession was the "appropriate remedy for the wrong" that Smith had perpetrated against the South.[98]

Another legal controversy directly linked to the Burns case also caught the attention of Virginian slaveholders and encouraged them to rethink their allegiance to the Union. Highly publicized in both the North and South, it involved demands for the removal of Loring as a Massachusetts judge of probate on the grounds that he had not obeyed the state's personal liberty law that, like similar laws in other Northern states, declared that Massachusetts officials were not to serve as slave commissioners who might have to return fugitive slaves under federal law. When Loring began Burns's hearing, abolitionists immediately demanded his dismissal, and they continued to do so until he was finally removed. On the eve of the decision against him, Garrison noted, "[T]here is not a slaveholder or slave-hunter in all the South, who is not anxiously watching to see how [the Loring removal case] will be disposed of."[99]

From the outset, the *Enquirer* denounced abolitionist criticism of Loring. It reported on a letter written by George T. Curtis, a relative of Loring and a well-known judge. The paper quoted Curtis as saying, "[T]he case of Burns had not been pending twenty-four hours before Judge Loring, when I saw that every effort would be made to drive him from the discharge of his duty, by exciting against him the worst passions of the community."[100] Passion there was. The Sunday after Burns was seized, Theodore Parker railed against Loring, noting that he was both "Judge of Probate *and* Slave Commissioner." Frederick Douglass published a letter from an enraged abolitionist saying, "OFF WITH HIS HEAD—Commissioner Loring, one of the kidnappers of Mr. Anthony Burns, is also a Judge of probate for the courts of Suffolk in the State of Massachusetts."[101] Slaveholding Virginians were also disturbed when some law students at Harvard boycotted Loring's lectures and when the commissioner was hanged in effigy.[102] So too were North Carolinians. When Harvard failed to renew Loring's contract, Holden "condemned" the university's administrators for not supporting the commissioner's enforcement of the Fugitive Slave Law. He concluded his defense of Loring by exclaiming, "Were we to shirk and cower under their [Northerners'] aggressions, insults, the manhood of their own region would despise us." He said, "This incident is one among many going to show the chain of intercourse and affection between the two sections, is growing weaker and weaker."[103] Charles Jones wrote to his parents, complaining about antislavery law students showing disrespect for Loring. "In our lecture room at Cambridge," noted Jones, "the viler species of abolitionists, members of the law school . . . indulge[d] their anserine propensities in hissing" at Loring as he entered the class to teach them.[104]

For many white Virginians and other slaveholding Southerners, Northerners' treatment of Loring served as another warning. The *Enquirer* concluded, "No sooner does a Southern man, in pursuit of his slave, present his claim under the law to a United States Commissioner, than efforts are made to intimidate the officer, and if he be an honest man, and fearlessly proceeds to the discharge of his duty, every species of embarrassment is thrown around his action, and every expedient is resorted to, that will protract, delay, and defeat the execution of justice."[105] Virginians read about numerous petitions to the Massachusetts House of Representatives and Senate, abolitionists' testimony before both houses, legislative debates on what abolitionists called "the petition of the people" to remove Loring, and his eventual removal as a judge of probate, a decision that Garrison claimed vindicated the will of the good people of Massachusetts.[106]

For many white Southerners, the clamor against Loring was rivaled only by the quashing of the indictments against the courthouse rioters on a legal technicality. Their trial on the indictments drawn up by U.S. district attorney Benjamin Hallett, which alleged that they had knowingly and willfully resisted, obstructed, and opposed U.S. marshals, ended with the dismissal of charges on grounds that the indictments "should have shown, by legal averments," that they emanated from a court or an officer of the court "empowered by law" to issue the writs. Abolitionists rejoiced, but the dismissal sent another message to the white South suggesting that the Fugitive Slave Law and the Compromise of 1850 could not be sustained in a Union ravaged by abolitionism.[107]

When the gates of Lumpkin's jail slammed shut on Anthony Burns, the *Enquirer* announced what it took to be the real meaning of the Burns drama—and it was one that other newspapers were also on the threshold of embracing. It was a message that certainly did not sit well with many Virginians steeped in the doctrines of liberty and limited government. The message was that they had not won the Burns case—not at all. "Such instances of the violent repression of the popular passions by military force as we have just seen in Boston, are terrible necessities in a republican Government," noted the Richmond paper, an assessment that echoed the thoughts Charles Jones relayed to his parents. "Despotism executes its purposes with the bayonet, but in free Governments the supremacy of law is dependent on the voluntary submission of public opinion." The *Enquirer's* editor continued, ominously: "The Institutions of liberty cannot co-exist with military violence, and when a free Government is driven to invoke the aid of the soldiery to carry out its laws, the day of its overthrow is not remote." Indeed, he warned, "Its decay has already begun, the contagion of insubordination will rapidly spread, and the exercise of military power in the repression of popular outbreaks will be no longer a remedy in great emergencies but an expedient of every day and [a] familiar resort. . . . [A] military despotism dominates, and the people are no longer free."[108] The *Enquirer* thus used the Burns drama to drive home how tenuous the position of the slaveholding South was in a Union supposedly infected by abolitionist sentiments. Remarkably, one of the first readers to pick up on the message was Frederick Douglass. He assailed the Pierce administration's support of Burns's return to bondage and reprinted the entire passage from the Richmond paper, echoing, though for reasons exactly opposite those of the *Enquirer,* the idea that "the people are no longer free."[109]

Perhaps knowing just how to irk slaveholding Southerners who believed in limited government, Douglass and others also seized upon the absurd cost of returning Burns. When Attorney General Cushing provided an initial estimate of the expenses incurred by the U.S. marshals, Douglass noted that as taxpayers, "we pay $50,000 and have Anthony Burns sent back; when we might have bought his freedom, the freedom of the three Pembrokes, the freedom of the nine Cincinnati Fugitives, and the freedom of every Fugitive that has ever been sent back under the law! [That sum] would have done all that and left a surplus besides."[110] When authorities published the amounts paid to various regiments and individuals a few months later, Garrison reminded the public of the high cost of returning Burns and insulted Southerners with his famous "Blood Money" article. Garrison said that those who cashed checks for having helped the forces of law and order ensure Burns's return to bondage had "taken part in a villainy," guaranteed "their infamy sure and lasting," and acted as "willing accomplices in kidnapping." The message for white Southerners was that the costs of returning Burns had been both exorbitant and, in the eyes of some Northerners, abhorrent.

As the *Enquirer* had said, the "decay [had] already begun."[111] It was a call to action. As Barbour put it in his address to the Literary Societies of the Virginia Military Institute, Virginians needed to act "while there is yet opportunity we should stand up." The alternative was "that greater evil," which he labeled "absorption"—absorption by a disorderly, unstable society ravaged by fanatical abolitionism.[112]

CHAPTER 6

Anthony Burns's St. Catharines
Safety under the "Lion's Paw"

I stand as a freeman along the northern shore of Old Erie, the freshwater sea,
And it cheers my very soul to behold the billows roll
And to know as a man I am free
Old Master and mistress, don't come after me,
For I won't be a slave any more;
I'm under British law safe beside the lion's paw
And he'll growl if you come near me sure.
—*Rev. Richard Ball*

The Fugitive Slave Law of 1850 changed the meaning of the North for runaway slaves and free blacks. African Americans had long suffered from endemic racism in the free states and from the plethora of discriminatory laws against blacks that such attitudes produced. These laws reflected in part white workers' fears of a flood of low-wage black laborers from the South. But at least blacks in the North had their freedom—however limited or tenuous it may have been. Yet when Senator Stephen Douglas guided the Compromise of 1850 through Congress, most observers viewed the new fugitive slave legislation as a major concession to Southern slaveholders. Antislavery activists in the North were especially alarmed. They denounced the act as proof that slavery was extending its tentacles into the free states. Rather than diminish gradually, as many Americans had expected, the peculiar institution now seemed poised for expansion.

In 1850, America took another giant step away from the course of events in Britain, where antislavery sentiment had risen steadily after Lord Mansfield's Somerset decision in 1772 effectively abolished slavery in England.[1] By the end of the eighteenth century, British public opinion had turned decidedly against slavery, and Britain officially ended its involvement in the still lucrative African slave trade in 1807. During the first decade of the nineteenth century, as cotton plantations using slave labor spread across the American South and new laws strengthened the institution's grasp, British abolitionists stepped up their campaign against slavery in their country's overseas possessions, helping to set the stage for imperial emancipation some three decades later.

When President Millard Fillmore's administration began enforcing the new fugitive slave legislation in September 1850, blacks and antislavery whites assailed provisions in the law that were designed to increase the efficiency of slave catching, arguing that they stacked the cards in favor of slaveholders. The act denied alleged fugitives the right of habeas corpus, excluded fugitive testimony in hearings before federally appointed slave law commissioners, and introduced hefty fines and jail terms for persons who assisted runaways. Critics also noted that the new legislation provided slave law commissioners with a financial incentive to rule in favor of individuals claiming ownership of alleged fugitives. When they validated a slaveholder's claim, slave law commissioners received fees twice that to which they were entitled when they ruled in favor of the purported fugitive.

Northern blacks maintained that the Fugitive Slave Law of 1850 created an open season for slave hunting throughout the free states; that perception boosted the number of fugitive slaves fleeing to Canada. At the beginning of the nineteenth century, most blacks probably would have seen little difference between Canada and the free American states, aside from the fact that north of the forty-ninth parallel, most of their white neighbors professed loyalty to the British monarch and flag. After the passage of the new fugitive slave legislation, however, the border took on new meaning. In the three months after Fillmore signed the Fugitive Slave Bill into law, some 3,000 fugitives— including many from the northern reaches of the free states—crossed the border. Nancy Howard, who had fled from Maryland and resided for seven years in Massachusetts, explained that she escaped to Ontario and settled in St. Catharines because of her "fear of being carried back" under the new legislation.[2] The migration to Canada was of such a magnitude that it threatened the survival of black communities and institutions in some areas of the United States. A Baptist church in Buffalo lost 130 members; another in Rochester reported losing 112 of its 114 worshippers; in Detroit, some 80 members of the city's black Baptist church were reported to have left in haste for Canada.[3]

Free blacks, as well as fugitives, felt threatened. They often had difficulty proving their free status, and they complained about the restriction on the testimony of alleged fugitives, noting that such curbs increased their chances of being wrongfully enslaved as a result of mistaken identity or kidnapping. These threats loomed especially large for free blacks who were new to an area or traveling through unfamiliar regions. When seized by slave catchers, they typically had nobody to speak on their behalf, and their own testimony was inadmissible.

Kidnappers used the new law to step up their illicit activities. Although kidnapping had always been a problem for free blacks—the free black musician Solomon Northup, for example, was abducted in New York in 1841 and wrongfully enslaved in Louisiana for some twelve years—the incidence of kidnapping increased significantly under the new law.[4] Free blacks found themselves at the mercy of men such as George F. Alberti, Philadelphia's most notorious kidnapper. In the early 1850s, he admitted to having abducted hundreds of free blacks. Most of his victims were captured around Philadelphia; many were young children, whom he easily overpowered or lured with candy-coated promises. Once they were in his custody, he claimed them as fugitive slaves. In areas bordering the Mason-Dixon line, organized groups such as the infamous Gap Gang in Lancaster County, Pennsylvania, reaped profits by seizing free blacks, claiming them as runaways, and selling them to traders in the Deep South, where the demand for labor remained strong.[5]

In this context, many free blacks perceived flight to Canada as their best insurance against falling prey to kidnappers. Indeed, some black migrants to Canada during this period reported that they had already experienced the misfortune of being abducted and sold into slavery. John Lindsey, perhaps the most prosperous black in St. Catharines on the eve of Anthony Burns's arrival, was a free black who had been kidnapped and forcibly enslaved in Tennessee prior to his escape to Canada. Henry Jackson, a fugitive who also settled on the Niagara Peninsula, was a literate free black from New York State. As a teenager, he had been kidnapped and sold in the South by the very man to whom he was apprenticed. After his escape from bondage, he too sought safe haven in Ontario, which was then officially known as Canada West.[6]

Rising prices for able-bodied slaves and the readiness of some Southern county courts to issue documents certifying ownership of slaves, which profiteers used to legitimate their claims, fueled abuses of the new Fugitive Slave Law. By some accounts, unscrupulous traders encouraged slave catchers to "go among the niggers [and] find their marks and scars" in order to supply exact descriptions for counterfeit ownership claims that county courts then certified. Such practices increased the number of free blacks who were wrongfully enslaved and suffered the trauma of separation from their families, the loss of their hard-earned property and homes, and, of course, abuse on and after the trek to the Deep South.[7]

Free black women and girls were as much at risk as males. Kidnappers grabbed Elizabeth Williams one night in West Chester, Pennsylvania, brought her before a slave law commissioner for a token fifteen-minute hearing, and then delivered her into bondage. Polly Seiper, a former slave who had been manumitted by her Virginian master, was seized and imprisoned as a fugitive slave in Washington, D.C. Her case illustrates a ruse sometimes employed by kidnappers who conspired with corrupt officials. Detained in a local jail and unable to pay the fees, Seiper and her child were forcibly hired out to cover their jail costs. Before long, they ended up back in slavery.[8]

On the eve of the Burns drama in Boston, many blacks considered Ontario attractive for additional reasons. The region benefited from a relatively temperate climate and the availability of fertile agricultural land. Furthermore, most residents spoke English and were Protestant. Most important, Canada was firmly embarked on the gradual elimination of slavery. Its flirtation with slavery had proved to be fleeting despite a 1790 imperial statute that had suggested that slaves could be legally held in "his Majesty's Colonies and Plantations in North America." Slavery failed to sink strong roots in Canada, although there was a temporary upsurge during the Revolutionary era associated with the arrival of a number of slaveholding Loyalists. Several factors limited the institution's expansion.[9] The lack of an agricultural staple for export; the predominance of small-scale farming; the high costs of sheltering, feeding, and clothing slaves during winter, even in temperate areas such as the Niagara Peninsula; and rising popular sentiment against an institution that smacked of Old World hierarchy checked the growth of slavery. Although some well-placed Loyalists vigorously lobbied colonial officials, demanding that slave property be protected, antislavery sentiment triumphed. Ontario's lieutenant governor, John Graves Simcoe, made sure of that.

An outspoken critic of slavery and a close friend of William Wilberforce, one of Britain's most prominent eighteenth-century abolitionists, Simcoe helped turn the tide against slavery when he arrived in Canada after the American Revolution. He declared that he would never assent to any law that "discriminates by dishonest policy between the natives of Africa, America, or Europe." In 1793, he seized the opportunity created by a crisis involving the fate of a young enslaved woman named Chloe Cooley. Cooley's master, William Vrooman, a resident of the Niagara Peninsula, had decided to sell her in the United States to take advantage of rising prices for slaves south of the border. However, when he carried her kicking and screaming to the docks to board a vessel about to cross the Niagara River, he stirred the wrath of bystanders and sparked a wave of antislavery sentiment. Simcoe quickly introduced legislation that sounded the death knell for slavery in Ontario.[10]

Simcoe's bill declared it "unjust that a people who enjoy freedom by law should encourage the introduction of slaves." Despite the opposition of some wealthy slaveholders, including recently arrived Loyalists who were members of his council, Simcoe pushed through the legislature a comprehensive package aimed at the gradual elimination of slavery. The statute provided for freeing the children of slaves when they reached the age of twenty-five, and it revoked all government-issued licenses to import persons of African descent as slaves. Stopping imports and freeing the children of slaves ensured the institution's demise. When Samuel Gridley Howe visited Ontario to assess the well-being of the free black population, he concluded that gradual elimination had been the most politically expedient way for Simcoe to abolish slavery while still supporting private property.[11]

In the early decades of the nineteenth century, Canadian recognition of black soldiers, court decisions favoring runaways, and the repeated refusal of British and colonial authorities to consent to the extradition of fugitive slaves all confirmed British North America's divergence from the United States' proslavery stance, thus reinforcing Canada's reputation as a safe haven.[12] During the War of 1812, British authorities reached out for the help of Ontario's growing population of black residents and formed the regiment known as the Coloured Corps, which played a central role in battles won by the British.[13] After the war, Ontario's new lieutenant governor, Sir Peregrine Maitland, recognized the contribution and valor of the Coloured Corps by offering black veterans land grants to establish homesteads on the eastern shore of Lake Huron between Lake Simcoe and Penetanguishene Bay. At about the same time, he refused U.S. senator Henry Clay's request to begin diplomatic talks on the extradition of fugitive slaves. Like Simcoe, Maitland embraced strong antislavery beliefs; he privately wrote that he wished "runaway slaves might find sanctuary" in Canada's unsettled regions.[14]

Maitland's rebuff to Clay was only the beginning of a lengthy stalemate on the extradition issue. In the 1820s, under pressure from Southern planters, Clay and Albert Gallatin, the U.S. ambassador to Britain at the time, lobbied imperial authorities for the "mutual surrender of all persons held to service or labor . . . who escape into the territory of the other." To their disappointment, officials in London responded that "it was utterly impossible" for the British government "to agree to a stipulation for the surrender of fugitive slaves." When Clay and Gallatin persisted in their demands, they received a terse message from Lord Aberdeen in 1828 stating "that the law of Parliament gave freedom to every slave who effected his landing upon British ground." A year later, the Executive Council in Quebec also took such a position. When an American slaveholder asked Canadian authorities to hand over his runaway slave, who had crossed the border with the aid of a Montrealer named Paul Vallard, they refused, arguing that "the state of slavery is not recognized by the Law of Canada." The council members deemed there had been no crime to justify the extradition of a fugitive.[15]

Reflecting growing antislavery sentiment in Britain and Canada, tensions on the extradition issue resurfaced in the early 1830s and threatened to jeopardize relations with the United States. Even before the abolition of slavery throughout the British Empire, the Ontario legislature took initiatives on the issue by appending a clause to an act dealing with fugitives from justice that authorized the lieutenant governor "not to deliver up a person if he deemed it inexpedient." The clause was designed to deal with fugitive slaves, and it was not long before it served as the basis for the next lieutenant governor, Sir John Colborne, to refuse to return Thorton Blackburn and his wife, two runaways from Kentucky who sought asylum in Ontario. Their master asked officials in Washington to demand their extradition. Responding to a growing antislavery constituency, Colborne refused the American request.[16]

Extradition became an even more contentious issue after the Imperial Emancipation Bill passed Parliament in 1833 and became effective on August 1, 1834. Britain's abolition of slavery accentuated Canada's status as a safe haven, thus encouraging fugitives to follow the North Star. Andrew Jackson's administration, still shaken in the aftermath of the Bank War and the Nullification Crisis, sought to appease Southern slaveholders by renewing American requests for an extradition treaty dealing with fugitives from bondage. Britain's continuing refusal frustrated slaveholders and pushed some to adopt more aggressive strategies to curb their losses, including kidnapping runaways on Canadian soil or charging them with felonies in order to extradite them as fugitives from justice. Such actions sometimes became international incidents and provoked public debates that pitted proslavery forces against abolitionists in Britain, Canada, and the free states. The three most notable events were the kidnapping of the Stanford family, the Solomon Moseby riot, and the Jesse Happy case, in which Canadian authorities refused an American request for Happy's extradition. These incidents not only forced British and Canadian officials to review their policies regarding the extradition of fugitive slaves but also encouraged blacks in Ontario to adopt a much more militant stance. These controversies also fueled abolitionist sentiment among Canadian whites. When Anthony Burns arrived in St. Catharines, the rising tide of antislavery sentiment ensured that neither kidnapping nor the extradition of fugitive slaves as felons was a viable expedient for slaveholders. Fugitives who made it across the Niagara River were safe under the "lion's paw," and slaveholders' attempts to abduct or extradite them only served to publicize the evils of the peculiar institution and strengthen the antislavery cause in Canada.

In 1835, the rescue of the Stanford family from kidnappers demonstrated the extent to which public opinion in Canada after imperial emancipation had turned against slavery. The Stanford incident also revealed that a growing number of blacks, supported by antislavery whites, were ready to take up arms to prevent their brethren from being returned to bondage. After the Stanfords escaped from a Kentucky plantation, a Nashville slave trader named Bacon Tate tracked the couple and their six-year-old child to the town that later became Anthony Burns's home. Tate hired six accomplices from upstate New York and two others from St. Catharines to help him seize the Stanfords and carry them back to the United States. His gang captured the family, put them in chains before onlookers, and then headed for Buffalo. But the word went out and blacks in St. Catharines and neighboring Niagara Falls responded immediately. Intent on saving the Stanfords, blacks "rallied their forces and rushed in pursuit." They joined antislavery militants from Buffalo led by the legendary William Wells Brown, a fugitive slave who had escaped from Kentucky in 1834, became a leading abolitionist, and is thought to be the first African American to have published a novel. The rescuers overtook the kidnappers outside the city. Although Tate and his assistants were assisted by a Buffalo sheriff's posse, the blacks reclaimed the Stanfords in a pitched battle, which Brown referred to as "one of the most fearful fights for freedom" that he ever witnessed. The triumphant blacks returned the Stanfords to the safety of St. Catharines. When Tate's Canadian accomplices returned home, St. Catharines police immediately charged them with kidnapping.[17]

The Stanford incident signaled to slaveholders the danger and costs of kidnapping expeditions in Canada. A local newspaper said it was a "fearful warning to all future kidnappers and their dupes."[18] The case also resulted in the increased vigilance of Canada's black residents and many of their white neighbors. Black newspapers counseled readers to be on the lookout for kidnappers and printed warnings whenever slave catchers were rumored to have crossed into Canada or to be combing the northern areas of neighboring states. White-controlled newspapers also frequently contained reports of kidnappers and warnings to black residents. In late 1852, for example, the *Brantford Herald* issued an alert that was picked up by the *St. Catharines Journal.* "Within the last few weeks, we have heard of two attempts in this vicinity, to carry off colored children," reported the *Journal.* "We would say to colored parents, *look out!*" The warning ended with a comforting message to blacks and a threat to kidnappers: "[T]he people of Canada will protect you with as much good will as they will punish the man stealer, if he is caught in any part of Canada."[19]

The fate of Solomon Moseby, a fugitive slave who arrived on the Niagara Peninsula in 1837, also affected public opinion. Moseby's case took a violent turn after his master traced his path to the Canadian border. American authorities contacted Canadian officials, alleging that the fugitive slave had stolen his master's horse when he escaped from Kentucky. They demanded his extradition as a felon. The Canadian authorities initially resisted, but when the U.S. State Department reiterated the extradition demand, Canadian officials agreed to arrest Moseby and hand him over as "a criminal for horse-stealing." Their decision, however, opened the floodgates of resistance among Canada's blacks. The black communities on the Niagara Peninsula, notably around St. Catharines, mobilized to resist his return, and many white sympathizers also rallied to his cause, voicing their opposition by petitioning the colonial legislature not to hand Moseby over.[20]

When officials ignored local sentiment and tried to surrender Moseby, a full-scale riot ensued. As a sheriff removed Moseby from the jail where he had been held and took him to a ferry that was to carry him across Lake Ontario to the United States, a black preacher named Herbert Holmes led some "two hundred determined black men" brandishing pitchforks, flails, and other makeshift weapons in an assault on the sheriff's wagon. Supported by their wives, who threw stones and other objects at the sheriff and his guards, the men were also joined by some of their white neighbors. The rescuers grabbed Moseby and took him to Montreal, where he boarded a ship about to set sail for London. Holmes and one of his supporters were killed during the skirmish.

The Moseby rescue precipitated considerable debate in the communities of Niagara Falls and St. Catharines. Initially the press coverage was mixed; some writers supported Holmes and the rescuers, but others denounced them, suggesting that their actions had been manifestations of mob rule. Very quickly, however, public opinion shifted solidly in favor of the black-led rescue, and authorities responded to growing demands for an inquest to determine whether charges should be laid against the sheriff and his men in

Holmes's death, and whether some of Holmes's accomplices who had been taken into custody should be released. Although the sheriff and his men were not indicted, the preacher's accomplices were acquitted of all charges and set free.[21]

If British authorities thought they had trouble on their hands with the Moseby riot, the extradition case of Jesse Happy, another Kentucky fugitive who escaped to Canada by stealing a horse from his master, Thomas Hickey, sent shock waves across the Atlantic. After receiving a carefully prepared request for Happy's extradition, Ontario's lieutenant governor, Sir Francis Bond Head, recognizing mounting antislavery sentiment after the Moseby affair, called for a commission of inquiry. The investigation uncovered facts that turned public opinion even more strongly in Happy's favor. The inquiry revealed that although Happy had used Hickey's horse to flee northward, he had left the horse on the American side of the border. He then wrote to his former master to tell him where he could recover his horse—and Hickey had done so. The investigation also revealed that Happy's flight had occurred more than four years earlier, which raised suspicions about Hickey's demands for the former slave's extradition as a criminal. Most observers in Canada concluded that Happy had borrowed, not stolen, the horse; that his former master had initially viewed his actions in this way; and that no felony had occurred.[22]

As public support for Happy increased, more Canadians questioned the wisdom of negotiating an extradition treaty with the United States. Many rejected the idea outright; they warned that Americans could use an extradition treaty dealing with criminal offenders to have fugitive slaves returned. Americans could simply lay criminal charges against runaway slaves, and Canadians would have to return them. Several whites rallied to Happy's cause and petitioned Bond Head, alleging that American authorities had charged the fugitive solely in order to have him returned to his master. They warned that if Canada entered into extradition arrangements with its Southern neighbor, injustice would be "perpetrated towards many unfortunate Individuals whose complexion differs from that of your Petitioners (freeholders and other white inhabitants of the province)."[23]

Bond Head and his Executive Council evidently recognized the risks. Their report, drafted by Chief Justice Beverley Robinson, emphasized what became known as the "double penalty," to which fugitives would be subjected if they were surrendered to American officials: as fugitives from bondage, they would invariably be returned to slavery whether or not they were guilty of an alleged crime, and if they were found guilty of a crime, they would suffer punishment on that account as well. The commission suggested that this double penalty distinguished extradition cases of runaway slaves from those of free persons alleged to have committed a crime. The double penalty, noted Robinson, made extradition procedures an ideal ruse for slaveholders. In fact, the Virginia-born chief justice concluded that most criminal allegations made by slaveholders, including allegations of horse stealing, were "mere contrivance to get the slave again within reach of his owner."[24] After the investigation, Bond Head's council announced its refusal to extradite Happy, but the council made the refusal subject to the approval of imperial authorities.[25]

That forced imperial authorities to initiate an in-depth review focusing on questions of imperial management, diplomacy, and both common and international law. The imperial review involved several prominent figures, including colonial secretary Lord Glenelg, British foreign secretary Lord Palmerston, and the law officers of the Crown—the British government's official attorneys. With both prominent British abolitionists and London businessmen who wanted closer trade ties with the United States watching, the cabinet ministers and leading lawyers dealt with Happy's fate.

Lord Glenelg searched in vain for statutes or legal precedents that might shed light on whether or not British authorities should extradite runaways alleged to be felons. He concluded that "in the case of fugitive Slaves, charged with crimes, there is no positive rule either in the British Statute Book or in the Law of Nations, requiring or forbidding the restitution of such Criminals, but that the Government must act according to their discretion." He believed that a case such as Happy's had to be resolved on its individual merit, and he supported the Canadian approach of granting the lieutenant governor discretion to decide whether or not to extradite fugitive slaves. But Glenelg hedged his bets; in the end, he indicated that he would defer to the expertise of foreign secretary Lord Palmerston and the law officers of the Crown.[26]

In their reviews, Palmerston and the law officers revealed antislavery leanings and introduced arguments that effectively provided "a sweeping defense" for fugitive slaves. Palmerston concluded that Happy had not "taken the horse with theft in mind." More important, he said that "the intentions of the offender," not only the actions he committed, had to be considered. In deciding that Canadian officials should not return Happy to the United States, Palmerston emphasized that reenslavement would certainly be part of any punishment that he would endure if Canadian authorities extradited him. Stressing that slavery had been abolished in the British Empire, Palmerston declared that even if Happy had stolen Hickey's horse, such punishment for horse stealing was "such as our principles of jurisdiction compell [sic] us to regard as indefensible and disproportionate to the crime."[27]

The law officers of the Crown, including Lord Mansfield's biographer, Attorney General John Campbell, endorsed the Canadian refusal to extradite Happy, and they did so in a manner that helped make Canada an even safer haven. They concluded that a fugitive slave should only be surrendered in instances where his or her crime would have warranted his or her apprehension if the crime had been committed in Canada. Since slavery was illegal in Canada, the law officers believed that flight from slavery did not constitute a crime. They also argued that in Happy's case, "what took place was not Horse Stealing according to the Laws of Upper Canada, but merely an unauthorized use of a Horse, without any intention of appropriating it."[28] Finally, they recognized that fugitive slaves might commit acts in attempts to escape that were inseparable from their primary act of self-liberation, or self-theft. Such action simply represented a form of self-defense—a defense of their right to liberty. On March 9, 1838, the law officers' opinion, embracing this broad definition of self-theft, became Britain's official policy. Palmerston immediately supported the law officers' interpretation, commenting also that a slave should not be surrendered "on the charge of having robbed his Master by carrying off the Clothes on his own back."[29] Imperial officials forwarded the law officers' report to Canada with instructions that Happy "ought to be set at liberty."[30] They were unaware that, despite the Executive Council's request for an imperial review, the Canadian authorities, faced with strong public sentiment in favor of rejecting the American extradition demand, had already freed Happy, citing the Executive Council's findings.

In the two decades before Burns's arrival in Canada, renewed American demands for the extradition of fugitive slaves severely tested the precedent established by the Happy case. Faced with the conflicting priorities of trying to improve relations with the United States but also responding to antislavery concerns in Britain and Canada, imperial officials walked a fine line on several occasions, including the *Creole* crisis and the Nelson Hackett affair, and during diplomatic talks between Lord Ashburton and Daniel Webster leading up to the Treaty of Washington in 1842.[31] The *Creole* incident and the Webster-Ashburton negotiations confirmed Canada's status as a safe haven, but in the Hackett case, Canadian authorities had little choice but to respond, albeit temporarily, to Southern interests.

In November 1841, slaves aboard the *Creole* killed two crew members as they took control of the American vessel and forced it to land at Nassau, in the Bahamas. Washington officials were aghast when the British refused to extradite the individuals involved. Reflecting the law officers' broad interpretation of self-theft, imperial officials indicated that "the intent and object of the slaves was not that of general Plunder on the High Seas"; rather, the slaves had acted "with the sole object of compelling the crew to take them . . . to some Port where they might obtain their Freedom." Southerners resented the British stance, considering it proof of London's increasing bias against slavery.[32]

Two months after the *Creole* incident, the British and the Americans found themselves involved in another controversy when U.S. officials alleged that a fugitive slave from Arkansas named Nelson Hackett, known to have fled to Canada, had stolen several items that were not necessary for his escape, including his master's gold watch. American authorities recognized that Hackett's theft could not be justified on the basis of a broad interpretation of self-theft and meticulously documented the crime, making it virtually impossible for the British and Canadian authorities to refuse extradition. For the Americans, it was an ideal test case; a fugitive slave had committed a crime unrelated to his quest for freedom. For British and Canadian authorities, the Hackett affair posed serious problems, and despite their antislavery bias, they felt that they had to act responsibly toward a friendly state and demonstrate their commitment to preventing Britain's northern possession from becoming "an asylum for the worst characters."[33] They surrendered Hackett.

Intent on demonstrating goodwill toward America, the British government also authorized Lord Ashburton to address the extradition issue in diplomatic negotiations with Secretary of State Daniel Webster—but in a way that ensured that the precedent established in the Happy case would not be compromised. Lord Stanley, Britain's new colonial secretary, instructed Ashburton to allow inclusion of neither "mutiny and Revolt on board Ship nor desertion" in the list of offenses that would require the surrender of fugitive slaves. Although Stanley authorized him to include robbery as an extraditable offense, he insisted that it be made clear that the British would continue to exercise discretion consistent with a broad interpretation of self-theft. He concluded that "a British Governor . . . will have carefully to consider whether the offence . . . [was] connected with the desire of freedom, necessary to its attainment and comparatively venial in its character."[34]

In these circumstances, Ashburton relied on the strength of his relationship with the American secretary of state and succeeded in getting Webster to agree to extradition terms, which became Article X of the Treaty of Washington of 1842. This article excluded mutiny, revolt, and desertion as extraditable offenses. Recognizing American concerns about fugitive slaves seeking asylum in Canada, Ashburton made two off-the-record promises to Webster. First, he guaranteed that henceforth *Creole*-type incidents would be reviewed in London. Second, he promised that imperial officials in London would instruct colonial governors not to interfere with American vessels driven into their waters by accident or violent means. Despite the exclusion of mutiny, revolt, and desertion, and probably in spite of a suspicion on Webster's part that the British intended to stand by a broad definition of self-theft, Ashburton's promises and the earlier extradition of Hackett apparently convinced the secretary of state that the interests of Americans, including slaveholders, would benefit from the agreement that became the Treaty of Washington. The agreement, also called the Webster-Ashburton Treaty, is best remembered today for having confirmed the border between Canada and the United States.[35]

The Treaty of Washington gave British and Canadian authorities substantial room to maneuver on the fugitive slave issue, and they clung to the legal precedent established in the Happy case, thus reinforcing Canada's reputation as a safe haven for blacks, fugitive and free. Indeed, after the passage of the American Fugitive Slave Law of 1850, British and Canadian officials broadened the range of crimes that could be forgiven as measures necessary to carry out self-theft. By the time Anthony Burns arrived in St. Catharines, they even refused to extradite fugitive slaves alleged to have committed serious crimes. In the most famous case, which occurred just prior to the outbreak of the Civil War, American officials alleged that a fugitive slave named Jack Burton, also known as John Anderson, had killed his master's neighbor as he fled to Canada, and they demanded his extradition.[36] Although Canadian authorities detained Anderson, and it initially appeared that they would extradite him, they bowed to Canadian public sentiment, which was "much aroused" in favor of Anderson. When antislavery activists filed a motion in the Canadian Court of Common Pleas requesting that Anderson be freed, and a judge ordered his release, Canadian officials seized the opportunity to refuse the American extradition request. British and Canadian authorities did not surrender a single fugitive slave under the terms of the Webster-Ashburton Treaty.[37]

Anthony Burns joined an antebellum Canadian black community that actively sought to advance its well-being under the protection of the "lion's paw." If Canada remained a beacon to blacks, it was to a great extent due to the actions of the blacks themselves. From imperial emancipation until the Civil War, blacks campaigned vigorously against proposed agreements between Britain and the United States that could have undermined their security or made it more difficult for their enslaved brethren to escape the South and join growing communities in Canada. Black Canadians publicized the horrors of slavery, including instances of kidnapping in the free states, and they exercised their rights as British citizens by taking a public stand against negotiations toward an extradition treaty.

Taking advantage of their improved access to literacy in Canada, blacks used both black and white newspapers to advance the antislavery cause. They organized antislavery conventions in several Canadian cities and towns, particularly after the passage of the American Fugitive Slave Law of 1850. Canada's black men also took advantage of their right to vote; in some electoral districts in Ontario, they held the balance of power. Often enjoying newfound independence associated with self-employment and land ownership, Canadian blacks lobbied provincial authorities and even imperial officials across the Atlantic. Their wide-ranging actions testified to their unrelenting desire to destroy an institution that degraded them and their determination to exercise their rights as British citizens. In early Ontario, the black community was much more than a population of fugitive slaves; it was a community of self-reliant individuals who embraced a very special mission—advancing and, as they perhaps saw it, even saving their race.

When Canadian blacks heard rumors that Americans wanted to renew talks toward an extradition treaty in the early 1840s, they immediately mobilized to prevent any agreement. Claiming the support of several thousand residents, they convened a "great meeting of Coloured People" in Toronto and approved a petition to be delivered to the British parliament by one Dr. Rolph of Ancaster, Ontario.[38] In the petition, they declared, "Satisfied as we are, with the protection we enjoy, and that no such infamous proposition will ever be listened to, by the Government of Great Britain, we only notice it to draw the attention of Government, and to pray that should it be made, that it will be treated with that contempt which so gross an insult to the cause of humanity, and to the honour and dignity of the British Crown, so well deserves."[39] They followed up this initiative with messages to both the queen and the provincial legislature, in which they emphasized that they expected their rights as British subjects to be respected. They also demanded that any fugitive charged with "the pretext of felony or other crime" in the United States be guaranteed a trial by jury in Canada in accordance with British law.[40] They stressed that because British law prohibited slavery, self-theft should not be recognized as a crime. Canadian blacks had their petitions printed in newspapers in order to sway public opinion in their favor and influence government policy. Such initiatives built on their earlier actions in the Moseby and Stanford affairs. Their efforts also served as a constant reminder to British and Canadian authorities, American officials, and

Southern slaveholders that a growing segment of the Canadian population, supported by many of their white neighbors, stood ready to resist the return of fugitive slaves to bondage.[41]

The actions of Canadian blacks also sent a special message to their brethren in the free states, and blacks such as the fugitive slave editor Henry Bibb became instrumental in building Ontario's reputation as the Promised Land and making Canada the beacon of freedom that it would become—especially after the enactment of the new Fugitive Slave Law. In his newspaper, the *Voice of the Fugitive,* Bibb portrayed the Niagara Peninsula and the area extending from Niagara Falls southwest toward Windsor, across the river from Detroit, as an especially appealing sanctuary for blacks. "My advice to all the colored people living in the states, the laws of which do not recognise them as citizens is to emigrate to Canada," declared Bibb. Railing against slavery in the South and restrictive laws against blacks in the North, he predicted that it would be "a long time if ever, before the wicked laws concerning coloured people which disgrace the statute books of these States will be erased and righteous ones occupy their place."[42]

Bibb portrayed Britain's northern possession as a land of liberty and opportunity. Most consequential, he said, was the fact that "the law of Canada respects [blacks] as men." Noting that the "laws of England or her province know no distinction as white or colored," he informed black men that if they came to Canada, they could serve on juries, sometimes even as foremen. He also told them that, like their white neighbors, they could vote for members of Parliament if they became landholders three months prior to an election and took an oath of allegiance to the government of Canada. He emphasized that white candidates seeking election to the provincial legislature often catered to the black vote, especially in areas where blacks represented a significant proportion of the population or held the balance of power. Reporting on an election campaign in the town of Sandwich, Bibb described white candidates "bowing to colored men, and enquiring after their health." He concluded that "the vote of the colored man is as mighty as that of a white man," and he held out hope that blacks would soon "send one of their own number to represent them in the Provincial Parliament." Self-help was one of Bibb's key themes. Bibb believed that the political gains he foresaw would be more likely if blacks sought to improve themselves and if they were "industrious and persevering in the acquisition of knowledge."[43] Bibb, however, perhaps might have added that not all white politicians believed in racial equality. Like their brethren in the free states, Canadian blacks sometimes faced challenges as a result of race prejudice, which some politicians sought to tap for their political advantage. The most notorious bigot in early Ontario in the 1850s was Edwin Larwill, a man who went down to defeat in 1857, partly as a result of the black vote, after he campaigned on a racist platform patterned on the Black Laws that existed in the free states.[44] His defeat was proof of the clout at the polls of a growing black community.

Bibb believed that slavery played a major role in debasing blacks, and he contended that until the hateful institution was extirpated, root and branch, it would continue to degrade his race. Therein lay the special importance of Bibb's adopted country of Canada. He argued that Britain's northern dominion was strategically well positioned to attack slavery, and that blacks in Ontario had a special role to play. He told them to "plant their feet firmly on [Canadian] soil where you can give aid and comfort to fleeing bondmen." He said that "one thousand intelligent enterprising colored men from the South would do more for the abolition of slavery by settling in Canada . . . than three times that number could effect by settling in the nominally free states." Some of Bibb's black neighbors shared these beliefs.[45]

In 1851, a few months after the passage of the Fugitive Slave Law of 1850, Bibb and several other Canadian blacks organized a North American Convention of Coloured People in Toronto. Inviting blacks from Canada and the free states, the organizers placed Canada at center stage in the fight to abolish slavery and elevate the black race. Their invitation, published in Bibb's newspaper, "emphatically" declared Canada "the only land of safety on the American continent for hunted refugees."[46] Choosing Toronto as the location underscored blacks' confidence in the protection afforded by British laws and institutions. Bibb and his fellow organizers asserted that the concentration of the free black population in British possessions such as Canada could serve as an effective means of undermining slavery and, at the same time, advance the "social, moral, political, and intellectual improvement" of blacks.[47] Bibb also stressed that migration to Canada was a much better alternative than returning to Africa, which proponents of African colonization recommended. He capped his argument in favor of Canada as the best destination for blacks by noting that the proslavery *Savannah Republican* had once concluded that "a colony [of free blacks in Canada] would be a fit nursery for the rearing of black soldiers to be turned loose upon the Southern States in a war between the U.S. and Great Britain."[48] Many Canadian whites also believed that Canada had a special role to play in bringing down slavery.[49]

Stressing that education would be instrumental in shaping the destiny of his race, Bibb argued that access to good schools was perhaps the most important advantage blacks could reap by crossing the forty-ninth parallel. He said that blacks could be "strengthened and elevated" by education. Using examples such as the tidy schoolhouse that William King erected in Ontario's all-black Elgin Association community and King's hiring of "a competent teacher," Bibb contrasted the opportunities for education available to blacks in British North America with the obstacles to black schooling in the United States, particularly in the South.[50] There were, however, times when Ontario blacks had to struggle for access to education. The Canadian safe haven was a paradise in comparison to areas from which many fugitives had fled, but its landscape too was occasionally blemished by racism. Sometimes in seeking to exercise their rights to education, black residents had to turn to the courts. For example, when Solomon Washington's son was repeatedly denied access to the common school in Charlottesville by trustees who gerrymandered the school district's boundaries to exclude Washington's farm, he took them to court. Although Chief Justice Beverley Robinson ruled in the blacks' favor in *Washington v. Trustees of Charlottesville*, his opinion did little to mask the racist sentiments that sometimes served as an obstacle to black children's access to education—a right so deeply valued by black migrants to Canada.[51] Like Frederick Douglass, Bibb argued that knowledge was the most effective weapon against slavery, and he told his readers that slaveholders feared the education of blacks more than they feared "bowie-knives or pistols."[52]

The recommendations adopted by the North American Convention of Coloured People reflected the worldview of Ontario's leading blacks and their goal of elevating their people. The convention participants believed that education and agriculture could combine to elevate blacks, especially on Canadian soil. Bibb reported that participants in the Toronto convention "strongly recommend the formation of a great Agricultural League of our people of the United States, the British American Provinces and the West Indies." Because they believed that land ownership provided independence and could serve as the economic means to advance blacks, they declared that the league should facilitate the purchase of "large tracts of land in Canada and Jamaica, with agricultural implements, and [establish] farms throughout these colonies, as far as it may be practicable for the purpose of encouraging industry among refugees from American slavery."[53]

Bibb frequently stressed the availability of prime agricultural land in Ontario, even for blacks who had only modest savings. He reported that, adjacent to Windsor, less than ten miles from Detroit, good farms could be purchased at rates varying from $9 to $40 an acre. Elsewhere in the Windsor-Niagara corridor, Bibb pointed out, prime agricultural lots of forty to one hundred acres were available for about $7 per acre. According to the black editor, fertile land near Sandwich, although not cleared, could be had for as little as $4 an acre. With land so cheap, he recommended that fugitives should not "stop short of Canada."[54] Land in that country could be both the "remedy for the physical wants" that haunted most fugitives from bondage and the means "to improve the moral, mental and political condition of a poverty stricken and degraded people."[55]

The success, social respectability, and improved quality of life of many black immigrants lent weight to Bibb's message and strengthened Canada's reputation as an attractive safe haven. Although some all-black settlements such as Wilberforce fell short of the expectations of their founders, who sought to develop communities of prosperous family farms, and others were sometimes fraught with internal division and allegations of corruption, still others such as William King's Elgin Association were resounding successes and saw the establishment of communities of self-sustaining family farms. The Elgin Association proved that free blacks, if given the opportunity, could fashion vibrant communities that contributed to their social and economic advancement.[56] Even in the less successful communities, however, Canadian blacks were no longer threatened by the specter of being returned to bondage or subjected to the extreme discrimination of the Black Laws prevailing in most free states. They could often build reasonably comfortable lives, enjoy peace of mind, and benefit from at least some measure of independence. Bibb, perhaps exaggerating, suggested that if black migrants to Canada were industrious, temperate, and determined, success would always be within their grasp. Any black "farmer who cannot live [well] in Canada West, with rich and fertile soil beneath his feet, with a mild climate, and an antislavery Government over his head," declared Bibb, "must be a little too lazy."[57]

At the same time, Bibb sought to discredit rumors about the depravity of blacks in Canada spread by Southern slaveholders intent on discouraging potential runaways, and by Northern confidence artists seeking to collect money and goods fraudulently on behalf of supposedly wretched fugitives in Canada. In early 1852, Bibb and several leading blacks signed a strongly worded open letter declaring that "the cry that has been raised that we could not support ourselves is a foul slander."[58] A few months later, Bibb published a letter from Frederick Douglass to the fugitive slave preacher the Reverend Jermain Wesley Loguen, who moved to Canada to avoid prosecution for his participation in the Jerry rescue in Syracuse. The letter indicated that members of St. Catharines's black community were "tired of being [wrongfully] represented as paupers and dependents."[59] After a stay in the town, Mary Ann Shadd, the founder of the antislavery newspaper the *Provincial Freeman* and the first black female editor in North America, confirmed that she had had "frequent opportunities of examining the general improvements of the place and was in no way more gratified than when viewing the snug homesteads of the colored people," which she viewed as refuting the falsehood that fugitives in St. Catharines needed to beg.[60]

Despite his interest in agriculture and advice to blacks about taking advantage of the vast expanses of virgin farmland, Bibb did not ignore the potential of Canada's rapidly growing towns. He argued that, in contrast to many American cities, Ontario's urban areas, particularly in the fastest-growing region between Toronto and Niagara Falls, offered blacks the opportunity to enjoy moral and economic elevation. The black editor thought that mid-nineteenth-century Toronto was already "a magnificent city" in which blacks could demonstrate their "industry and moral worth." He noted that Toronto's two antislavery societies included leading citizens who were committed to "the elevation of the colored population." Bibb especially admired George Brown, Ontario's leading Reform Party politician and the publisher of Toronto's *Globe and Mail*. Brown had established himself as one of Canada's most outspoken antislavery men. Brown constantly denounced American slavery and attacked the Fugitive Slave Law. He reported on British, American, and Canadian antislavery conventions and encouraged his readers to support government policies that advanced the interests of Canada's black population.[61] Bibb believed that Toronto could serve as a model of race relations for other North American cities, noting that the races amicably shared social and geographic space in the city. "We are happy to say that there are no colored schools," wrote Bibb, "and where there are colored churches there is no necessity for them, for the schools and churches are open to all alike without regard to color."[62]

Though smaller, the city of Hamilton, some fifty miles southwest, tended to follow Toronto's lead in race relations. In this growing industrial center, which by midcentury had become the heart of Canada's iron industry, whites generally welcomed blacks in most walks of life. The Reverend Geddes, the minister of Hamilton's Anglican church, reported that his congregation included blacks, and they apparently worshipped alongside their white neighbors, who usually followed the example of their pastor, a man who encouraged black participation in church activities. "I have always taken an interest in the improvement of their condition, socially and religiously," said the minister. While he reported that race prejudice was uncommon, he nevertheless admitted that a few whites in his congregation had complained about two black women teaching Sunday school.[63]

Although the principal of a Hamilton school supported the Reverend Geddes's view that discrimination was the exception, not the rule, it certainly had not always been the case. For example, in 1843, some Hamilton blacks petitioned Governor-General Charles Metcalfe, saying that although they were taxpayers, their children had been refused access to public schools. Nevertheless, a decade later, race relations had apparently improved and children of both races seemed to benefit in the classroom and the school yard. The Hamilton school principal claimed that "little white children do not show the slightest repugnance to playing with colored children, or coming into contact with them. We give the children their seats according to their credit-marks in the preceding month, and I never have had the slightest difficulty. The moral conduct of the colored children is just as good as that of the others."[64] By the early 1850s, some two hundred blacks had made Hamilton their home. After visiting the city, Bibb recounted that many blacks were "doing good business, and [were] much respected, not only for their wealth but for their moral and intellectual worth."[65] In 1852, the Reverend Samuel R. Ward spent time in Hamilton and confirmed that most blacks were in "comfortable circumstances," some of them "much better off than a number of Europeans."[66] The same was true in neighboring St. Catharines, soon to be Anthony Burns's home.

Situated on the western shore of Lake Ontario between Hamilton and Niagara Falls, St. Catharines emerged as a special haven for black migrants to Canada. For many, the town served as a way station, a place to recover from the arduous journey northward before settling elsewhere in British North America. For others, including Anthony Burns, St. Catharines became a final destination, an adopted home. With a population of about 7,000, it was one of early Ontario's larger towns and had much in common with cities such as Toronto and Hamilton, which on the eve of the American Civil War had populations of about 30,000 and 10,000, respectively. St. Catharines's growth was spurred in part by the construction of the Welland Canal, which gave the town a role in Great Lakes shipping. At midcentury, St. Catharines had a flourishing labor market and a wide range of specialized trades.[67] Discovery of mineral waters in the vicinity, coupled with the picturesque countryside along Lake Ontario and the nearby Niagara Falls, also boosted tourism and led to the construction of resort hotels, which created new jobs.[68] For blacks eager to build new lives, St. Catharines had much to offer.

In the decade before Burns arrived, the town's blacks numbered about seven to eight hundred, about one-tenth of the city's population. Most lived near the town's center in an area known as St. Paul's Ward. Similar to Ontario's all-black communities such as Elgin, St. Catharines's black community was tightly knit.

Surrounded by some of the finest agricultural land on the Niagara Peninsula, St. Catharines was also a market town. Henry Bibb noted that more than two-thirds of the blacks migrating to Ontario in the early 1850s had spent most of their lives in agriculture. For them, farming was a vocation, a way of life.[69] With a relatively mild climate, rich soil, and a growing urban population in the Toronto–Niagara Falls corridor that provided a ready market for farm products, the St. Catharines vicinity had everything enterprising blacks needed to carve out independent livelihoods. Many did.

Although the area offered much in terms of natural amenities and economic opportunity, the initiative of black residents, aided by sympathetic whites, particularly distinguished Anthony Burns's St. Catharines. Its reputation as the "City of Refuge" was established in the 1850s after several high-profile individuals, including the radical white abolitionist Hiram Wilson and fugitive slave preachers Jermain Wesley Loguen and Alexander Hemsley, moved to the town and devoted themselves to the advancement of its black community. Wilson was one of the so-called Lane rebels expelled from Oberlin College for having defied the directive of the seminary's board of trustees ordering faculty and students not to engage in antislavery activities. He moved to the Ontario town of Amherstburg, where he stepped up his antislavery fight. In 1842, with the aid of Josiah Henson, a fugitive slave from Montgomery County, Maryland, who was once thought to have been the inspiration for Harriet Beecher Stowe's Uncle Tom, and a $1,500 donation from James C. Fuller, an English Quaker, Hiram Wilson established the famous vocational school for blacks known as the British American Institute. Wilson's work at the institute proved to be only the beginning of his efforts to improve black education in early Ontario. He eventually had a hand in establishing some fifteen schools.[70]

A fugitive slave, Loguen had fled north to Syracuse, where he became a renowned preacher and antislavery militant. In 1851, after his indictment as an organizer of the Jerry rescue, he crossed Lake Ontario and settled in St. Catharines. He continued to wage his campaign against slavery and developed a reputation as a forceful and eloquent speaker. He cared for fugitives and devoted time to schooling black children and adults. In 1852, he gained fame as a result of his open letter to the governor of New York demanding "exact and equal justice to all men" and calling for the legislature to repudiate the Fugitive Slave Act by recognizing the "God-given guarantee of [the black man's] right to freedom." Loguen's letter also focused on his own plight—his forced migration to Canada to avoid arrest and his separation from his family and friends in Syracuse.[71]

Hemsley, too, had been at the center of much controversy. A fugitive slave from Maryland, he was seized by slave catchers in Northampton, Massachusetts, where he lived for several years. He narrowly escaped being returned to slavery thanks to Justice Joseph C. Hornblower's recognition of a writ of habeas corpus filed in the New Jersey courts by antislavery activists, who rallied to Hemsley's cause after his capture. When his captors failed to prove his identity as the slave of one Isaac Baggs, Justice Theodore Frelinghuysen of the New Jersey Supreme Court ruled that Hemsley should be set free. Still fearing kidnapping and another attempt by slave catchers to prove his status as another man's property, Hemsley sought asylum in St. Catharines.[72]

Wilson, Loguen, and Hemsley helped make St. Catharines the veritable bastion of antislavery activity that it became in the mid-nineteenth century. Constantly attacking the peculiar institution and the Fugitive Slave Law of 1850, these militants also helped found local institutions to meet the needs of the steady stream of black immigrants arriving in the town. In addition, they forged links with antislavery activists in other communities in Canada and the northeastern United States, where activists helped furnish St. Catharines with money, clothing, and school supplies to assist new arrivals. Equally important, Wilson, Loguen, and Hemsley developed strong ties and good working relationships with the town's leading whites, men who had the wealth and political clout to assist a growing number of fugitives.

Harriet Tubman, the most famous conductor of the Underground Railroad, also contributed to St. Catharines's reputation as the City of Refuge. In the 1850s, Tubman, known as the "Black Moses," adopted St. Catharines as her home, making it her Canadian headquarters and the Underground Railroad's northern terminus. She made an estimated nineteen trips to the South and led some 312 blacks to freedom in Ontario. On her first trip in 1851, she brought eleven fugitives to the Niagara Peninsula. After that, she continued to lead freedom seekers to the area until 1858, the same year that she met with the fiery John Brown in St. Catharines before he headed south to Harper's Ferry.[73]

Tubman became involved in community affairs with Wilson, Loguen, and Hemsley. She participated in the interracial Refugee Slaves' Friends Society (RSFS), founded in 1852 by members of the black community and leading whites; the latter included the Niagara Peninsula's most powerful politician, William Hamilton Merritt. Tubman also rented a house to shelter fugitives adjacent to the British Methodist Episcopal (BME) Church, where she worshipped. The basement of the BME Church served as a temporary shelter for fugitives arriving on the Underground Railroad. Tubman's activities, coupled with the steady migration of individuals and families arriving on their own, fueled the growth of the town's black population. When Anthony Burns arrived, the St. Catharines assessment roll identified more than 350 black households, numbering almost 1,000 persons.[74] The town had two flourishing black churches, Tubman's BME Church and Burns's Zion Baptist Church.[75] The RSFS worked with both congregations.

From its inception, the RSFS, assisting fugitives after their arrival in the town, played a major role in advancing the well-being of St. Catharines's blacks. The society's members defined their mission as "bear[ing] testimony against slavery" and "extending sympathy and friendly aid to those who have escaped [from slavery] and are taking refuge in this section of Canada."[76] The RSFS boasted an initial membership of seventy persons, including the town's member of Parliament, William Hamilton Merritt; the mayor of St. Catharines, Elias Adams; Canadian customs collector John Clark; and the editor of the *St. Catharines Journal,* James Lamb. The members elected Lamb chairman at the society's first meeting on April 16, 1852, and during the next several months, he used his newspaper to publicize the RSFS's aims. Lamb portrayed the RSFS's role as a humanitarian duty—a God-given mission. Providence had made St. Catharines a "City of Refuge to the oppressed and afflicted," wrote Lamb. Members of the RSFS encouraged participation in their society by setting membership dues at levels that ordinary people could afford. They also benefited from the town leaders' willingness to let them meet in the St. Catharines town hall. Black participation was significant, and three blacks served on the society's five-member executive committee.[77]

Wilson reported that despite the assistance fugitive slaves received on the Underground Railroad, when they reached St. Catharines, they invariably suffered from "exposure occasioned by the hellish national slave hunt" and often from serious illness. Most arrived undernourished, scantily clad, and penniless after a journey that in some cases exceeded a thousand miles by foot with little food and the constant fear of recapture.[78] Writing to Frederick Douglass, Loguen said most fugitives arrived "ragged, lonely, homeless, hungry and forlorn."[79] Many came in late autumn or early winter, making it difficult for them to find employment in an often snow-covered land, where work followed a seasonal pattern.[80] This resulted in serious problems prior to

1852, when the RSFS had not yet been organized but the new Fugitive Slave Law was boosting new arrivals. Henson reported that many were forced to subsist on roots and herbs. To survive, some fugitives engaged in petty theft in the countryside. When they were arrested, sympathetic whites, including Lamb, came to their defense. William Hamilton Merritt also often defended fugitives and called for residents to help, not condemn, fugitive slaves.[81]

In addition to facing the elements, new arrivals typically suffered emotional trauma associated with separation from loved ones. At its first meeting, the RSFS passed a resolution recognizing Loguen's trials and extending their "deepest sympathies, in his present suffering, separated as he is from his wife and family and home."[82] Almost all of St. Catharines's black residents left loved ones, usually members of their immediate families, when they fled north. The fugitive slave Dan Josiah Lockhart recalled that he began his journey northward by looking at his wife and two small children sleeping before he quietly slipped away. Christopher Nichols fled from a master who constantly whipped him; he agonized about his separation from his wife, three children, and three grandchildren—"loved ones he never expect[ed] to see again in this world." David West escaped to Canada from a Virginian plantation to avoid being sold to the Deep South; he longed for his wife and four children. So too did Jamie Macie, who wrote to his wife, "I have arrived in St. Catharines this morning after a journey of two weeks. Tell father and mother that I am safe and hope that they will not mourn after me. I shall ever remember them and if we do not meet on earth, I hope that we shall meet in heaven."[83]

That most observers, including Frederick Douglass, who visited St. Catharines in the 1850s, "saw no destitution, misery, [or] starvation" is testimony to the determination of the fugitives who made the trek northward, the commitment of those who received them, and the strength of early Ontario's black institutions.[84] In St. Catharines, the black churches were instrumental in meeting the needs of new arrivals and helping them build new lives in a strange land. Located almost side by side in St. Paul's Ward, the BME Church and the Zion Baptist Church, where Burns preached during the last two years of his life, constituted the heart of the community. Most St. Catharines blacks lived in the immediate vicinity. In a tightly knit black community, the two congregations cooperated with each other and maintained close links with the town's leading whites.[85]

The BME Church was an outgrowth of the African Methodist Episcopal (AME) Church, which Richard Allen founded in Philadelphia in 1816. During the 1820s, the AME expanded northward in an effort to respond to the needs of the growing population of free blacks and fugitives in the free states. After imperial emancipation, AME conference members turned their attention to Canada and vowed to help fugitives crossing the border. In 1834, they sent missionaries to Ontario; when the Reverend Richard Williams formed a congregation in St. Catharines three years later, the town became the site of the first permanent AME church in Canada. Initially, the congregation numbered about seventy persons. In 1838, the Canadian Conference was established, and it presided over remarkable growth. In the mid-1850s, under the leadership of the Reverend Benjamin Stewart, the Canadians severed ties with the American association. This move reflected disaffection among Canadian blacks with political developments in the United States, particularly the Fugitive Slave Law of 1850. They wanted to "identify themselves more closely with the British ideals and government," including imperial emancipation and the extension of citizenship rights to blacks. In 1856, the BME Church of Canada came into being, and Chatham, Ontario, was chosen as its headquarters.[86]

Established in 1838 as a small log structure on the corner of Geneva and North streets on a lot provided *"free from all charge . . .* to the *Methodist* people of color" by William Hamilton Merritt, the BME Church in St. Catharines was rebuilt in the 1850s with Gothic windows and white clapboard siding. The reconstruction, completed in 1855, reflected "the memory of the churches" most members of the congregation had "left behind in the Southern States."[87] Although Merritt donated the land, the chapel's initial construction and its major renovation both represented the efforts of the black congregation. In the 1850s, John Lindsey, perhaps the wealthiest black in St. Catharines, played a key role and managed the building fund. He sometimes advanced his own money and provided resources such as horses, wagons, and tools free of charge to avoid delays in completing the work. The renovated church, christened the Salem Chapel, opened for worship on November 4, 1855.[88]

St. Catharines's second black meetinghouse, the Zion Baptist Church, arose from the vision and perseverance of elder Washington Christian, the pastor of the black Abyssinia Baptist Church in New York City. In the 1820s, he moved to Toronto with the intention of building meetinghouses for the increasing population of fugitive slaves who had fled to Ontario.[89] Over the next decade, his efforts resulted in the formation of several Baptist congregations as well as the construction of churches in Toronto and Hamilton. Shortly after he founded the St. Catharines Baptist Society in 1838, construction of another church began in the town.

Like their neighbors at the BME Church, the black Baptist congregation, consisting mostly of fugitive slaves and their families, turned to William Hamilton Merritt for assistance. He gave them two lots on Geneva Street, about one hundred yards from the Salem Chapel. On the first, they began construction of their chapel. In an open letter published in the *St. Catharines Journal,* Henry Gray, one of the congregation's most active members, thanked the town's leading merchant and politician for his support and praised Merritt's goodwill. "This poor man's benefactor" had provided the congregation with not one lot but two.[90] Completed in 1844, the Zion Baptist Church was a small, plain structure with three rows of pews that could seat "about sixty people." John Anderson, the first pastor, preached to a congregation of about forty-six. In the mid-1850s, membership stood at some sixty. On the second lot, the Zion Baptists built a small house in which Anthony Burns would reside.[91]

The RSFS and these two black churches provided the institutional framework for a range of antislavery activities in St. Catharines. Town leaders joined Wilson, Loguen, Hemsley, and others in organizing antislavery meetings and inviting well-known orators, including legendary figures such as Frederick Douglass, H. F. Douglass, and William H. Day. Lamb publicized the meetings in the *St. Catharines Journal.*[92] Canadian activists, including the president of the Upper Canadian Anti-Slavery Society, the Reverend Dr. Michael Willis of Toronto, also often made the trip to St. Catharines to attend meetings. Willis typically emphasized the horrors of slavery and the injustice of America's new Fugitive Slave Law. He also argued that Canadians, "bordering as we do on the country where man is chattel, and from which he is daily running to us for protection, and seeing as we do the accumulated misery," had a unique responsibility to help bring down slavery and aid fugitives from bondage in their quest to realize their "inherent and inalienable right to freedom" and "the intellectual and moral elevation of themselves and their children."[93]

St. Catharines antislavery gatherings were usually held in the town hall and attracted large audiences. They typically included performances by St. Catharines's black choir, which served to boost attendance. The largest antislavery get-together was the annual celebration of the British abolition of slavery on August 1. A committee invariably consisting of leading members of the black community such as John Lindsey and Henry Gray organized festivities and publicized events. They set the tone for the celebrations, remembered their brethren still held in bondage in the South, and reminded fellow Canadian blacks of their individual responsibilities. In the 1840 celebrations, the committee resolved, "May we, by good conduct, honesty and integrity always maintain the good name which the inhabitants of St. Catharines have kindly bestowed upon us."[94]

As demonstrated previously, schools were especially valued in most Canadian black communities, and St. Catharines was no exception. The town's blacks had a great "esteem for instruction," observed Samuel Gridley Howe after visiting the Niagara Peninsula. "They all wish to have their children go to school."[95] Although many families depended on their children's labor on their farms or in their businesses, they made every effort to send them to school. Blacks' resentment of their lack of schooling in the South made them appreciate even more their children's access to education in Ontario. "I feel that I have been wrongfully deprived of the knowledge of writing," declared David West. "I could have done better for myself in every way had I known how to write." William Grose, a fugitive from Harper's Ferry, Virginia, said, "I don't intend to let my children come up as I did. I'll give them a good education, which I could not do in the southern portion of the United States."[96]

Although after his visit to Anthony Burns's adopted home, Howe stressed that the laws governing common schools in Canada West made "no distinction of color" and noted that about 70 percent of the black school population regularly attended school, the same proportion as that for white children, St. Catharines, like Hamilton, did not have a perfect record on equal education.[97] In the 1840s, the option of separate schooling, initially developed to meet the interests of Ontario's Catholic minority, was extended to the black population. In St. Catharines, blacks requested their own school, and for about a decade, education in the town was mostly segregated, although black families still had the option of sending their children to integrated common schools.[98] By the 1850s, however, most blacks recognized that a separate school typically did not benefit from the same level of funding as the common schools, and that teaching standards and the quality of facilities therefore fell below common school norms. When blacks sought to return their children to the common schools, they sometimes faced resistance. Nevertheless, by the time Burns moved to St. Catharines, the situation seems to have been settled in favor of racial harmony. By then, most of the town's blacks believed that "they [had] made a mistake in asking for separate schools" and had successfully returned their children to the regular schools. Records show that in the second half of the 1850s, about 80 percent of black students attended the town's integrated schools.[99]

In addition to focusing on their children's education, many St. Catharines blacks sought to make up for their own earlier lack of schooling. Adults attended evening classes, which were usually offered in churches. Writing to Bibb in the early 1850s, Hiram Wilson reported that he and his wife were busy helping many black residents learn to read and write. He was "teaching a class of adults in the evening and [his] wife another."[100] Given the remarkable growth of the building trades as a result of construction of the Welland Canal, hotels, and manufacturing concerns, it is also likely that some St. Catharines blacks attended the British American Institute to learn carpentry, bricklaying, and other manual skills that would allow them "to become productive members of a free society."[101]

Temperance societies also loomed large in the institutional fabric of St. Catharines's black community, another reflection of the commitment to moral elevation, as the concept was understood at the time. Temperance meetings were held in the churches, but gatherings appear to have been interdenominational. In early 1852, Wilson said that he and Loguen had "lectured the people several times" on temperance, and he proudly reported that they had succeeded in encouraging some fifty people to take the temperance pledge. Overall, the temperance efforts of the St. Catharines black leaders appear to have made some headway.[102] In 1856, the fugitive slave William Johnson recounted that upon his arrival in St. Catharines, he found the town's blacks very industrious and frugal. Perhaps exaggerating slightly, he added, "No person has offered me any liquor since I have been here: I have seen no colored person use it."[103]

In light of the exclusion of blacks from the militia south of the border, one of the most interesting black institutions in St. Catharines was the Coloured Corps, which was established on the suggestion of Richard Pierpoint, a black who fought with the British during the American Revolution. Pierpoint received a land grant in St. Catharines in recognition of his service. Most Canadians apparently admired the unit's military skills.[104] Numbering some one hundred men in the 1840s, the Coloured Corps was stationed at nearby Port Robinson from 1841 to 1851. For blacks, the unit evinced whites' recognition of their participation in the defense of Canada and their valor in the War of 1812. Serving initially under Captain Robert Runchey, a white officer, and later under James Robertson, a black, members of the Coloured Corps distinguished themselves in two key battles of that war on the Niagara Peninsula, Queenston Heights and Lundy's Lane. St. Catharines blacks were also proud of the Coloured Corps' support of the imperial authorities during the Rebellion of 1837, when William Lyon Mackenzie and his followers sought to overthrow the colonial administration with some—albeit unofficial—American support. Some 150 blacks participated in the standoff with Mackenzie's rebel forces near Navy Island in the Niagara River.[105] In a speech to the Provincial Parliament after the rebellion, Sir Francis Bond Head paid "striking tribute" to the black population, who had demonstrated their loyalty and desire "to be foremost to defend the glorious institutions of Great Britain."[106]

Members of the black community also remembered the Coloured Corps' contribution during the 1840s, when escalating tensions between Irish Catholics and Protestant Orangemen working on the Welland Canal threatened to erupt in widespread violence and endanger other St. Catharines residents. Canadian authorities summoned the black unit to restore peace—and they did so on several occasions. The most notable incident was the so-called Battle of Slabtown, the shantytown on the outskirts of St. Catharines. Some one hundred former residents of Connaught clashed with forty to fifty former residents of County Cork celebrating Orangemen's Day. Hearing that five men had been killed and some thirty injured, authorities called on the Coloured Corps to restore order. Although the black regiment "fearlessly, conscientiously, and honourably discharged their duties," the task of maintaining order proved to be a thankless job, and blacks paid dearly for their efforts as a result of the backlash that followed. Their peacekeeping efforts placed them in conflict with both groups of Irish immigrants, who often competed with blacks for jobs. After the Battle of Slabtown, a large number of Irish workers participated in a racist assault on members of the Coloured Corps as they paraded on militia training day in 1852. Afterward, they destroyed the homes of several members of the Coloured Corps. St. Catharines's white leaders denounced the attack, raised funds to cover the damage to the property of the black residents, and worked closely with members of the black community in an effort to restore the racial harmony that had been instrumental in making the town the northern terminus of the Underground Railroad.[107] Estimates suggest that by the late 1850s, the town's black population had reached almost 1,500, indicating that despite the racial turmoil, St. Catharines remained a City of Refuge for fugitive slaves and free blacks from the Northern states.[108]

Even so, the second half of the 1850s proved to be a difficult period for the town's Zion Baptist Church, which suffered under the inept leadership of one Brother Richard Godfrey. By 1860, the church was struggling with increased debt, and members found themselves embroiled in controversy when it was discovered that the Reverend Godfrey had a wife in St. Catharines and another in Lockport, New York.[109] A distraught congregation sought to rescue their house of worship and find a new pastor capable of renewing their church at a critical time. In 1860, they turned to Anthony Burns. After completing his studies at Oberlin College, Burns had accepted a position with a Baptist church in Indianapolis, but he remained "ever fearful" of the state's Black Laws and the threat of being returned to slavery.[110] When the St. Catharines Zion Baptists reached out to him, he accepted their invitation and moved to the City of Refuge.

On becoming pastor in St. Catharines, Burns demonstrated remarkable "promise" and began ministering to a congregation that, according to some estimates, reached almost three hundred members as he put the church's affairs in order.[111] "His gentle, unassuming and yet manly bearing secured him many friends." He became known as a good speaker and had a reputation of being a "fine-looking man, tall and broad shouldered, but with a slight stoop, indicating a weak chest." He quickly became a "respected citizen" in St. Catharines and was reputed to be "very popular with both whites and blacks." Despite his failing health and his responsibilities to the church, Burns helped ensure that the town remained the bastion of antislavery that it had become, and he spoke frequently at antislavery meetings.[112] Within two years, he had renewed the church and reestablished its reputation in the St. Catharines community, not only ridding it of debt but "succeed[ing] in making some important repairs [and] improvements."[113]

But Burns's health steadily deteriorated—much to the chagrin of a devoted and thankful congregation. On July 27, 1862, despite the "best medical care" available in the city, he died of consumption (tuberculosis). An interdenominational funeral service attended by many townspeople—blacks and whites alike—was held. After the service, a large and very impressive funeral procession wound its way from the meetinghouse to the cemetery now known as Victoria Lawn Cemetery, which at the time was on the outskirts of St. Catharines. At the graveside, it was the local St. Catharines Methodist minister who "thanked God, on behalf of Brother Burns, for taking him where he could no longer hear the clanking of the chains of slavery." Among the onlookers were many fugitive slaves who, like Anthony Burns, had "fled from bondage," sought refuge under the lion's paw, and helped popularize the Underground Railroad song:

I'm on my way to Canada, that cold and dreary land,
The dire effects of slavery I can no longer stand.
My soul is mixed within me so, to think that I'm a slave,
I'm now resolved to strike the blow,
For freedom or the grave.

Chorus: Oh Righteous Father, wilt Thou not pity me,
    And aid me on to Canada, where coloured men are free?
I heard old Queen Victoria say if we would all forsake
Our native land of slavery and come across the lake.
That she was standing on the shore, with arms extended wide,
To give us all a peaceful home, beyond the rolling tide.
Chorus: Farewell old master, this is enough for me,
    I'm going straight to Canada, where coloured men are free.
I've served my master all my days without a dime's reward,
And now I'm forced to run away to flee the lot abhorred.
The hounds are baying on my track, the master's just behind,
Resolved that he will bring me back before I cross the line.
Chorus: And so, old master, don't come after me,
    I'm going straight to Canada, where coloured men are free.[114]

Thus began Anthony Burns's passage into historical memory, one that has been rekindled a century and a half later by a handful of St. Catharines blacks seeking to pay tribute to the beloved preacher of their forefathers. They erected a historical plaque to commemorate Burns's short yet full and significant life, a gesture that helps to ensure him a place at center stage in Canadian blacks' memory of the trials and challenges of their ancestors, which at times have been overlooked or forgotten, partly because so many Canadian blacks returned to the United States after the Civil War and the Thirteenth Amendment abolished slavery. Like Harriet Tubman, the Reverend Jermain Wesley Loguen, and others who pioneered the Niagara Freedom Trail, Anthony Burns lives in historical memory as a champion and a legendary figure who helped to make the Niagara Peninsula a beacon of freedom and, despite incidents that marred its record, a special and relatively harmonious biracial community.

In 1999, members of the St. Catharines black community successfully petitioned Canadian government authorities to establish Anthony Burns's grave as a joint Canadian-American heritage site. Restored and cherished by descendants of fugitive slaves who followed the North Star and created a vibrant community and a vision for their people, Anthony Burns's resting place is now a time-honored site.[115] His tombstone reads:

In Memoriam.
Rev. Anthony Burns
The Fugitive Slave of the Boston Riots, 1854.

Pastor of the Zion Baptist Church.
Born in Virginia, May 31, 1834.
Died in the Triumph of Faith in St. Catharines,
July 27, A.D. 1862.

Nevertheless, Anthony Burns, the time he spent in Ontario, and the character of the community he joined there still constitute a largely forgotten chapter in the historical memory of black striving on the North American continent. Many blacks who went to Canada in the antebellum period sought an opportunity not only to secure their liberty but also to do significant deeds and thereby prove their worth. Many, including Burns, did just that. In a new land, they met the challenges before them, and through their determination, efforts, and constructive self-assertion as citizens of early Ontario, they made a place for themselves and their children while earning the respect of their new neighbors.

These remarkable early Canadian blacks seized upon the opportunity to expand the antislavery arsenal. They did so in a variety of ways. They organized antislavery rallies; they helped establish antislavery networks on an international scale; when they had to, they took up arms to prevent their brethren from being returned to bondage; and they even petitioned the queen and the imperial parliament in London in order to ensure that their rights as citizens were protected. While representing at most only about 10 percent of the population in towns such as St. Catharines, through their initiative and relationships with white neighbors, they influenced politics and policies, particularly and to a surprising extent on the extradition issue. Their efforts ensured that Canada remained a safe haven for their people.

All these activities evince the determination of a people to shape their world. Anthony Burns and the blacks of St. Catharines were not merely fugitives; they were fighters and builders—and they worked with local whites to form a biracial community while retaining their own identity. Burns became an integral and influential part of this world; the recognition of his efforts to renew the St. Catharines Zion Baptist Church and the coming together of blacks and whites for his funeral are evidence of this. Burns was much more than a fugitive slave, more than an object of other people's actions, more than a mere symbol. Anthony Burns fled the yoke of slavery, but not the issue of human bondage: even after his horrendous trials in Boston, and later in Richmond, he willingly assumed a role in the struggle against the institution of slavery. He spent his last days in a place where he could effectively fight slavery with a devoted group of militants and minister to many—like him—who bore its scars. His life, and those of his compatriots, reminds us that the struggle against slavery spanned the forty-ninth parallel, and in many instances, the struggle was conducted by remarkable black men and women who sought American liberties for themselves and for their offspring. They, too, should be remembered as American Revolutionaries.

Anthony Burns, Past and Present

... And, as I thought of Liberty
Marched handcuffed down that sworded street,
The solid earth beneath my feet
Reeled fluid as the sea.
I felt a sense of bitter loss,—
Shame, tearless grief, and stifling wrath,
And loathing fear, as if my path
A serpent stretched across.
All love of home, all pride of place,
All generous confidence and trust,
Sank smothering in that deep disgust
And anguish of disgrace.
Down on my native hills of June,
And home's green quiet, hiding all,
Fell sudden darkness like the fall
Of midnight upon noon!
And Law, an unloosed maniac, strong,
Blood-drunken, through the blackness trod,
Hoarse-shouting in the ear of God
The blasphemy of wrong. ...
　　　—John Greenleaf Whittier, "The Rendition"

[We] have therefore Resolved, Unanimously, that he [Anthony Burns] be excommunicated from the communion and fellowship of this church. ... Done by order
of the church in regular church meeting, this twentieth day of October, 1855.
　　—Wm. W. West, Clerk

Hearing of Anthony Burns's death, William Lloyd Garrison commented
that the case of the last fugitive slave returned from Boston had "become
historic," and he predicted that Burns would "form a conspicuous figure in
the drama of the times."[1] The legendary abolitionist was only partially right.
Burns's case has become historic, but his story has yet to find its rightful
place in mainstream history alongside those of other Americans who stirred
hearts and inspired dreams—sometimes on the streets of Boston. Although

Burns has captured the attention of several brilliant scholars, his story remains unknown to many Americans and certainly to most Canadians—even if he is, to the present day, perhaps the most famous refugee who ever made Canada his adopted home. The Burns drama can tell Americans and Canadians much about their histories and the people who shaped them.

Anthony Burns's story has also been misinterpreted and sometimes misused. Influenced by Burns's first chronicler, Charles Emery Stevens, scholars who have focused on the drama have suggested that it precipitated an antislavery groundswell, or even a pocket revolution, in Emerson's Boston that spread throughout the North, making the Civil War and the extirpation of slavery on American soil almost inevitable. Some scholars have argued that the Burns rendition was a watershed that changed the way many ordinary Americans in the North viewed slavery and the federal government's support of it; others have said that, at a minimum, it encouraged Bostonians to embrace principles of equality and natural rights, which lay at the heart of the Revolutionary heritage handed down to them from their forefathers. The image of Burns being escorted down the hallowed streets of Boston clashed with notions of a city on a hill embellished by the memory of the Adamses, Paul Revere, and their Revolutionary compatriots.

But such conclusions ignore the complexity; the confusion and chaos; and, above all, the racial, ethnic, and class tensions in mid-nineteenth-century Boston. Not everyone prayed for Burns as he was held in the courthouse awaiting Commissioner Loring's decision on his fate; not everyone shared his anguish as he passed through the city's narrow streets under heavy guard, wearing coattails like a domestic slave being auctioned in a Southern slave pen; not everyone cared about him as he reportedly languished in isolation with little water or food in Robert Lumpkin's infamous prison after he was returned to Richmond, Virginia. Indeed, in midcentury Boston, antislavery feelings competed with a wide range of other concerns, and it is far from clear that abolitionist sentiments were on the rise during or immediately after the drama.

Most white Bostonians went about their business as usual, stopping only to gaze at a grand spectacle around two o'clock on a beautiful day in early June 1854. Most, including several leading antislavery figures, identified little or not at all with Burns. Many whites simply regarded the drama, America's greatest show of force in peacetime, as a novelty, as a source of excitement or entertainment, as a spectacle. The outcome also satisfied their underlying concerns with law and order. Many white Bostonians had been strong supporters of the recently deceased Daniel Webster, the "Great Orator." Like him, they sought to conserve the Union, the fruit of their fathers' Revolution. This meant respecting the laws of the Union and standing by the compromises of the Constitution. Most white Bostonians did not seek to extend the fruits of the Revolution to an unfortunate bondsman, to his enslaved brethren, or even to their free black neighbors. Indeed, many Boston whites believed that they had redeemed their city when Thomas Sims, the fugitive slave from Georgia, was returned to Savannah a few years earlier, and they wanted to keep it that way.

The Burns drama, however, had a very different meaning for black Bostonians. It confirmed that President Franklin Pierce's administration, like Millard Fillmore's before it, was committed to enforcing the new fugitive slave legislation and stood ready to defend the interests of Southern slaveholders. Equally important, it confirmed black Bostonians' suspicions that many of their supposedly antislavery white neighbors could not be depended on to take a meaningful stand against the Fugitive Slave Law and prevent slavery from extending its tentacles onto free soil. The message for blacks across the North was that they had to unite and look out for their own interests. As Frederick Douglass put it, blacks had "a special mission to perform in the United States—a mission which none but themselves could perform."[2] It was up to them to extend the fruits of the Revolution to members of their race; for them, the Revolution was not yet finished. Moreover, like Charles Lenox Remond, they believed they had every right to share in the heritage of Lexington and Concord. Anthony Burns certainly believed this. When he heard that some proslavery whites sought to return him to bondage after he had gained his freedom, he declared that "should [someone] attempt to deprive me of my liberty as before, then I would enforce the motto of Patrick Henry, '*Liberty or Death.*'"[3]

Anthony Burns clearly embraced the missions of which both Patrick Henry and Frederick Douglass spoke—something that has been largely overlooked by most scholars, who have tended to see him only as a victim of oppression— even a "piteous" object, to use Richard Henry Dana's description.[4] He was much more than that, however, and he had been so from childhood, when he seized on every opportunity that he had to become literate, to learn the ways of the world, and to understand the scriptures. When the Baptist church in Fauquier County banned him from membership, he defended himself before God and before man. "Thus you have excommunicated me, on the charge of 'disobeying both the laws of God and men,' in absconding from the service of my master, and refusing to return voluntarily," declared Burns. He then framed his defense on the basis of natural and divine rights, again claiming the fruits of the American Revolution. "Look at my case," wrote Burns. "I was stolen and made a slave as soon as I was born. No man had any right to steal me. That manstealer who stole me trampled on my dearest rights. He committed an outrage on the law of God; therefore his manstealing gave him no right in me, and laid me under no obligation to be his slave. God made me a man—not a slave. . . . I utterly deny that those things which outrage all right are laws. To be real laws they must be founded in equity."[5] After the drama in Boston, Anthony Burns and many African Americans embraced a new militancy aimed at asserting their rights and sharing in the results of the American Revolution; more than 180,000 black men would put their lives on the line for this cause between 1863 and 1865.[6]

Despite Commissioner Loring's decision in favor of Colonel Charles F. Suttle, the Burns crisis served as a call to action to many slaveholding Virginians. The show of force required to ensure Burns's return to bondage grated against the inherited political culture of many white Virginians who embraced Jeffersonian ideals of limited government. It also seemed to reinforce their suspicions that antislavery sentiments were on the rise in the rapidly expanding North. Reminding them of John C. Calhoun's warning that population growth in the free states undermined the "equilibrium between the sections," the Burns drama had a two-sided message for white Virginians: although Franklin Pierce had firmly defended the interests of a Southern slaveholder, they could not depend on future presidents to do likewise.[7]

Furthermore, unlike the Kansas-Nebraska crisis, which concerned the prospect of slavery in a distant, undeveloped western territory, the Burns drama focused attention on Southern society and institutions, and it accentuated differences between the North and the South. This process hastened the rise of a new generation of proslavery Southern thinkers who argued that slavery was a positive good, not merely a necessary evil tacitly recognized by the Constitution. The Burns affair served as a real test of their arguments, and many white Virginians quickly came to view the Union differently. Despite their previous commitment to the Union and their support of the Compromise of 1850, many interpreted the Burns crisis as a signal that it was now time to think about the South, and they began to support measures to distance themselves from the North. The major impact of the Burns crisis on the coming of the Civil War appears to have been in the South, not in the North, as has been suggested by many scholars.

Once freed, Anthony Burns never relinquished his people's fight for freedom. In moving to St. Catharines, Ontario, he joined a vibrant black community committed to resisting slavery and elevating the black race.

Building strong institutions, fostering good relations with prominent whites, taking advantage of access to education, and achieving independence and new prosperity through landownership and gainful employment, Ontario's early blacks asserted their rights as British subjects and citizens. From the 1830s until the eve of the Civil War, these enterprising black men and women demonstrated militancy similar to that shown by Frederick Douglass in his battle against slavery, the Reverend Jermain Wesley Loguen in the Jerry rescue, and Harriet Tubman on her many trips to the South to lead her people to freedom in St. Catharines.

There in the City of Refuge, alongside the likes of Harriet Tubman, the Reverend Loguen, and the white abolitionist Hiram Wilson, Anthony Burns established himself as a leader in a truly remarkable community, if only for a short while because of his untimely death. Descendants of those who knew Anthony Burns in St. Catharines not only remember him as "the fugitive slave of the Boston riots, 1854," they recognize him as a central figure on their Freedom Trail and a symbol of all that it represented. Determined to preserve his place in their historical memory, as well as in the story of the broader North American past, they have established both Anthony Burns's gravesite and Harriet Tubman's BME Church as official heritage sites. These places represent points and people not to be forgotten in American and Canadian history; they also remind us that the struggle against American slavery spanned the forty-ninth parallel and that Anthony Burns was both a freedom seeker and a fighter for freedom; he sought the extension of American liberties to himself and his people. He was an American Revolutionary.

Notes

PROLOGUE

1. Albert Réville, *The Life and Writings of Theodore Parker* (London: Simpkin, Marshall, 1865), 116.

2. Charles Emery Stevens, *Anthony Burns: A History* (Boston: John P. Jewett, 1856).

3. Stanley W. Campbell, *The Slave Catchers: Enforcement of the Fugitive Slave Law, 1850–1860* (Chapel Hill: Univ. of North Carolina Press, 1968), 81; Jane H. Pease and William H. Pease, *The Fugitive Slave Law and Anthony Burns* (Philadelphia: Lippincott, 1975).

4. Jane H. Pease and William H. Pease, "Confrontation and Abolition in the 1850s," *Journal of American History* 58, no. 4 (1972): 923–37, esp. 925–26.

5. Harold Schwartz, "Fugitive Slave Days in Boston," *New England Quarterly* 27, no. 2 (1954): 211; Stanley Shapiro, "The Rendition of Anthony Burns," *Journal of Negro History* 44, no. 1 (1959): 37.

6. David R. Maginnes, "The Case of the Court House Rioters in the Rendition of the Fugitive Slave Anthony Burns, 1854," *Journal of Negro History* 56, no. 1 (1971): 31–42.

7. James Oliver Horton and Lois E. Horton, *Black Bostonians: Family Life and Community Struggle in the Antebellum North* (New York: Holmes and Meier, 1979), esp. 113–14. In *Slavery and the Making of America* (New York: Oxford Univ. Press, 2005), the Hortons emphasize that "the sight of a fugitive guarded by federal troops being marched to the wharf in Boston, the stronghold of abolition, was proof that the federal government was in the hands of an increasingly aggressive 'slave power.' . . . The South's recovery of Anthony Burns and other fugitives from northern cities raised awareness of many northern whites to the evils of slavery" (156). Charles Johnson, Patricia Smith, and WGBH Series Research Team, *Africans in America: America's Journey through Slavery* (New York: Harcourt Brace, 1998), 401, 403.

8. David Herbert Donald, *Charles Sumner* (New York: Da Capo, 1996), esp. 260–67; Albert J. Von Frank, *The Trials of Anthony Burns: Freedom and Slavery in Emerson's Boston* (Cambridge, Mass.: Harvard Univ. Press, 1998), esp. xiii, 322–33.

9. Although both Sumner and Garrison opposed slavery on moral grounds, they expressed their opposition very differently. Sumner embraced politics as a means to bring down the slave power; Garrison advocated disengagement from the American political system and direct confrontation with slavery, which led to his rejection of the Constitution.

10. W. E. B. Du Bois, *Black Reconstruction in America* (New York: Russell and Russell, 1935).

11. William E. Gienapp, "Abolitionism and the Nature of Antebellum Reform," in *Courage and Conscience: Black and White Abolitionists in Boston,* ed. Donald M. Jacobs (Indianapolis: Indiana Univ. Press, 1993), 20–46, esp. 42.

12. Eric Foner, *Free Soil, Free Labor, Free Men: The Ideology of the Republican Party before the Civil War* (New York: Oxford Univ. Press, 1995), 262–65.

127

13. Ira Berlin, "Who Freed the Slaves? Emancipation and Its Meaning," in *Union and Emancipation: Essays on Politics and Race in the Civil War*, ed. David W. Blight and Brooks D. Simpson (Kent, Ohio: Kent State Univ. Press, 1997), 105–21.

14. David W. Blight, *Beyond the Battlefield: Race, Memory, and the American Civil War* (Amherst: Univ. of Massachusetts Press, 2002), 37.

15. Eric Foner uses the term "unfinished" in his *Reconstruction: America's Unfinished Revolution, 1863–1877* (New York: Harper & Row).

16. Anthony Burns to Richard Henry Dana Jr., Aug. 30, 1857, Massachusetts Historical Society Archives, Boston. Implicitly I am arguing that for many blacks, the American Revolution extended beyond the Jackson years, as has been suggested by Gordon S. Wood in *The Radicalism of the American Revolution* (New York: Vintage Books, 1991). I argue that for many African Americans, the Revolution was not complete until they shared in American liberties.

1. PERCEIVING THE NORTH STAR

1. Charles Emery Stevens interviewed Anthony Burns and remains the best available source on his early life. See Charles Emery Stevens, *Anthony Burns: A History* (Boston: John P. Jewett, 1856). The Burns family appears to have conformed to patterns of family development described by Herbert Gutman: family ties were strong, Burns's mother had a large number of children, and she was serially monogamous. See Herbert G. Gutman, *The Black Family in Slavery and Freedom, 1750–1925* (New York: Vintage Books, 1977).

2. Walter Johnson stresses that slaves acquired a "double consciousness" at a very young age. Young males could enjoy their growing strength and females could take pride in the development of their bodies as they reached puberty, but black youths, male or female, could not ignore the fact that these very qualities increased their value at auction. Walter Johnson, *Soul by Soul: Life in the Antebellum Slave Market* (Cambridge, Mass.: Harvard Univ. Press, 1999).

3. Frederick Douglass frequently addressed the issue of slave literacy. He covertly educated himself after his master, Hugh Auld, reprimanded his wife for giving Douglass lessons and succeeded in convincing her that "slavery and education were incompatible with each other." Douglass said his master's opposition only encouraged him to learn, and he "set out with high hope, and a fixed purpose, at whatever the cost of trouble, to learn how to read." *Narrative of the Life of Frederick Douglass* (New York: Dover, 1995), 20.

4. Stevens, *Anthony Burns*, 154–55.

5. This formative period for Burns on the Brent plantation substantiates John Blassingame's views of the importance of life in the slave quarters away from the master's surveillance. See John W. Blassingame, *The Slave Community: Plantation Life in the Antebellum South* (New York: Oxford Univ. Press, 1979), esp. 249–83.

6. Stevens, *Anthony Burns*, 155–57.

7. An expression used by Kenneth M. Stampp, *The Peculiar Institution: Slavery in the Ante-bellum South* (New York: Knopf, 1956), 141.

8. Stevens, *Anthony Burns*, 151.

9. Ibid., 161–67; Peter Kolchin, *American Slavery, 1619–1877* (New York: Hill and Wang, 2003), 143.

10. Stevens, *Anthony Burns*, 174. In his study of Gabriel (sometimes called Gabriel Prosser), the leader of the failed Gabriel's Rebellion in 1800, Douglas Egerton stresses the influence of free blacks and whites on slaves hired out in the Richmond market. See Douglas R. Egerton, *Gabriel's Rebellion: The Virginia Slave Conspiracies of 1800 and 1802* (Chapel Hill: Univ. of North Carolina Press, 1993), esp. x–xi.

11. Stevens, *Anthony Burns*, 174–75.

2. The Elusive North Star over the Cradle of Liberty

1. Charles Emery Stevens, *Anthony Burns: A History* (Boston: John P. Jewett, 1856), 178–79. Stevens remains the best source on Burns's escape.

2. George A. Levesque, *Black Boston: African American Life and Culture in Urban America, 1750–1860* (New York: Garland, 1994), tables I-8, I-13.

3. Albert J. Von Frank, *The Trials of Anthony Burns: Freedom and Slavery in Emerson's Boston* (Cambridge, Mass.: Harvard Univ. Press, 1998), 13–15.

4. For a discussion of William Cooper Nell and the Franklin Medal, see Stephen Kendrick and Paul Kendrick, *Sarah's Long Walk: The Free Blacks of Boston and How Their Struggle for Equality Changed America* (Boston: Beacon Press, 2004), 67–69.

5. Charles Sumner, "Brief for Public School Integration," in *Brown v. Board of Education: A Brief History with Documents*, ed. Waldo E. Martin Jr. (Boston: Bedford/St. Martin's, 1998), 47.

6. Kendrick and Kendrick, *Sarah's Long Walk*, xv; Sumner, "Brief for Public School Integration," 59.

7. Sumner, "Brief for Public School Integration," 59.

8. David Herbert Donald, *Charles Sumner* (New York: Da Capo, 1996), 181–82. For a concise discussion of the issue of interracial marriage, discrimination against blacks in public transportation, and racist policies in awarding the Franklin Medal, see Kendrick and Kendrick, *Sarah's Long Walk*, 53–69.

9. Kendrick and Kendrick, *Sarah's Long Walk*, 17, 21.

10. Stevens, *Anthony Burns*, 179–80.

11. Von Frank, *The Trials of Anthony Burns*, 126–27. Von Frank describes the busy atmosphere in Boston during Anniversary Week.

12. [Anonymous], *Boston Slave Riot and Trial of Anthony Burns Containing the Report . . .* (1854; Northbrook, Ill.: Metro Books, 1972), 15. See also Stevens, *Anthony Burns*, 180.

13. In 1851, Asa Butman was deputized under the new Fugitive Slave Law (1850) and arrested the fugitive slave Thomas Sims, who was later returned to Georgia. In the eyes of Massachusetts abolitionists, Butman became a much-hated symbol of the federal government's support for slavery. For descriptions of the arrest of Burns, see *Frederick Douglass' Paper*, June 16, 1854; *Boston Slave Riot*, 21; Stevens, *Anthony Burns*, 16; Jane H. Pease and William H. Pease, *The Fugitive Slave Law and Anthony Burns* (Philadelphia: Lippincott, 1975), 28.

14. By midcentury, vigilance committees had been formed in leading Northern cities. The Boston Vigilance Committee was interracial and included several of the city's antislavery leaders. It provided food, clothing, and shelter to fugitives arriving in the city. As a result of their contacts with abolitionists in Canada and Britain, members of the Boston Vigilance Committee were positioned to assist fugitives seeking refuge in these areas.

15. The Fugitive Slave Law of 1850 set up special tribunals to hear fugitive slave cases, which were presided over by federally appointed slave commissioners who enjoyed arbitrary authority. See the discussion of the Fugitive Slave Law of 1850 in chap. 3. Partly because of his leading role in the Jerry rescue in Syracuse in 1851, May was regarded as one of New England's most prominent abolitionists.

16. Quoted in Charles Johnson, Patricia Smith, and WGBH Series Research Team, *Africans in America: America's Journey through Slavery* (New York: Harcourt Brace, 1998), 399.

17. Leonard W. Levy, "Sims' Case: The Fugitive Slave Law in Boston in 1851," *Journal of Negro History* 35, no. 1 (1950): 44.

18. *The Journal of Richard Henry Dana, Jr.*, ed. Robert F. Lucid (Cambridge, Mass.: Belknap Press of Harvard Univ. Press, 1968), 2:625–26. It is interesting to note that Frederick Douglass initially criticized Burns's remarks of despair, which he seemed to think indicated

an unwillingness on Burns's part to fight for liberty. See *The Frederick Douglass Papers*, ed. John W. Blassingame (New Haven, Conn.: Yale Univ. Press, 1985), 3:88. Douglass's overall reaction to the Burns rendition is discussed in chap. 4.

19. *Monthly Law Reporter*, Aug. 1854, 181–82.

20. Ibid., 182; *Journal of Richard Henry Dana, Jr.*, 625–26.

21. Henry Steele Commager, *Theodore Parker: Yankee Crusader* (Boston: Beacon Press, 1960), 233. See also Von Frank, *The Trials of Anthony Burns*, 10.

22. Von Frank, *The Trials of Anthony Burns*, 9.

23. For a copy of the writ of personal replevin, see Stevens, *Anthony Burns*, 249–51. For discussion of these events, see also *Journal of Richard Henry Dana, Jr.*, 627.

24. Several scholars have touched on the division of the Boston Vigilance Committee. See Von Frank, *The Trials of Anthony Burns*, 11–12, and Harold Schwartz, "Fugitive Slave Days in Boston," *New England Quarterly* 27, no. 2 (1954): 191–212. Gary L. Collison provides several insights into the law-and-order bias of the Boston Vigilance Committee. See Gary L. Collison, "The Boston Vigilance Committee: A Reconsideration," *Historical Journal of Massachusetts* 12, no. 2 (1984): 104–16, and *Shadrach Minkins: From Fugitive Slave to Citizen* (Cambridge, Mass.: Harvard Univ. Press, 1997), esp. 84. Martin Stowell also participated in the Jerry rescue.

25. *Boston Evening Transcript*, May 27, 1854.

26. *Journal of Richard Henry Dana, Jr.*, 628–29.

27. *Boston Slave Riot*, 8. See also *Frederick Douglass' Paper*, June 9, 1854; Von Frank, *The Trials of Anthony Burns*, 55.

28. *Boston Morning Journal*, May 27, 1854. See also Pease and Pease, *The Fugitive Slave Law*, 31; *Boston Slave Riot*, 8–10. The issue of higher law assumed great importance after William Seward's "Higher Law" speech in the Great Debates on slavery in 1850.

29. Von Frank, *The Trials of Anthony Burns*, 56.

30. *Boston Slave Riot*, 8–9; Stevens, *Anthony Burns*, 41; *Frederick Douglass' Paper*, June 9, 1854; *Boston Morning Journal*, May 27, 1854; Von Frank, *The Trials of Anthony Burns*, 57–58, 61.

31. *Boston Morning Journal*, May 27, 1854; *Boston Slave Riot*, 8–9.

32. *Boston Morning Journal*, May 27, 1854. See also *Boston Slave Riot*, 10; *Frederick Douglass' Paper*, June 9, 1854.

33. *Boston Morning Journal*, May 27, 1854; Von Frank, *The Trials of Anthony Burns*, 62–63. Higginson's reaction to the crisis is also addressed in Samuel Shapiro, "The Rendition of Anthony Burns," *Journal of Negro History* 44, no. 1 (1959): 38, and in Commager, *Theodore Parker*, 235–36.

34. Describing the assault on the courthouse, the Peases write that "hoisting a battering ram, a dozen or more men, mostly black, charged repeatedly, smashing the timber against the door till it gave way." Pease and Pease, *The Fugitive Slave Law*, 33. The assault is also dealt with in Von Frank's *The Trials of Anthony Burns* and in *Boston Slave Riot*.

35. David R. Maginnes, "The Case of the Court House Rioters in the Rendition of the Fugitive Slave Anthony Burns, 1854," *Journal of Negro History* 56, no. 1 (1971): 31.

36. *Boston Morning Journal*, May 27, 1854; *Boston Evening Transcript*, May 27, 1854; Stevens, *Anthony Burns*, 44. See also Commager, *Theodore Parker*, 236; *Provincial Freeman*, June 3, 1854.

37. When the west side door broke open, Batchelder suddenly cried out that he had been stabbed. With blood gushing from his groin, he was taken by fellow guards into an adjacent room, where he died shortly thereafter. There was much confusion surrounding his death. Until the announcement several days later of the results of a coroner's inquest, which confirmed that Batchelder died from a knife wound that severed his femoral artery, most people—including Stowell and Hayden, who both had fired pistols during the assault—presumed that the guard had

been killed by gunfire. *Boston Morning Journal,* May 27, 1854; *Boston Evening Transcript,* May 27, 1854; Stevens, *Anthony Burns,* 43–44; *Boston Slave Riot,* 12; *Provincial Freeman,* June 3, 1854.

38. Charles Sumner, *The Works of Charles Sumner* (Boston: Lee and Shepard, 1873), 457.

39. *Boston Evening Transcript,* May 27, 1854. The Peases describe the square shortly after midnight as "deserted." Pease and Pease, *The Fugitive Slave Law,* 33.

40. Roy Franklin Nichols, *Franklin Pierce: Young Hickory of the Granite Hills* (Philadelphia: Univ. of Pennsylvania Press, 1969), 361. See also the *Richmond Enquirer,* June 2, 1854; *National Era,* June 1, 1854; Commager, *Theodore Parker,* 236–37.

41. *Journal of Richard Henry Dana, Jr.,* 629.

42. *Monthly Law Reporter,* Aug. 1854, 184.

43. This purchase attempt was reported in several newspapers, including the *Boston Evening Transcript,* May 29, 1854, and the *National Era,* June 1, 1854. See also *Boston Slave Riot,* 18–19, and Stevens, *Anthony Burns,* 60–79. The failure of the purchase attempt is discussed in chap. 4.

44. *Boston Evening Transcript,* May 29, 1854.

45. *Richmond Enquirer,* June 2, 1854.

46. *Boston Evening Transcript,* May 29, 1854; *Richmond Enquirer,* June 2, 1854.

47. Collison, "The Boston Vigilance Committee," 110.

48. *New York Daily Times,* June 1, 1854, also quoted in Shapiro, "The Rendition of Anthony Burns," 41.

49. Stevens, *Anthony Burns,* 86; *Monthly Law Reporter,* Aug. 1854, 182.

50. *Monthly Law Reporter,* Aug. 1854, 185–86. See also Stevens, *Anthony Burns,* 85–87; *Boston Slave Riot,* 45, 47.

51. *Monthly Law Reporter,* Aug. 1854, 188.

52. Ibid., 188–91, 198–99. See also Stevens, *Anthony Burns,* 92–94; *Boston Slave Riot,* 64–65; *Journal of Richard Henry Dana, Jr.,* 632.

53. *Boston Evening Transcript,* May 31, 1854.

54. Ibid.

55. *Journal of Richard Henry Dana, Jr.,* 632.

56. George Ticknor Curtis was appointed executor of Webster's estate. He also was a slave law commissioner. His brother, Benjamin Robbins Curtis, was the attorney who prosecuted the case against the fugitive slave Thomas Sims. Loring was the stepbrother of Christopher Pelham Curtis and Thomas B. Curtis, distant cousins of George and Benjamin. Thomas Curtis, a wealthy merchant, was instrumental in organizing a joint letter with more than nine hundred signatures commending Webster on the Compromise of 1850 and the new Fugitive Slave Law. Von Frank, *The Trials of Anthony Burns,* 116–17.

57. *Frederick Douglass' Paper,* June 9, 1854; *Boston Morning Journal,* June 3, 1854; *Boston Slave Riot,* 76–77. See also *Journal of Richard Henry Dana, Jr.,* 634.

58. *Monthly Law Reporter,* Aug. 1854, 203–7.

59. Ibid., 207–10. Implicitly, Loring adopted a narrow interpretation of fugitive testimony under the new Fugitive Slave Law, excluding statements made out of court by the alleged fugitive as "testimony."

60. Ibid. See also *Boston Slave Riot,* 82–83; Stevens, *Anthony Burns,* 120–212. Burns's departure had to be delayed an hour in order to clear the streets between the courthouse and the harbor.

61. *Boston Morning Journal,* June 3, 1854; *Boston Evening Transcript,* June 2, 1854; *Boston Slave Riot,* 77–78; *Richmond Enquirer,* June 3, 1854.

62. *Boston Evening Transcript,* June 2, 1854.

63. *Frederick Douglass' Paper,* June 9, 1854.

64. *Boston Evening Transcript,* June 3, 1854.

65. Ibid.

66. *Boston Evening Transcript,* June 2 and 3, 1854; *Boston Morning Journal,* June 3, 1854. See also *Boston Slave Riot,* 84–86; *Richmond Enquirer,* June 2, 1854; *Frederick Douglass' Paper,* June 9, 1854.

67. *Boston Evening Transcript,* June 2, 1854.

68. *The Journal of Charlotte L. Forten: A Free Negro in the Slave Era,* ed. Ray Allen Billington (New York: Collier Books, 1961), 46.

69. *Boston Slave Riot,* 85.

70. Shapiro, "The Rendition of Anthony Burns," 45.

71. *Boston Morning Journal,* June 3, 1854; Shapiro, "The Rendition of Anthony Burns," 45; *Frederick Douglass' Paper,* Dec. 22, 1854; Commager, *Theodore Parker,* 241; *Journal of Richard Henry Dana, Jr.,* 634, 636. See also *Frederick Douglass' Paper,* June 9, 1854; Von Frank, *The Trials of Anthony Burns,* 215.

72. *Boston Morning Journal,* June 3, 1854, also quoted in *Boston Slave Riot,* 84–86.

73. *Richmond Enquirer,* June 2, 1854, also quoted in *Frederick Douglass' Paper,* June 9, 1854; *Boston Evening Transcript,* June 3, 1854.

74. *Boston Evening Transcript,* June 3, 1854. Dana also mentions the countermanding of the order. *Journal of Richard Henry Dana, Jr.,* 635.

75. *Boston Evening Transcript,* June 3, 1854.

76. Ibid.

77. *Boston Morning Journal,* June 3, 1854.

78. *Frederick Douglass' Paper,* Mar. 16, 1855; *Provincial Freeman,* Mar. 17, 1855. In *Anthony Burns: A History,* Stevens also mentions the ill treatment of Burns in Lumpkin's prison.

3. The Background to the Spectacle

1. Bruce Laurie has also focused on the number of curious spectators. See Bruce Laurie, *Beyond Garrison: Antislavery and Social Reform* (New York: Cambridge Univ. Press, 2005), 241.

2. Stanley W. Campbell, *The Slave Catchers: Enforcement of the Fugitive Slave Law, 1850–1860* (Chapel Hill: Univ. of North Carolina Press, 1968), 5. Campbell emphasizes that many Southerners were "particularly anxious" for the Fugitive Slave Law to be enforced. In fact, the Georgia Platform (see chap. 5) took the position that "faithful execution" of the law was essential if the Union were to be preserved.

3. For a summary of events leading to the Compromise of 1850 and the adoption of the new Fugitive Slave Law, see John C. Waugh, *On the Brink of Civil War: The Compromise of 1850 and How It Changed the Course of American History* (Wilmington, Del.: Scholarly Resources, 2003). See also Jane H. Pease and William H. Pease, *The Fugitive Slave Law and Anthony Burns* (Philadelphia: Lippincott, 1975), 6–12.

4. Quoted in Hudson Strode, *Jefferson Davis: American Patriot, 1808–1861* (New York: Harcourt Brace, 1955), 222.

5. Dayton quoted in *Congressional Globe,* 31st Congress, 1st sess., Aug. 1850, 1584.

6. *Jefferson Davis, Constitutionalist: His Letters, Papers and Speeches,* ed. Dunbar Rowland (Jackson: Mississippi Department of Archives and History, 1923), 520.

7. Clemens quoted in *Congressional Globe,* 31st Congress, 1st sess., Feb. 22, 1850, appendix, 305.

8. V. Jacque Voegeli, *Free but Not Equal: The Midwest and the Negro during the Civil War* (Chicago: Univ. of Chicago Press, 1967), 5.

9. *The Life and Writings of Frederick Douglass,* ed. Philip S. Foner (New York: International Publishers, 1950), 2:127; [Frederick Douglass], *The Life and Times of Frederick Douglass* (New York: Cosimo, 2008), 213.

10. Frederick Douglass, *My Bondage and My Freedom* (New York: Miller, Orton & Mulligan, 1853), 453. For a summary of executive policies toward enforcement of fugitive slave legislation during the Pierce and Buchanan administrations, see Campbell, *The Slave Catchers,* 104–9.

11. Wilmot and Seward are both quoted in George M. Fredrickson, *The Black Image in the White Mind: The Debate on Afro-American Character and Destiny, 1817–1914* (New York: Harper & Row, 1971), 140–41.

12. *Life and Times of Frederick Douglass,* 208.

13. Quoted in W. E. B. Du Bois, *Black Reconstruction in America* (New York: Russell and Russell, 1935), 22.

14. Voegeli, *Free but Not Equal,* 6.

15. Campbell, *The Slave Catchers,* 60–61.

16. Leon Litwack, *North of Slavery: The Negro in the Free States, 1790–1860* (Chicago: University of Chicago Press, 1961), 97.

17. Ibid., 115.

18. Ibid.

19. C. Vann Woodward, *American Counterpoint: Slavery and Racism in the North-South Dialogue* (Boston: Little, Brown, 1971), 97.

20. Quoted in Philip S. Foner, *History of Black Americans: From the Compromise of 1850 to the End of the Civil War* (Westport, Conn.: Greenwood Press, 1983), 145–46.

21. Fredrickson, *The Black Image,* 92.

22. Ibid., 95.

23. Ibid., 52, 74, 94–95.

24. Litwack, *North of Slavery,* 98. In this context, black men in the antebellum North strove "to affirm their manhood," a movement that is particularly well documented in James Oliver Horton and Lois E. Horton, "The Affirmation of Manhood," in *Courage and Conscience: Black and White Abolitionists in Boston,* ed. Donald M. Jacobs (Indianapolis: Indiana Univ. Press, 1993), 127–54. The Hortons highlight how this affirmation contributed to splits between pacifist abolitionists and militant Northern blacks. Anthony Burns embraced this mission; he declared that he wanted to prove he was a man.

25. Melvin Patrick Ely, *Israel on the Appomattox: A Southern Experiment in Black Freedom from the 1790s through the Civil War* (New York: Knopf, 2004), 284, 442, 440. For background, see also 70–94 and 284–301.

26. George A. Levesque, *Black Boston: African American Life and Culture in Urban America, 1750–1860* (New York: Garland, 1994), 71–111.

27. Voegeli, *Free but Not Equal,* 5. C. Vann Woodward also has emphasized this consideration. See Woodward, *American Counterpoint,* 157.

28. Du Bois, *Black Reconstruction in America,* 18; *National Era,* Nov. 15, 1855.

29. Leonard P. Curry, *The Free Blacks in Urban America, 1800–1850* (Chicago: Univ. of Chicago Press, 1981), 104.

30. Gary B. Nash, *Forging Freedom: The Formation of Philadelphia's Black Community, 1720–1840* (Cambridge, Mass.: Harvard Univ. Press, 1988), 278.

31. Du Bois, *Black Reconstruction in America,* 18. On the impact of antebellum racial strife, see also James Oliver Horton and Lois E. Horton, *In Hope of Liberty: Culture, Community, and Protest among Northern Free Blacks, 1760–1860* (New York: Oxford Univ. Press, 1997), 210; Curry, *Free Blacks in Urban America,* 104–5, 107.

32. Horton and Horton, *In Hope of Liberty*, 233–34.

33. Grier quoted in the *American Law Journal*, Apr. 1852, 459. For summaries of the Christiana affair, see Foner, *History of Black Americans*, 50–60; Pease and Pease, *The Fugitive Slave Law*, 19. The federal response to the affair continued to incense antislavery activists long after and to be assailed in the abolitionist press years later.

34. *National Era*, Apr. 20, 1855.

35. Marion Gleason McDougall, *Fugitive Slaves, 1619–1865* (New York: Bergman, 1967), 49.

36. For a discussion of such sentiments in Syracuse, see W. Freeman Galpin, "The Jerry Rescue," *New York History* 26 (Jan. 1945): 19, 30.

37. *New York Herald*, July 10, 1853, reprinted in the *National Era*, July 28, 1853.

38. On the fate of Elijah Lovejoy, see Horton and Horton, *In Hope of Liberty*, 240.

39. *New York Daily Times*, May 29, 1854.

40. Samuel May, *Recollections of Our Antislavery Conflict* (Boston: Fields, Osgood, 1869), 127–28.

41. Quoted in Campbell, *The Slave Catchers*, 73–74, 55.

42. Quoted in ibid., 65–66.

43. Quoted in ibid., 69.

44. Quoted in ibid., 122.

45. Quoted in ibid., 69.

46. *American Law Journal*, Apr. 1852, 458; Pease and Pease, *The Fugitive Slave Law*, 14; Campbell, *The Slave Catchers*, 74.

47. Leonard W. Levy, "Sims' Case: The Fugitive Slave Law in Boston in 1851," *Journal of Negro History* 35, no. 1 (1950): 40.

48. *National Era*, May 10, 1855, and Dec. 30, 1858.

49. *Frederick Douglass' Paper*, Dec. 22, 1854.

50. Quoted in Pease and Pease, *The Fugitive Slave Law*, 28.

51. Henry Mayer, *All on Fire: William Lloyd Garrison and the Abolition of Slavery* (New York: St. Martin's, 1998), 407.

52. The American Presidency Project, "Millard Fillmore: Second Annual Message, Dec. 2, 1851," accessed at www.presidency.ucsb.edu/ws/index.php?pid=29492.

53. Webster quoted in Galpin, "The Jerry Rescue," 19.

54. In his current research on Concord, Massachusetts, focusing on the antislavery stance of the *Yeoman's Gazette*, Robert A. Gross uncovers conflicts between antislavery sentiments of abolitionists and other residents' concerns about the stability of the Union and law and order in general. See Robert A. Gross, "Humanitarian Interests: Antislavery Activism in Concord, Massachusetts" (unpublished manuscript, Jan. 7, 2007).

55. Foner, *History of Black Americans*, 37–38; Austin Bearse, *Reminiscences of Fugitive-Slave Days in Boston* (1880; New York: Arno Press, 1969), 17. All quotes are from Levy, "Sims' Case," 41–42.

56. Winthrop and Lawrence quoted in Thomas H. O'Connor, *Lords of the Loom: The Cotton Whigs and the Coming of the Civil War* (New York: Charles Scribner's Sons, 1968), 97.

57. Vincent Y. Bowditch, *Life and Correspondence of Henry Ingersoll Bowditch* (Boston: Houghton, Mifflin, 1902), 1:212; Parker quoted in John White Chadwick, *Theodore Parker: Preacher and Reformer* (Boston: Houghton Mifflin, 1900), 252.

58. *Monthly Law Reporter*, May 1851, 1.

59. Under the Fugitive Slave Law of 1850, individuals had to cooperate with authorities in apprehending fugitive slaves. To arrest a fugitive officially, however, an individual needed to be deputized as a federal marshal. Invoking the philosophy that led to the passage of "personal liberty laws" in several Northern states, including Massachusetts, antislavery activists

in Boston opposed the deputation of state and city police as federal marshals. They asserted that deputation of city and state police was contrary to the Massachusetts personal liberty law that expressly disallowed "any state officials or facilities to be used in the capture and rendition of fugitive slaves"—this after the contentious U.S. Supreme Court ruling in *Prigg v. Pennsylvania* (1842). See discussion in James Oliver Horton and Lois E. Horton, *Slavery and the Making of America* (New York: Oxford Univ. Press, 2005).

60. All quotes from Levy, "Sims' Case," 51, 69, 72.

61. *National Era*, Apr. 10, 1851; *Liberator*, Apr. 18, 1851; Bearse, *Reminiscences*, 25; Mayer, *All on Fire*, 411–12; Levy, "Sims' Case," 50–72; Bowditch, *Life and Correspondence*, 1:217.

62. Fillmore quoted in Pease and Pease, *The Fugitive Slave Law*, 19.

63. Quoted in the *Liberator*, May 23, 1851. Campbell also notes that the abolitionists did not command the support of most Bostonians. See Campbell, *The Slave Catchers*, 119.

64. Bearse, *Reminiscences*, 32 and 35, also quoted in Harold Schwartz, "Fugitive Slave Days," *New England Quarterly* 27, no. 2 (1954): 199.

65. Wendell Phillips, *Speeches, Lectures, and Letters* (Boston: J. Redpath, 1863), 57.

66. Quoted in Schwartz, "Fugitive Slave Days in Boston," 199. Higginson's labeling of abolitionists as "irresolute and hopeless" was consistent with his frustration with the Boston Vigilance Committee's unwillingness to support a rescue of Burns at its meetings immediately following Burns's arrest.

67. See Roy E. Finkenbine, "Boston's Black Churches: Institutional Centers of the Anti-slavery Movement," in *Courage and Conscience: Black and White Abolitionists in Boston*, ed. Donald M. Jacobs (Indianapolis: Indiana Univ. Press, 1993), esp. 170–83.

68. James Oliver Horton and Lois E. Horton, *Black Bostonians: Family Life and Community Struggle in the Antebellum North* (New York: Holmes and Meier, 1979), 94.

69. Gary L. Collison, "The Boston Vigilance Committee: A Reconsideration," *Historical Journal of Massachusetts* 12, no. 2 (1984): 111.

70. Horton and Horton, *In Hope of Liberty*, 221. On black Boston's initiatives, and the eventual overturn of school segregation in 1855, see also *Black Bostonians*, 115–28.

71. Albert Réville, *The Life and Writings of Theodore Parker* (London: Simpkin, Marshall, 1865), 117.

72. Horton and Horton, *Black Bostonians*, 103.

73. Finkenbine, "Boston's Black Churches," 174. The increasing militancy of Frederick Douglass in these circumstances is highlighted in chap. 4.

74. *National Era*, Nov. 15, 1855.

75. Curry, *Free Blacks in Urban America*, 100.

76. On the political and economic climate, see Levesque, *Black Boston*, 21–39.

4. The Meaning of the Spectacle

1. Charles Emery Stevens, *Anthony Burns: A History* (Boston: John P. Jewett, 1856), 291, also 289–95. Stevens reproduces Parker's speech in Appendix M. See also Albert J. Von Frank, *The Trials of Anthony Burns: Freedom and Slavery in Emerson's Boston* (Cambridge, Mass.: Harvard Univ. Press, 1998), 58–59, and Albert Réville, *The Life and Writings of Theodore Parker* (London: Simpkin, Marshall, 1865), 119.

2. *Boston Morning Journal*, May 27, 1854. The denunciation of this policy by the prominent abolitionist Francis W. Bird was criticized in a *Boston Courier* editorial and in the *New York Times* of May 29, 1854.

3. *Boston Post*, May 27, 1854, reprinted in *New York Daily Times*, May 29, 1854.

4. *Boston Post*, June 3, 1854.

5. *Boston Daily Courier,* May 27, 1854, reprinted in *New York Daily Times,* May 29, 1854.

6. *Boston Evening Transcript,* May 30, 1854. Whittier's rejection of violence was also consistent with his Quaker beliefs.

7. *Boston Evening Transcript,* June 6, 1854.

8. *Boston Evening Transcript,* May 30, 1854.

9. *Boston Evening Transcript,* May 27, 1854, and May 29, 1854. The Columbian Artillery incurred the wrath of abolitionists, as seen in a broadside from the archives of the Massachusetts Historical Society:

AMERICANS TO THE RESCUE! IRISHMEN UNDER ARMS! AMERICANS! SONS OF THE REVOLUTION!! A body of SEVENTY-FIVE IRISHMEN, known as "COLUMBIAN ARTIL-LERY!" Have volunteered their services to SHOOT DOWN THE CITIZENS OF BOSTON, aided by a company of the UNITED STATES MARINES, nearly all of them are IRISH-MEN!! And are now under arms to defend Virginia IN KIDNAPPING A CITIZEN OF MASSACHUSETTS!!! AMERICANS! These Irishmen have called us "Cowards! And Sons of Cowards!!" SHALL WE SUBMIT TO HAVE OUR CITIZENS SHOT DOWN BY A SET OF VAGABOND IRISHMEN!

10. *Boston Evening Transcript,* June 1, 1854.

11. Quoted in Harold Schwartz, "Fugitive Slave Days in Boston," *New England Quarterly* 27, no. 2 (1954): 209.

12. *Liberator,* June 9, 1854.

13. E. B. Willson, *The Bad Friday: A Sermon Preached in the First Church, West Roxbury, June 4, 1854: It being Sunday after the Return of Anthony Burns* (Boston: John Wilson & Son, 1854), 5-7, in the Massachusetts Historical Society Archives, Boston.

14. E. H. Gray, *Assault upon Freedom! or [Kidnapping an Outrage upon Humanity and Abhorrent to God] A Discourse, Occasioned by the Rendition of Anthony Burns* (Shelburne Falls, Mass.: D. B. Gunn, 1854), 12, in the Massachusetts Historical Society Archives, Boston.

15. *Boston Evening Transcript,* June 6, 1854.

16. *Boston Evening Transcript,* Aug. 17, 1854.

17. John R. Mulkern, *The Know-Nothing Party in Massachusetts: The Rise and Fall of a People's Movement* (Boston: Northeastern Univ. Press, 1990), 68.

18. *Liberator,* Dec. 15, 1854.

19. For a discussion of Gardner's win, see Mulkern, *The Know-Nothing Party,* 75-82.

20. *Boston Evening Transcript,* Nov. 6, 1854.

21. *Boston Daily Atlas,* Oct. 3, 1854; *Boston Post,* Nov. 14, 1854.

22. Mulkern, *The Know-Nothing Party,* 73-80.

23. *Boston Evening Transcript,* Sept. 14, 1854. See also Henry Gardner, *Address of His Excellency Henry J. Gardner, to the Two Branches of the Legislature of Massachusetts, January 9, 1855* (Boston: William White, Printer to the State, 1855), in the Massachusetts Historical Society Archives, Boston. The term "progressive nativism" has been used by Steven Taylor, "Progressive Nativism: The Know-Nothing Party in Massachusetts," *Historical Journal of Massachusetts* 28 (2000): 165-85.

24. *National Era,* Nov. 15, 1855. Attitudes such as those demonstrated by Gardner and Smith provoke questions about the motivations for the antislavery legislation passed by Massachusetts's Know-Nothing legislature. I contend that to realize their revolution, the Know-Nothings forged temporary alliances with antislavery men who shared nativist and anti-Catholic sentiments, and they had to deliver on some antislavery promises to them. As Bruce Laurie has so adeptly shown, politics in Massachusetts during this period was "eclectic"—not just Free-Soil politics, but all politics. For the Know-Nothings, the greatest menace was that "the Irish

began to vote in greater numbers after 1852." Bruce Laurie, *Beyond Garrison: Antislavery and Social Reform* (New York: Cambridge Univ. Press, 2005), 288, 274. Their blend of xenophobia, anti-Catholicism, and antislavery heavily favored the two first sentiments and very quickly dispensed with the last. Gardner's political record during his term as governor indicates that while his political scheming, including his willingness to regress on slavery issues, may have been morally repulsive, it served him well. Although his margin of victory slipped in 1855, he still won, and the following year, he registered another triumph at the polls.

25. *Boston Post*, reprinted in the *Liberator*, June 9, 1854.

26. Gary L. Collison, "The Boston Vigilance Committee: A Reconsideration," *Historical Journal of Massachusetts* 12, no. 2 (1984): 109; Von Frank, *The Trials of Anthony Burns*, 69.

27. Charles Emery Stevens, *Anthony Burns: A History* (Boston: John P. Jewett, 1856), 35.

28. Schwartz, "Fugitive Slave Days," 209–10.

29. [Anonymous], *Boston Slave Riot and Trial of Anthony Burns Containing the Report . . .* (1854; Northbrook, Ill.: Metro Books, 1972), 8.

30. Vincent Y. Bowditch, *Life and Correspondence of Henry Ingersoll Bowditch* (Boston: Houghton, Mifflin, 1902), 1:265–66.

31. Phillips quoted in *Boston Slave Riot*, 9; Henry Steele Commager, *Theodore Parker: Yankee Crusader* (Boston: Beacon Press, 1960), 236; Alcott and Higginson quoted in Von Frank, *The Trials of Anthony Burns*, 70, 217.

32. Von Frank, *The Trials of Anthony Burns*, 54, 193–94.

33. *Boston Evening Transcript*, June 2, 1854.

34. *Boston Morning Journal*, June 3, 1854.

35. *Boston Slave Riot*, 85.

36. Von Frank, *The Trials of Anthony Burns*, 193–94. Stowe's profile is consistent with Henry Mayer's description of her earlier behavior. Mayer suggests that "[u]nlike Lydia Maria Child, who sacrificed her popularity for the [antislavery] movement," Stowe "remained as remote from social agitation as her father and husband had long thought all Christians should be." Her antislavery sentiments were "too 'Abolitiony' for her family's comfort." See Henry Mayer, *All on Fire: William Lloyd Garrison and the Abolition of Slavery* (New York: St. Martin's, 1998), 407.

37. Von Frank, *The Trials of Anthony Burns*, 214.

38. Collison, "The Boston Vigilance Committee," 110.

39. James Freeman Clarke, *The Rendition of Anthony Burns: Its Causes and Consequences: A Discourse on Christian Politics Delivered in Williams Hall, Boston on Whitsunday, June 4, 1854* (Boston: Crosby, Nichols and Prentiss & Sawyer, 1854), 16–17.

40. Ibid., 17.

41. Ibid., 17–20.

42. *Liberator*, July 21, 1854.

43. The Boston Vigilance Committee roster kept by Austin Bearse, the committee's doorkeeper from 1850 to 1860, contained 209 names. See Austin Bearse, *Reminiscences of Fugitive-Slave Days in Boston* (1880; New York: Arno Press, 1969), 3–5. Perhaps the following radical Locofoco Democrat's description of Boston's prosperity in 1854 highlights the absurdity of Bostonians not coming up with the money to purchase Burns that Saturday, if they did embrace antislavery sentiments. "Why, Sir, . . . here [in Boston] are our merchant princes, with their elegant and powerful bearing, our wealthy capitalists, with their all-controlling banking system and operations, our immense railroads, and manufacturing corporations; an empire—yes, sir, an EMPIRE of business men are here in the city of Boston." In Mulkern, *The Know-Nothing Party*, 20–21.

44. *Boston Evening Transcript*, May 30, 1854. For Boston Vigilance Committee membership and structure, see Bearse, *Reminiscences*, 3–6.

45. On the purchase attempt, see Jane H. Pease and William H. Pease, *The Fugitive Slave Law and Anthony Burns* (Philadelphia: Lippincott, 1975), 39–40; Stanley Shapiro, "The Rendition of Anthony Burns," *Journal of Negro History* 44 (1959): 37–38; *The Journal of Richard Henry Dana, Jr.*, ed. Robert F. Lucid (Cambridge, Mass.: Belknap Press of Harvard Univ. Press, 1968), 2:629; Von Frank, *The Trials of Anthony Burns*, 78–84; Charles Emery Stevens, *Anthony Burns: A History* (Boston: John P. Jewett, 1856), 61–79.

46. Quoted in Von Frank, *The Trials of Anthony Burns*, 234–35.

47. Anthony Burns to Richard Henry Dana Jr., Aug. 23, 1854, Massachusetts Historical Society Archives, Boston.

48. David Herbert Donald, *Charles Sumner* (New York: Da Capo, 1996), 166.

49. *Richmond Enquirer*, June 20, 1854.

50. Samuel May, *Recollections of Our Antislavery Conflict* (Boston: Fields, Osgood, 1869), 127–28.

51. *Liberator*, June 23, 1854.

52. Ibid.

53. Ibid.

54. Ibid.

55. Paul Tweed, "'A Brave Man's Child': Theodore Parker and the Memory of the American Revolution," *Historical Journal of Massachusetts* 29, no. 2 (2001): 184. For recent discussion of black participation in the American Revolution and historical memory, see also Joyce Lee Malcolm, *Peter's War: A New England Slave Boy and the American Revolution* (New Haven, Conn.: Yale Univ. Press, 2009).

56. *Journal of Richard Henry Dana, Jr.*, 671–73.

57. Wendell Phillips, *Argument of Wendell Phillips Esq. before the Committee on Federal Relations, (of the Massachusetts Legislature) in support of the Petitions for the removal of Edward Greely Loring from the Office of Judge of Probate, February 20, 1855* (Boston: J. B. Yerrinton & Son, Printers, 1855), 24–25.

58. *Liberator*, June 30, 1854; *Monthly Religious Magazine*, July 1854; *Liberator*, June 9, 1854; *Frederick Douglass' Paper*, Mar. 16, 1855.

59. Quoted in Schwartz, "Fugitive Slave Days," 210.

60. *Liberator*, Mar. 9, 1855. Burns's refusal is quoted in Von Frank, *The Trials of Anthony Burns*, 302.

61. Josiah Quincy, *Address Illustrative of the Nature and Power of the Slave States; delivered at the Request of the Inhabitants of the Town of Quincy, Mass., on Thursday, June, 1856* (Boston: Ticknor and Fields, 1856), 3–4.

62. Josiah Quincy, *Speech Delivered by Hon. Josiah Quincy, Senior, Before the Whig State Convention, Assembled at the Music Hall, Boston, August 16, 1854* (Boston: John Wilson & Son, 1854), 7–8.

63. Laurie, *Beyond Garrison*, 269.

64. See Roy E. Finkenbine, "Boston's Black Churches: Institutional Centers of the Antislavery Movement," in *Courage and Conscience: Black and White Abolitionists in Boston*, ed. Donald M. Jacobs (Indianapolis: Indiana Univ. Press, 1993), 179–83.

65. To use Bruce Laurie's expression, most of black Bostonians' friendly white neighbors had "turned out to be summer soldiers." Laurie, *Beyond Garrison*, 293.

66. *Boston Evening Transcript*, May 29, 1854.

67. *Boston Evening Transcript*, May 31, 1854.

68. *Richmond Enquirer*, June 6, 1854.

69. *Boston Slave Riot*, 76.

70. Von Frank, *The Trials of Anthony Burns*, 135.

71. *Boston Slave Riot*, 78.

72. *Boston Evening Transcript,* June 3, 1854.

73. *New York Daily Times,* May 30, 1854; *Richmond Enquirer,* June 2, 1854.

74. *Boston Slave Riot,* 84. See also *Provincial Freeman,* June 10, 1854; Von Frank, *The Trials of Anthony Burns,* 135, 208; *Journal of Richard Henry Dana, Jr.,* 636–37.

75. *Boston Evening Transcript,* June 3, 1854. Theodore Parker and Wendell Phillips actually sought protection from angry proslavery Irishmen who wanted to avenge the death of Batchelder, an issue that was picked up by some Southern papers such as the *Daily South Carolinian* (May 31, 1854).

76. *National Era,* June 1, 1854.

77. Shapiro, "The Rendition of Anthony Burns," 45; *Frederick Douglass' Paper,* Dec. 22, 1854; Commager, *Theodore Parker,* 241; *Journal of Richard Henry Dana, Jr.,* 634, 636. See also *Frederick Douglass' Paper,* June 9, 1854; Von Frank, *The Trials of Anthony Burns,* 215.

78. *Boston Slave Riot,* 85; *Frederick Douglass' Paper,* June 23, 1854; *Boston Morning Journal,* June 3, 1854.

79. James Oliver Horton and Lois E. Horton, *Black Bostonians: Family Life and Community Struggle in the Antebellum North* (New York: Holmes and Meier, 1979), 3; Schwartz, "Fugitive Slave Days," 193. These findings are consistent with Robert A. Gross's recent work on Concord, Massachusetts, in which he questions the existence of an antislavery "rank and file" and also demonstrates how other social, political, and economic interests shaped the antislavery attitudes of residents in "the New England town, once the focus of Puritan life and the crucible of the Revolution." Robert A. Gross, "A Petitioner's Tale: Antislavery Activism in Thoreau's Concord" (unpublished manuscript, July 7, 2006), 4 and 14–15.

80. *Boston Slave Riot,* 17, 34, 42. On these dealings, see Stevens, *Anthony Burns,* 202–17; Von Frank, *The Trials of Anthony Burns,* 290. The $1,300 payment to McDaniel was covered by the $676 that had already been collected by the Reverend Grimes when the actual purchase took place and $624 advanced on Grimes's behalf by Charles C. Barry. Barry, a member of the Boston Vigilance Committee, was the cashier at Boston's City Bank.

81. Gayle T. Tate, "Free Black Resistance in the Antebellum Era, 1830 to 1860," *Journal of Black Studies* 28, no. 6 (1998): 767.

82. Quoted in *Frederick Douglass' Paper,* Aug. 18, 1854.

83. *The Frederick Douglass Papers,* ed. John W. Blassingame (New Haven, Conn.: Yale Univ. Press, 1985), 3:3, 123.

84. *Frederick Douglass' Paper,* June 9, 1854.

5. A CALL TO ACTION IN VIRGINIA

1. Some scholars stress that Pierce responded to slaveholders' demands, tailored policies to their interests, and "fulfilled southern expectations." James M. McPherson, *Battle Cry of Freedom: The Civil War Era* (New York: Oxford Univ. Press, 1988), 119. Pierce's enforcement of the Fugitive Slave Law does not, however, necessarily mean that the Union managed to fulfill the expectations of white Southerners.

2. Quoted in David M. Potter, *The Impending Crisis, 1848–1861* (New York: Harper & Row, 1876), 128.

3. *Southern Literary Messenger,* Nov. 1850. In the 1850s, Thompson became a strong defender of Southern rights. He promised to "show our Northern brethren that Southern learning can think for itself," and when Harriet Beecher Stowe published *Uncle Tom's Cabin,* he came out with a review "as hot as hellfire, blasting and searing the reputation of the vile wretch in petticoats who could write such a volume." Quoted in John McCardell, *The Idea of a Southern Nation: Southern Nationalists and Southern Nationalism, 1830–1860* (New York: Norton, 1979), 74, 212.

4. *Lynchburg Republican,* June 7, 1854.

5. Quotations from William W. Holden originally appeared in the *Standard,* May 3, 1851, and were reprinted in Horace W. Raper, *William W. Holden: North Carolina's Political Enigma* (Chapel Hill: Univ. of North Carolina Press, 1985), 19.

6. *Fayetteville Observer,* June 5, 1854.

7. Allen's letter to the *Boston Post* highlighted Bostonians' embrace of law and order: "To the United States marshal, to the civil and military authorities, to the United States district attorney, to his counsel, and to the citizens who took an interest in executing the laws of the land, in the name of Virginia and the South, Col. Suttle returns his warmest thanks. The South will never forget this act of justice; and when I return to my own state, I can say to Louisianians that Boston is a law-abiding city, and that I have seen the rights of Southern men respected and firmly maintained—that the *order-loving* citizens of Boston, in the broad noon of day, executed the *constitutional law of the land.*" *Liberator,* June 9, 1854.

8. Upon hearing of the dinner for the U.S. marshals, Frederick Douglass criticized the Virginians who had arranged the affair. He said, "Slavery, being the sum total of all villany [*sic*], this dinner of course, was the sum total of all happiness to the Prince of Darkness." *Frederick Douglass' Paper,* June 30, 1854.

9. Robert Manson Myers, ed., *The Children of Pride: A True Story of Georgia and the Civil War* (New Haven, Conn.: Yale Univ Press, 1972), 37.

10. *The Works of John C. Calhoun,* ed. Richard K. Crallé (New York, 1854), 4:542, 550, 558. Calhoun's speech, titled "On the Slavery Question," revealed his tendency to overestimate the strength of abolitionism and underestimate the South's political strength within the Union; Calhoun's estimate of relative power has been stressed by scholars, including David Brion Davis and Brian Holden Reid. See David Brion Davis, *Challenging the Boundaries of Slavery* (Cambridge, Mass.: Harvard Univ. Press, 2003), 77; Brian Holden Reid, *The Origins of the American Civil War* (New York: Longman, 1996), 119.

11. The *Richmond Enquirer* treated Virginians to some of the most vehement attacks, including the following paragraph of Theodore Parker's famous sermon:

> I deliberately charge it upon you, Edward Greeley [*sic*] Loring, Judge of Probate, for the county of Suffolk, United States Commissioner, before the citizens of Boston, on this Ascension Sunday, assembled to worship God—I charge you deliberately with the murder of a man on Friday night last. I charge you with putting in peril the lives of nine men, who were arrested, charged with that murder. I charge you with filling Boston Court-house with one hundred and eighty-four ruffians, and alarming not only our own citizens, but stirring up the whole population of this Commonwealth, and filling them with indignation, the results of which no man has yet seen the end.—That my friends, is my morning lesson—let us sing the 168th hymn.

Frank E. Vandiver highlighted the importance of speeches, newspaper articles, and editorials in "coalescing" Southern opinion in the late antebellum period. Frank E. Vandiver, "The Confederacy and the American Tradition," in *The Civil War: A Second American Revolution?* ed. William E. Parrish (New York: Holt Rinehart, 1970), 132.

12. *Southern Literary Messenger,* Sept. 1854.

13. Henry T. Shanks points out that Hunter, of Essex County, Virginia, was very much under the influence of Calhoun and Mason. After the Wilmot Proviso controversy, he became a fire-eater. See Henry T. Shanks, *The Secession Movement in Virginia, 1847–1861* (New York: Da Capo, 1970), 27.

14. *Raleigh Daily Register,* June 14, 1854; *Weekly Register,* June 7, 1854.

15. *Savannah Daily Morning News,* June 2, 1854.

16. *Charleston Mercury,* Jan. 1, 1856.

17. *Daily South Carolinian,* May 30, 1854; June 6, 1854; and June 14, 1854. Sometimes reports of abolitionists' activity were obviously sensational and exaggerated. On May 29, 1854, for example, the *Lynchburg Republican* reported that after the courthouse riot, "six or eight hundred of the most violent [members of the mob] lingered around the building."

18. *Charleston Mercury,* July 21, 1854, in *The Diary of Edmund Ruffin,* ed. William Kaufman Scarborough (Baton Rouge: Louisiana State Univ. Press, 1976), 1:629.

19. *Richmond Whig,* Oct. 28, 1854.

20. *Lynchburg Virginian,* June 7, 1854, and June 23, 1854.

21. Myers, *Children of Pride,* 37, 44.

22. When antislavery supporters focused on slavery in the District of Columbia during the late 1840s, they too had turned the gaze on Southern society and thus encouraged slaveholders' defense of their peculiar institution, which was heightened during the Great Debates of 1850. On this issue, see Shanks, *The Secession Movement,* 26–28. The much stronger reaction of some Virginians to abolitionist attacks on slavery in D.C. and other areas in the South than to attacks on the expansion of slavery to Kansas also stemmed from their concerns about the viability of slavery in Kansas. Craig M. Simpson has argued that Henry A. Wise and Robert M. T. Hunter, for example, both "believed that Kansas did not represent a substantive issue because slavery could not exist there." Craig M. Simpson, *A Good Southerner: The Life of Henry A. Wise of Virginia* (Chapel Hill: Univ. of North Carolina Press, 1985), 99.

23. *The Works of John C. Calhoun,* 2:631.

24. Potter argues that in the Deep South the Southern rights case for disunion faltered after the Compromise of 1850. He stresses that after the Compromise, by the time Mississippi elected Unionist Henry S. Foote as governor over Jefferson Davis, the call for disunion had diminished to a whimper. He also suggests that for many white Southerners, this probably came as a relief. Often their flirting with secession from their beloved Union during the tension-filled days prior to the passage of the Compromise had been somewhat hedged by remarks such as it should only be "the last extremity" or "May God forever avert the necessity." Potter, *The Impending Crisis,* 123.

25. *The Works of John C. Calhoun,* 2:631. The term "armistice" is used by Potter in *The Impending Crisis.*

26. *Richmond Enquirer,* May 26, 1854. William Barney argues that in looking at factors that fueled the "secessionist impulse," scholars should not dismiss the strength of the Southern economy during most of the 1850s, with the exception of the downturn in 1857. Many Southerners believed that they had the economic strength to prosper independently of the North. In Mississippi, Barney notes that rising cotton production and prices, coupled with investments in manufacturing, boosted fortunes, and that "this very prosperity imparted to the state's leaders a confidence that was lacking a decade earlier." William L. Barney, *The Secessionist Impulse: Alabama and Mississippi in 1860* (Princeton, N.J.: Princeton Univ. Press, 1974), 4.

27. *Daily South Carolinian,* June 14, 1854.

28. *Richmond Enquirer,* May 26, 1854. Contrary to Stanley Shapiro's view, it was in the South, not the North, that the Burns crisis fanned the flames of Nebraska. Shapiro, "The Rendition of Anthony Burns," 37.

29. In taking this stance, the *Enquirer* subtly addressed the divisions that typically characterized Virginia politics at midcentury. These had included divisions between Tidewater planters and western farmers, Democrats and Whigs, and so-called Southern Rights Whigs and unionist Whigs. For a discussion of these issues, see Shanks, *The Secession Movement,* 1–84, and McCardell, *Idea of a Southern Nation,* 11–80.

30. *Richmond Enquirer,* May 26, 1854.

31. *Richmond Enquirer,* June 2, 1854.

32. Myers, *Children of Pride,* 37, 44, 37.

33. *Richmond Enquirer,* June 2, 1854.

34. *Weekly Raleigh Register,* June 7, 1854; *Lynchburg Republican,* June 1, 1854.

35. *Richmond Enquirer,* June 2, 1854.

36. Myers, *Children of Pride,* 45.

37. *Richmond Enquirer,* June 16, 1854, and June 6, 1854. Suggesting that the slain guard James Batchelder was the unfortunate victim of unrestrained abolitionist fury, the Elizabeth City County residents also called on Virginians to make donations to his family.

38. For brief summaries of the individual views of these men, see Eugene H. Berwanger, *As They Saw Slavery* (Minneapolis: Winston Press, 1973), 83–103.

39. Had he lived, Nathaniel Beverley Tucker, a member of one of Virginia's leading families and a renowned legal scholar, would certainly have carried the Southern rights torch during the Burns crisis; he died in 1851. In the post-Burns period, Wise adopted political positions that set precedents for later actions. By 1856, he advocated succession "if a Black Republican was elected" and boasted that "if Fremont were elected he could 'arm and equip 50,000 men the next morning ready for revolution." Shanks, *The Secession Movement,* 53.

40. Thomas Jefferson, *Notes on the State of Virginia,* ed. William Peden (Chapel Hill: Univ. of North Carolina Press, 1954), 138.

41. George Fredrickson underlines Dew's importance in strengthening and shifting the Southern defense of slavery in the 1820s. George M. Fredrickson, *The Black Image in the White Mind: The Debate on Afro-American Character and Destiny, 1817–1914* (New York: Harper & Row, 1971), 43–70.

42. Ibid. Dew focused on the remarkable growth of the slave population and concluded that the logistics and costs of transporting emancipated blacks to Africa would be exorbitant. For him, the idea of colonization was not bad, but it had become unrealistic. He argued that the idea of colonizing about 6,000 slaves, the estimated annual increase of the slave population in Virginia, had become "vain and fruitless . . . stupendously absurd." Thomas R. Dew, "Review of the Debate in the Virginia Legislature," reprinted in Eric L. McKitrick, ed., *Slavery Defended: The Views of the Old South* (Englewood Cliffs, N.J.: Prentice-Hall, 1963), 29. Drew Gilpin Faust notes Dew's emphasis on how the demographic profiles of the North and of Europe differed from that of the South. See Thomas Roderick Dew, "Abolition of Negro Slavery," in *The Ideology of Slavery: Proslavery Thought in the Antebellum South, 1830–1860,* ed. Drew Gilpin Faust (Baton Rouge: Louisiana State Univ. Press, 1981), 21–77.

43. *The Pro-Slavery Argument; As Maintained by the Most Distinguished Writers of the Southern States, Containing the Several Essays, on the Subject, of Chancellor Harper, Governor Hammond, Dr. Simms, and Professor Dew* (New York: Negro Universities Press, 1968), 437, 443.

44. James Oliver Horton and Lois E. Horton highlight the impact of Walker's *Appeal* and note his criticism of colonization schemes and advice to blacks: "Let no man of us budge one step . . . and let slave-holders come to beat us from our country. America is more our country, than it is the whites'—we have enriched it with our *blood and tears.*" Quoted in James Oliver Horton and Lois E. Horton, *Slavery and the Making of America* (New York: Oxford Univ. Press, 2005), 111–12. For details on Nat Turner, see Stephen B. Oates, *The Fires of Jubilee: Nat Turner's Fierce Rebellion* (New York: Harper, 1990).

45. Jefferson Davis was among the Southern leaders who embraced this view and used the term "fanatic." See *The Papers of Jefferson Davis,* ed. Linda Lasswell Crist (Baton Rouge: Louisiana State Univ. Press, 1983), 4:33.

46. When the Republican Party emerged, some Southerners immediately described it as an instrument of anarchy or social degeneracy. For example, the *Augusta Chronicle and Sentinel* labeled it "a menace to Society, to Liberty, and to Law. It has drawn to it the corrupt, the vile,

the licentious, the profligate, the lawless. . . . It is a fiend, the type of lawless Democracy, a law unto itself, its only Lord King Numbers, its decrees but the will of a wild mob." Quoted in Michael F. Holt, *The Political Crisis of the 1850s* (New York: John Wiley & Sons, 1978), 241.

47. George Fredrickson discusses the emergence of Richard Colfax and his publication of *Evidence against the Views of the Abolitionists, Consisting of Physical and Moral Proofs of the Natural Inferiority of the Negroes* in New York in 1833. See Fredrickson, *The Black Image*, 43–70.

48. Perhaps the best example of this is Jefferson Davis's letter to Malcolm Haynes, the Virginia-born state treasurer of Mississippi during the 1840s. Davis described a sort of domino effect set in motion by abolitionists, who he said targeted one area after another. He argued that to protect the South, a line in the sand needed to be drawn. He said:

> When the fanatics of England had completed their task of West India emancipation, they rested not, content with their impoverishment of the distant Islanders, who unknown, unheard, uncared for, had been the victims of the home agitation, but came as missionaries to the United States, colaborers [*sic*] in the work of Northern abolitionists. Ignorant of our federative relations, and the mutual restraints and obligation growing out of them, and devoid of American sympathies, they were fit ministers of a sect the cardinal points of whose creed are the destruction of the guarantees of the constitution, and violation of the property rights of Southern citizens. . . . The fraternity due to our Union would have repelled such approaches, national pride would have driven these foreign emissaries away, common justice, human charity would have turned from such teachers to those who at least had an opportunity to know the truth. Not thus did our Northern brethren act. They struck hands with the stranger and entered into a league with the foreigner against us. (*Papers of Jefferson Davis,* 4:33)

Paul Gilje notes the importance of the Atlantic context and the impact of "French Negroes" in the nineteenth-century race riots. Paul Gilje, *Rioting in America* (Indianapolis: Indiana Univ. Press, 1996), 90.

49. *Southern Literary Messenger,* July 1854.

50. See Faust, *The Ideology of Slavery,* 1–2 and 274.

51. *Charleston Mercury,* Jan. 17, 1854, and Jan. 8, 1854.

52. I argue that this movement triggered individual reactions among Virginians that encouraged them to participate in strengthening the defense of slavery as a positive good and also forced them to look at options for the South, including disunion.

53. C. Vann Woodward stresses that Fitzhugh "deplored" race hatred and theories that suggested blacks were subhuman, as such notions encouraged mistreatment of slaves and violated scripture, "which teaches that the whole human race descended from a common parentage." Fitzhugh's views distanced him from those who embraced theories that advanced notions of black inferiority. George Fitzhugh, *Cannibals All! or Slaves without Masters,* ed. C. Vann Woodward (Cambridge, Mass.: Belknap Press of Harvard Univ. Press, 1960), xi. John Ashcroft makes the point that proslavery theory was not "monolithic" and focuses on Fitzhugh's belief in the superiority of slave labor independent of any consideration of race. John Ashcroft, *Slavery, Capitalism, and Politics in the Antebellum Republic* (Cambridge: Cambridge Univ. Press, 1995), 1:194, 228.

54. Fitzhugh's *Sociology for the South* was the first American publication with the word "sociology" in the title. See George Fitzhugh, *Sociology for the South, or The Failure of Free Society* (Richmond, Va.: Morris, 1854), xvii, and Woodward's introduction to *Cannibals All!*

55. By midcentury, Jefferson Davis embraced this view. He argued that slavery had morally and socially elevated blacks, allowing them to become docile, intelligent, and civilized agricultural laborers. This idea is similar to the view later adopted by the historian Ulrich

Bonnell Phillips, who portrayed slavery as a benign institution, and plantations as "the best schools yet invented for the mass training of that sort of inert and backward people." Ulrich Bonnell Phillips, *American Negro Slavery: A Survey of the Supply, Employment and Control of Negro Labor as Determined by the Plantation Régime* (New York: D. Appleton, 1918), 343. These arguments were consistent with Fitzhugh's views. For Jefferson Davis's view, see his speech to the Confederate Congress, Apr. 29, 1861, reprinted in Edwin C. Rozwenc, *The Causes of the American Civil War* (Boston: Heath, 1961), 32. For a concise summary of George Fitzhugh's thought, see C. Vann Woodward, *American Counterpoint: Slavery and Racism in the North-South Dialogue* (Boston: Little, Brown, 1971), 107–39. Woodward emphasizes Fitzhugh's rejection of Adam Smith, John Locke, and other Enlightenment thinkers who influenced Thomas Jefferson as well as many prominent Northerners. He highlights Fitzhugh's views on subordination and caste and notes that family lay at the heart of Fitzhugh's fundamentally Filmerian perspective.

56. George Fitzhugh, *Sociology for the South,* reprinted in McKitrick, *Slavery Defended,* 35. Fitzhugh used the example of the destitution of the Irish in Ireland, as well as after their migration to England and the North, to argue against free and so-called equal societies. "A half million died of hunger in one year in Ireland—they died because in the eye of the law they were equals, and liberty had made them enemies, of their landlords and employers. Had they been vassals or serfs, they would have been beloved, cherished and taken care of by those same landlords and employers. Slaves never die of hunger, scarcely ever feel want" (38).

57. *Charleston Mercury,* Jan. 8, 1854.

58. Fitzhugh, *Cannibals All!* 17–19.

59. *Southern Literary Messenger,* July 1854.

60. Edmund Ruffin, *The Political Economy of Slavery* ([Washington]: L. Towers, [1857]), 8.

61. James Henry Hammond, "Mud-Sill Speech," reprinted in McKitrick, *Slavery Defended,* 122–23.

62. *Richmond Enquirer,* June 7, 1854, quoted in H. Robert Baker, *The Rescue of Joshua Glover: A Fugitive Slave, the Constitution, and the Coming of the Civil War* (Athens: Ohio Univ. Press, 2006), 13. Barney links the antislavery cause and urbanization, arguing also that Southerners drew this connection. He says that "the most unsettling of the nagging fears that the city instilled in the planter was the conviction that 'every city was destined to be the seat of freesoilism.'" Barney, *The Secessionist Impulse,* 37. It is not surprising that the editorial did not draw attention to the fact that in cities in slaveholding states, serious riots had also been experienced, many of them instigated by proslavery mobs. The *Pearl* affair riot in Washington was a prime example, but there were others as well in St. Louis, Louisville, New Orleans, and Baltimore. For details of these riots, see Gilje, *Rioting in America,* 90–91, and David Grimsted, *American Mobbing, 1828–1861: Toward Civil War* (New York: Oxford Univ. Press, 1998).

63. *Richmond Enquirer,* June 7, 1854.

64. *Lynchburg Virginian,* June 7, 1854.

65. *Richmond Enquirer,* June 7, 1854. Statements such as these suggest that the editor embraced Fitzhugh's doctrines and the notion of slavery as a positive good. He argued that continued exposure to abolitionist forces would cause Southern society to degenerate and Southerners would eventually be forced to adopt the less stable structures that prevailed in the North.

66. *Richmond Enquirer,* June 7, 1854.

67. *Lynchburg Virginian,* June 7, 1854.

68. Before writing the Articles of Confederation, John Dickinson was famous for his "Letters from a Pennsylvania Farmer," which fueled debate and colonial resistance after the British parliament's passage of the Declaratory Act of 1766.

69. *Richmond Enquirer,* June 20, 1854.

70. *Lynchburg Virginian,* June 1, 1854. It was at this time that the *Lynchburg Republican* began to adopt a firmer stance against the Northern disrespect of Southern rights. It stated, "[T]he South cannot expect to remain content under such outrages and injuries."

71. *Richmond Enquirer,* June 20, 1854.

72. Ibid.

73. Myers, *Children of Pride,* 44.

74. *Richmond Enquirer,* June 20, 1854.

75. *Lynchburg Virginian,* June 23, 1854.

76. *Richmond Enquirer,* June 20, 1854. One product, among several, that the Virginia farmer mentioned, recognizing the midcentury trend toward the standardization of work and the increasing importance of measuring time, was clocks. He called for "Open manufactories of cotton in all its branches; of iron in all its branches; of wood; including . . . clocks." He also suggested that more trade with Europe could lead to new opportunities for high-value manufacturing activity in the South, including the production of "finer fabrics" through the processing of semifinished linens from the Continent.

77. *Richmond Enquirer,* June 14, 1854. The *Enquirer* also argued that Southern universities, notably the University of Virginia and the College of South Carolina, were better than the leading Northern institutions.

78. *Richmond Whig,* Mar. 17, 1854, quoted in Shanks, *The Secession Movement,* 77; *Lynchburg Republican,* June 23, 1854; *Southern Literary Messenger,* Sept. 1854.

79. Quoted in Raper, *William W. Holden,* 24.

80. Quoted in McCardell, *Idea of a Southern Nation,* 207.

81. *Southern Literary Messenger,* Sept. 1854. Barbour regarded Britain as a model that Virginia should follow and suggested that the diversification of British industry had been instrumental in the creation of wealth.

82. Revealing a gender bias, the Virginia farmer argued that women should assume the less noble commercial pursuits of running dry-goods stores—traditionally a male occupation in Virginia. He said men should not be "vending tape and ribbon." Interestingly, he did not promote the mechanical arts among blacks. White Southerners were hesitant about the idea of blacks entering skilled trades and socializing with white artisans. James Hammond said, "Whenever a slave is made a mechanic, he's more than half freed, and soon becomes, as we all too well know, and all history attests, with rare exceptions, the most corrupt and turbulent of his class." Quoted in Barney, *The Secessionist Impulse,* 17. Hammond may have been thinking about Gabriel, the blacksmith who led the attempted uprising in 1800 commonly known as Gabriel's Rebellion. Douglas Egerton stresses how slaves who hired themselves out were influenced by free blacks and white workers. See Douglas R. Egerton, *Gabriel's Rebellion: The Virginia Slave Conspiracies of 1800 and 1802* (Chapel Hill: Univ. of North Carolina Press, 1993).

83. *Richmond Enquirer,* June 20, 1854. Such views were often shared by politicians. Robert M. Hunter, for example, believed that "if secession were accomplished, Virginia as a member of a Southern confederacy would supplant New England as the manufacturing section for the South." Shanks, *The Secession Movement,* 74.

84. *Richmond Enquirer,* June 20, 1854.

85. *Savannah Daily Morning News,* June 2, 1854.

86. This consideration has been emphasized by scholars who have argued that the Burns crisis led to a groundswell of antislavery sentiment. Avery O. Craven and James G. Randall, usually associated with the repressible conflict school of Civil War interpretation, stressed that the renewed abolitionist attacks "helped to pound the South into self-consciousness." Thomas J. Pressly, *Americans Interpret Their Civil War* (New York: Free Press, 1962), 316.

87. Charles Sumner, "Speech of Hon. Charles Sumner at the Republican Convention at Worcester, September 7, 1854," reprinted in *Frederick Douglass' Paper,* Sept. 24, 1854.

88. John Weiss, *Reform and Repeal: A Sermon . . .* (Boston: Crosby, Nichols, 1854), in the Massachusetts Historical Society Archives, Boston.

89. *New York Daily Times,* June 1, 1854. Although some of these Northern newspaper reports may obviously have contributed to Northern cities'—and especially Boston's—reputations as centers of "mad abolitionism," much of the evidence presented in this chapter suggests that the reputations of Northern cities such as Boston as bastions of antislavery feeling, both in the Burns affair and in general, actually owed a lot to assertions by white Southerners—often in newspapers such as the *Enquirer.* A critical question thus becomes "Did white Boston maintain its liberal patina less by dint of what it did than by what secessionists said it did?" In other words, to what extent was Boston's antislavery reputation a Southern construct?

90. *Richmond Daily Whig,* Sept. 27, 1855.

91. Although Douglass distanced himself from Garrison's pacifism, the latter continued to publicize Douglass's activities in the *Liberator.* For example, Garrison reported that at an anniversary celebration of the Jerry rescue in October 1854, the first after the Burns crisis, Douglass outlined his opposition to the "doctrine of non-resistance." He also described in detail how the black orator "carried the *feelings* of the audience by his irresistible wit and touching appeals." The latter, Garrison noted, included Douglass's holding up the very fetters that had manacled Jerry. *Liberator,* Oct. 13, 1854.

92. *Freeman's Journal,* quoted in the *Liberator,* Sept. 29, 1854. This was especially true of Jefferson Davis.

93. *Virginia Gazette,* June 22, 1854. Jane and William Pease cite Garrison's actions at the Framingham picnic. Pease and Pease, "Confrontation and Abolition," 926.

94. *Lynchburg Republican,* June 15, 1854.

95. Baker, *The Rescue of Joshua Glover,* 118–25. Baker provides an excellent description of the rescue of Joshua Glover and an analysis of Smith's decision.

96. *Ibid.*

97. *Richmond Enquirer,* June 16, 1854. Congressional authority to legislate on slavery was also a most contentious issue that widened the rifts between slaveholders and abolitionists, particularly after Chief Justice Roger Taney's ruling in the case of Dred Scott in 1857.

98. *Richmond Enquirer,* June 6, 1854, and June 16, 1854.

99. *Liberator,* Jan. 15, 1858. In the *Liberator* the week before, Garrison carefully explained that the Massachusetts personal liberty law stipulated that "No person who holds any office under the laws of the United States, which qualifies him to issue any warrant or other process, or to grant any certificate under the acts of Congress named in the 9th section of this act, or to serve the same, shall, at the same time, hold any office of honor, trust, or emolument under the laws of this Commonwealth." *Liberator,* Jan. 8, 1858.

100. *Richmond Enquirer,* June 17, 1854.

101. *Frederick Douglass' Paper,* June 23, 1854.

102. *Richmond Enquirer,* June 6, 1854. The effigy of Judge Loring bore the inscription "The Slave Catcher of 1854." *Boston Evening Transcript,* June 8, 1854.

103. *Standard,* Feb. 21, 1855, reprinted in Raper, *William W. Holden,* 24.

104. Myers, *Children of Pride,* 45.

105. *Richmond Enquirer,* June 17, 1854. Antislavery activists made every effort to embarrass Loring and cast doubt on his impartiality. Wendell Phillips, for example, told the legislative committee of inquiry on Loring's case that the commissioner had said to him the day after Burns's arrest, "Mr. Phillips, I think this case is so clear that you will not be justified in placing any obstacle in the way of this man's going back [to slavery] as he probably will." *Frederick Douglass' Paper,* Mar. 9, 1855.

106. *Liberator,* Apr. 2, 1858. Antislavery petitioners frequently raised the issue of a conflict of interest between the position of judge of probate and slave commissioner. An example of this was the following argument presented to the Massachusetts House of Representatives: "[A] single illustration will suggest the conflict which might arise in the exercise of the power and duties of the two offices. A slave mother dies in Massachusetts, and her children are brought before the Court of Probate for the appointment of a guardian. The Judge of Probate, by the laws of Massachusetts, is for the time their *protector* and friend, and while the hearing is pending, the same Judge, in the capacity of Commissioner, is called upon to issue a warrant for their seizure, as the property of a Southern slave-owner." *Liberator,* Mar. 12, 1858.

107. *Frederick Douglass' Paper,* Apr. 20, 1855. Although Douglass remained cautious throughout this period, he printed a letter that reflected the sentiments of many abolitionists who interpreted the dismissal of Loring as evidence that "a revolution [was] taking place." *Frederick Douglass' Paper,* Apr. 20, 1855.

108. Quoted in *Frederick Douglass' Paper,* June 30, 1854.

109. Ibid.

110. Ibid.

111. *Liberator,* Dec. 29, 1854; *Frederick Douglass' Paper,* June 30, 1854.

112. *Southern Literary Messenger,* Sept. 1854.

6. Anthony Burns's St. Catharines

1. The Somerset case was filed by British antislavery activists on behalf of James Somerset, who had arrived in London two years earlier with his master, Charles Stewart. In his ruling, Chief Justice Lord Mansfield declared that Somerset could not be taken to Jamaica and sold as a slave; his opinion was generally interpreted as abolishing slavery in England. Although Mansfield's decision saved Somerset from being sold, the chief justice actually said nothing about the legality of slavery in Britain's colonies, including Canada. For a discussion of the case, see James Oliver Horton and Lois E. Horton, *Slavery and the Making of America* (New York: Oxford Univ. Press, 2004), 56–57.

2. Nancy Howard interview in Benjamin Drew, *The Refugee, or The Narratives of Fugitive Slaves in Canada. Related by Themselves, with an Account of the History and Condition of the Colored Population of Upper Canada* (Boston: John P. Jewett, 1856), 50.

3. Data on migration are from Fred Landon, "The Negro Migration to Canada after the Passing of the Fugitive Slave Act," *Journal of Negro History* 5, no. 1 (1920): 22–24. Landon discusses Pittsburgh, where, two weeks after the new Fugitive Slave Act became law, it was reported that "nearly all the waiters in the hotels have fled to Canada. Sunday 30 fled; on Monday 40; on Tuesday 50; on Wednesday 30 and up to this time the number that has left will not fall short of 300." Landon, "The Negro Migration," 24.

4. See Horton and Horton, *Slavery and the Making of America,* for a good discussion of Northup's experience. Northup is also well covered in Carol Wilson, *Freedom at Risk: The Kidnapping of Free Blacks in America, 1780–1865* (Lexington: Univ. Press of Kentucky, 1994), 11–12. Wilson focuses on events in Kentucky and Pennsylvania and substantiates David Potter's argument that kidnapping was "undoubtedly accentuated by the new law." See Wilson, *Freedom at Risk,* 40–66, and David Potter, *The Impending Crisis, 1848–1861* (New York: Harper & Row, 1976), 131.

5. Wilson, *Freedom at Risk,* 53.

6. Drew, *The Refugee,* 77, 92. Free blacks who had been abducted or who had escaped to Canada to avoid abduction represented twelve of Drew's interviews in Canada West. John Lindsey was reputed to have property worth between $8,000 and $10,000 in the mid-1850s, a significant amount at the time. He was among the twelve interviewed by Drew. In *The Blacks*

in Canada: A History (Montreal: McGill-Queen's Univ. Press, 1997), 243–44, Robin W. Winks also stresses this motivation for flight and notes that several prosperous black residents in early Canada had been free blacks who migrated to avoid the risk of being kidnapped and sold into slavery.

7. Philip S. Foner, *History of Black Americans: From the Compromise of 1850 to the End of the Civil War* (Westport, Conn.: Greenwood Press, 1983), 16–17. It should be noted that many white Southerners regarded the kidnapping of free blacks as abhorrent and saw those involved in such schemes as unscrupulous profiteers. Foner points out that Gerrit Smith stressed profiteers' use of counterfeit transcripts to facilitate the abduction of free blacks.

8. Foner, *History of Black Americans*, 16; Wilson, *Freedom at Risk*, 45.

9. "Crusade against Slavery," *St. Catharines Standard*, Jan. 14, 1995, in *Blacks in the Niagara Peninsula*, scrapbook, St. Catharines Public Library Special Collections. Some prominent Loyalist slaveholders were Mohawk chief Joseph Brant, Christopher Robinson, Peter Russell, William Jarvis, and Richard Cartwright.

10. Peter Martin, a black member of Butler's Rangers who fought for the British during the American Revolution, brought the incident before Simcoe's Executive Council. An infuriated Simcoe wanted to prosecute Vrooman, but in the end he could not do so because legally slaves were, at the time, deemed to have no rights. As one scholar has pointed out, "In law, Vrooman had no more committed a breach of peace than if he had been handing over his heifer to a new owner." Frustrated, Simcoe moved to eliminate slavery. Daniel G. Hill, *The Freedom-Seekers: Blacks in Early Canada* (Toronto: Stoddart, 1992), 15–16. See also "Crusade against Slavery," *St. Catharines Standard*, Jan. 14, 1995, in *Blacks in the Niagara Peninsula*.

11. One of Simcoe's strongest critics was Christopher Robinson, a loyalist from Virginia who tried to pass a bill in 1798 that would have permitted immigrants to bring slaves into Canada. The proposal was blocked in the upper house of the colonial legislature. "Crusade against Slavery," *St. Catharines Standard*, Jan. 14, 1995, in *Blacks in the Niagara Peninsula*; Samuel Gridley Howe, *Report to the Freedmen's Inquiry Commission, 1864: The Refugees from Slavery in Canada West* (1864; New York: Arno Press, 1969), 9–10.

12. In 1803, Quebec or Lower Canada's Chief Justice William Osgoode delivered the first Canadian opinion suggesting that slavery was inconsistent with British law, which left slave-holders in British North America with virtually no protection in the courts. See Winks, *The Blacks in Canada*, 96–113.

13. Black participation in the War of 1812 was not confined to this unit. In fact, Ron Dale, superintendent of the Niagara Historic Sites of Canada, has records of blacks in most militia regiments, including the highly respected Glengarry Light Infantry Fencibles. Dale, letter to author, Aug. 22, 2005.

14. Hill, *The Freedom-Seekers*, 18–19. See also Maggie Parnall, "Black History in the Ni-agara Peninsula" (unpublished manuscript, 1996), 14–15, in Special Collections and Archives, James A. Gibson Library, Brock University, St. Catharines. Parnall highlights the valor demonstrated by black soldiers at the Battle of Queenston Heights, Oct. 13, 1812, and notes that in 1813 the black Lieutenant James Robertson took command of the Coloured Corps, which had previously been led by white officers. She emphasizes that three blacks—Edmund Gough, William Thompson, and James Waters—held the rank of sergeant and five others were corporals—Robert Jupiter, Isaac Lee, John Vanpatten, Humphrey Waters, and Francis Wilson. She lists fifty-three privates, including Richard Pierpoint, who initially proposed the formation of the Coloured Corps.

15. Winks, *The Blacks in Canada*, 102. The Vallard case is also dealt with by William R. Riddell, "An International Complication between Illinois and Canada Arising out of Slavery," *Journal of the Illinois State Historical Society* 25 (1932): 123–26. In the early 1800s, Lower Canada comprised the territory covered by modern-day Quebec.

16. Winks, *The Blacks in Canada*, 168–69. Later Colborne also turned down an American request to return a fugitive slave from Virginia.

17. "Kidnapping of Freed Slaves," *St. Catharines' British American Journal*, July 23, 1835, in *Blacks in the Niagara Peninsula*.

18. Ibid.

19. *St. Catharines Journal*, Nov. 4, 1852, and Aug. 30, 1853. Newspaper coverage of kidnapping was not restricted to incidents in Canada; it covered the free states as well. For example, the *St. Catharines Journal* printed reports titled "Kidnapping in Pennsylvania" (Jan. 10, 1856) and "Bold and Deliberate Attempt at Kidnapping a Negro" (Jan. 14, 1860) about a kidnapping in Cincinnati. Not surprisingly, the *St. Catharines Journal* printed an extensive review of *Twelve Years a Slave: Narrative of Solomon Northup, a Citizen of New York, Kidnapped in Washington City in 1841, and Rescued in 1853.* See *St. Catharines Journal*, July 21, 1853.

20. Janet Carnochan, "A Slave Rescue in Niagara Sixty Years Ago" (paper delivered to the Canadian Institute, the Lundy's Lane Historical Society, and the Niagara Historical Society, 1897), 12, in *Blacks in the Niagara Peninsula*.

21. Ibid., 12–17. Winks points out that after the inquest, Moseby, also known as Mosely, was allowed to return to the Niagara area. Winks, *The Blacks in Canada*, 169–70.

22. For summaries of the Happy case, see J. Mackenzie Leask, "Jesse Happy: A Fugitive Slave from Kentucky," *Ontario History* 54 (1962): 87–106, and Alexander L. Murray, "The Extradition of Fugitive Slaves from Canada: A Re-evaluation," *Canadian Historical Review* 43 (1962): 298–314.

23. Leask, "Jesse Happy," 88.

24. Quoted in ibid., 97.

25. In rendering its decision, the council also spelled out its argument of the double penalty, stressing that even if Happy were acquitted of horse theft, he would be returned to slavery if he were extradited. The council suggested too that Happy's letter was proof that he had not taken the horse with "felonious intentions." See Murray, "Extradition of Fugitive Slaves," 299.

26. Quoted in Leask, "Jesse Happy," 94–95.

27. Quoted in Murray, "Extradition of Fugitive Slaves," 299–300.

28. Quoted in Leask, "Jesse Happy," 96. This was especially important, as Palmerston's approach took account of intentions rather than actions committed, making it difficult to apply and somewhat suspect in an era of positive law that emphasized statutes and evidence.

29. Quoted in Murray, "Extradition of Fugitive Slaves," 302.

30. Quoted in Leask, "Jesse Happy," 96. See also Fred Landon, "The Fugitive Slave in Canada," *University Magazine* 18 (1919): 270–79.

31. After the War of 1812, official British policy shifted steadily toward what one noted Canadian historian has called *entente*, which became increasingly important when Britain experimented with free trade in the 1840s. Imperial authorities were also increasingly determined to come to an agreement on the boundary issues. For a summary of the British position, see J. M. Bumstead, *The Peoples of Canada: A Pre-Confederation History* (Toronto: Oxford Univ. Press, 1992), 283.

32. Quoted in Murray, "Extradition of Fugitive Slaves," 304.

33. Quoted in Winks, *The Blacks in Canada*, 172.

34. "Lord Stanley apprehends that on the one hand, there can be no desire to protect from punishment . . . a person who had been legally and on credible evidence, charged with a heinous [sic] offence," wrote one of Stanley's aides. "Yet on the other, not only must the British Government repudiate any proposal to surrender up a person charged with the mere offence of escaping from Slavery, but if a discretionary power be left, the exercise of that discretion must, in a free country, be influenced by the consideration of the motive which led to the commission of the offence." Quoted in Murray, "Extradition of Fugitive Slaves," 306.

35. Murray argues in "Extradition of Fugitive Slaves" that Webster was aware of "the British intention to consider the motives of every escaped slave but preferred, by keeping silent, to secure the passage of the treaty" (309). See also Richard N. Current, "Webster's Propaganda and the Ashburton Treaty," *Mississippi Valley Historical Review* 34 (1947): 187–200.

36. After escaping to Canada, Anderson also apparently used the name William Jones. Fred Landon, "The Anderson Fugitive Case," *Journal of Negro History* 7 (1922): 233–42.

37. Landon, "The Negro Migration," 36. Both abolitionists and proslavery advocates fueled public debates surrounding the Webster-Ashburton discussions, which were reported in the press. Later extradition cases renewed debates. In 1849, referring again to the Happy case, one member of Parliament summed up what appears to have been the general sentiment in Canada at the time: "The mere act of stealing a horse would not . . . be sufficient for this country to give a slave up." See coverage of legislative debates in the *Globe and Mail,* Feb. 10, 1849.

38. *St. Catharines Journal,* Apr. 22, 1840.

39. *St. Catharines Journal,* Oct. 1, 1840.

40. Howe, *Report to the Freedmen's Inquiry Commission,* 12–14.

41. *St. Catharines Standard,* Jan. 14, 1995. After Rolph's return, Canadian blacks convened meetings to discuss his trip to London. *St. Catharines Journal,* Oct. 1, 1840.

42. *Voice of the Fugitive,* Mar. 12, 1851.

43. Ibid. Bibb often discussed blacks' right to vote, their eligibility to serve on juries, and their political influence. See the July 2, 1851; Jan. 1, 1852; and Mar. 12, 1851, editions of the *Voice of the Fugitive.*

44. Winks, *The Blacks in Canada,* 213–14.

45. *Voice of the Fugitive,* Feb. 12, 1852.

46. *Voice of the Fugitive,* Aug. 13, 1851.

47. *Voice of the Fugitive,* Oct. 22, 1851.

48. *Voice of the Fugitive,* Feb. 12, 1852. On Mar. 12, 1851, Bibb discussed ways blacks in Canada could advance themselves, emphasizing access to land and education. In the early 1850s, many blacks who sought to leave the United States saw moving to Canada as a much more attractive alternative than African colonization, and as the best means to elevate their race and confront the slave power.

49. For example, Charles Lamb, editor of the *St. Catharines Journal,* quoted Dr. Michael Willis, president of the Upper Canadian Antislavery Society, as saying:

> It may be asked what has Canada to do with the slavery existing in the States of America? We answer—Canada is not, as we know of, separated by any national boundaries from human feelings or human sympathies. Slavery is an outrage on humanity, and therefore, all nations and people are interested in its exposure and termination. But in addition to this apology for anti-slavery meetings on British soil, we have this also—that bordering as we do on this country where man is chattel, and from which he is daily running to us for protection, and seeing as we do the accumulated misery borne by these poor hunted wretches, we should be less than human if we did not give expression to our feelings of condemnation of this monster crime. (*St. Catharines Journal,* Apr. 8, 1852)

50. *Voice of the Fugitive,* Jan. 15, 1851.

51. For an excellent discussion of this case and others involving blacks' access to education, see Claudette Knight, "Black Parents Speak: Education in Mid-Nineteenth-Century Canada West," *Ontario History* 89, no. 4 (1997): 269–84. She also highlights the strategy used by some racist whites of claiming that their local common school was private, thus denying access to black children.

52. *Voice of the Fugitive,* Jan. 15, 1851. Frederick Douglass discussed slaveholders' fears of literacy among their slaves in recounting his early instruction from Mrs. Auld when he arrived in Baltimore. *Narrative of the Life of Frederick Douglass,* 19–20.

53. *Voice of the Fugitive,* Oct. 22, 1851. Although Mary Ann Shadd often argued with Bibb, she agreed with him on the question of land ownership and the independence it provided to fugitives. Discussing the blacks of St. Catharines, she noted that "the desire and determination of all is to become possessors of the soil or [in the case of the town's shopkeepers and tradesmen] have some kind of property." *Provincial Freeman,* May 6, 1854.

54. *Voice of the Fugitive,* Mar. 12, 1851; Apr. 9, 1851; and Oct. 22, 1851; land prices from Jan. 15, 1852, and June 18, 1852.

55. *Voice of the Fugitive,* June 18, 1851. Fugitive slaves who settled in towns also sought the independence of owning their homes.

56. In the mid-nineteenth century, observers often spoke of moral elevation as well, which usually embraced notions of frugality, industry, and patterns of social behavior consistent with Christian teachings.

57. Bibb argued that if a black man could not succeed in Canada, he would "die a pauper" even if he were "placed in a country flowing with milk and honey." *Voice of the Fugitive,* Apr. 8, 1852.

58. *Voice of the Fugitive,* Jan. 1, 1852. In their letter, they also dispelled notions that the climate in Ontario was too severe by comparing temperatures recorded in Ontario with those in Boston, Cleveland, Chicago, Philadelphia, and Baltimore. They argued that the climate in Southern Ontario was milder than that in many American cities.

59. *Voice of the Fugitive,* Apr. 8, 1852. The letter from Frederick Douglass appeared in the *Voice of the Fugitive,* Sept. 9, 1852.

60. *Provincial Freeman,* Nov. 3, 1855.

61. In the 1840s, Brown escalated his campaign against slavery, exploiting a wide range of issues, including the Mexican War, slavery in the District of Columbia, fugitive slave crises, attacking churches and religious denominations that did not denounce slavery, and French emancipation of slavery in the West Indies. He also opposed Canadians who favored annexation to the United States, arguing that Canada would be subjugated to the slave power. See *Globe and Mail,* Oct. 27, 1847, and May 20, 1848.

62. *Voice of the Fugitive,* Oct. 8, 1851.

63. Howe, *Refugees of Slavery in Canada West,* 46–47.

64. Quoted in ibid.

65. *Voice of the Fugitive,* Oct. 8, 1852. Claudette Knight discusses the petition to Metcalfe in "Black Parents Speak," 274.

66. *Voice of the Fugitive,* Oct. 8, 1851, and Feb. 26, 1852.

67. Mary Ann Shadd reported that in St. Catharines, "work is abundant and wages are good. Many of them [blacks] are owners of real estate property and in comfortable circumstances." *Provincial Freeman,* May 6, 1854.

68. A famous nineteenth-century visitor to St. Catharines's spas was Mary Todd Lincoln. Seeking to recover her mental and physical health after her husband's assassination and the death of her son, she visited in 1873 and 1881. In 1873, she caused a stir when she stayed in the town's first spa, the Stephenson House, which was managed by Nathaniel Beverley Tucker, a former Confederate. Owen Thomas, *Niagara's Freedom Trail: A Guide to African-Canadian History on the Niagara Peninsula* (Niagara: Ontario Heritage Foundation, 1995), 46–47.

69. *Voice of the Fugitive,* June 18, 1851.

70. Wilbur H. Siebert, *The Underground Railroad from Slavery to Freedom* (North Stratford, N.H.: Ayer, 2000), 206.

71. *St. Catharines Journal,* Jan. 22, 1852, and Sept. 30, 1852. Loguen's letter was published in the *Journal* of Jan. 22, 1852.

72. Drew, *The Refugee*, 33–36.

73. After Brown's raid, residents of St. Catharines speculated on whether he had made the final arrangements while he was in St. Catharines. The Nov. 3, 1859, *Journal* published the following report:

The organization of which Brown was the head, which caused the disturbance at Harper's Ferry on the 16th inst . . . we believe was got up in this Town last summer, when, we also feel inclined to think, the pamphlet containing the "Constitution of the Provisional Government of the United States," was printed. In May or June, 1858, Captain John Brown, or "Osawatomie Brown," was stopping at Gross' Saloon in this place, and was accompanied by a mulatto, who was a printer, and during this time they were engaged in printing a pamphlet, which we saw, and on reading the "Constitution" as published in the *Baltimore Weekly Exchange,* we at once became convinced that the pamphlet we then saw and the "Constitution" were one and the same. The party who was then with Brown is now in Europe, and will probably remain there until the result of the trial is known. . . . Whether the organization had any great number of adherents in Canada we are unable to state; but Brown and his companions were extremely active during their sojourn here, and it is altogether likely that they succeeded in receiving promises of both money and men, and had any success attended the crude attempt at Harper's Ferry, there can be no doubt that thousands of refugees now in Canada would have proceeded to the scene of the hostilities.

74. For estimates of the black population and the number of black households and a discussion of Tubman in Canada, see Rosemary Sadlier, *Harriet Tubman and the Underground Railroad: Her Life in the United States and Canada* (Toronto: Umbrella Press, 1997); *St. Catharines Standard,* Feb. 7, 1993, and Feb. 18, 2003.

75. *St. Catharines Standard,* Feb. 22, 2003; undated British Methodist Episcopal Church pamphlet in *Blacks in the Niagara Peninsula; St. Catharines Standard,* June 18, 1989, and Feb. 7, 1993.

76. *St. Catharines Journal,* Apr. 22, 1852.

77. *St. Catharines Journal,* Sept. 30, 1852. The town's blacks were deeply committed to the RSFS. As Hiram Wilson put it, they were "heart in hand in the cause." *Voice of the Fugitive,* May 6, 1852, reprint in *Blacks in the Niagara Peninsula.*

78. *Voice of the Fugitive,* Feb. 26, 1852, reprint in *Blacks in the Niagara Peninsula.*

79. Quoted in Siebert, *The Underground Railroad,* 198.

80. Even fugitives from the Upper South who left in early summer only reached Ontario late in the year.

81. *St. Catharines Journal,* Dec. 12, 1850, and Apr. 15, 1852; Siebert, *The Underground Railroad,* 198.

82. *St. Catharines Journal,* Apr. 22, 1852.

83. Drew, *The Refugee,* 46, 71–72, and 87–88; *St. Catharines Standard,* Feb. 3, 1996, reprint in *Blacks in the Niagara Peninsula.*

84. Frederick Douglass, letter published in the *Voice of the Fugitive,* Sept. 9, 1852.

85. "Most St. Catharines blacks lived near the intersection of Geneva and North Streets, just south of Welland Avenue." *Toronto Star,* Feb. 8, 1993, and *St. Catharines Standard,* June, 8 1989, both in *Blacks in the Niagara Peninsula.*

86. The creation of an independent Canadian Conference reflected the antislavery sentiments of many Canadian churchmen and also their rejection of religious arguments that slavery was a positive good. The *St. Catharines Constitutional* reported: "We had no idea

then as we since now have—that to such an extent the Christian and divine religion of Christ would be prostituted to such a vile purpose as that of making it a foundation or creed for enslaving mankind or for creating a positive *chattel* property by man in man." *St. Catharines Constitutional,* July 6, 1856.

87. Undated pamphlet of the British Methodist Episcopal Church of Canada, 92 Geneva Street, St. Catharines, in *Blacks in the Niagara Peninsula; Toronto Star,* Feb. 7, 1993; *St. Catharines Journal,* Mar. 11, 1841. See the article by Dennis Gannon in the *Toronto Star,* Feb. 8, 1993, in *Blacks in the Niagara Peninsula.* The BME Church still stands today. In 1993, the Ontario government made it an official heritage site with a plaque honoring Harriet Tubman reading:

> A legendary conductor of the Underground Railroad, Harriet was born into slavery on a Maryland plantation and suffered brutal treatment from numerous owners before escaping in 1849. Over the next decade she returned to the American South many times and led hundreds of freedom seekers north. When the Fugitive Slave Act of 1850 allowed slave owners to recapture runaways in the Northern free states, Tubman extended her operation across the Canadian border. For eight years she lived in St. Catharines and at one point rented a house in this neighbourhood. With the outbreak of the Civil War, she returned to the U.S.A. to serve the Union Army.

On February 7, 1990, the mayor of St. Catharines declared an official Harriet Tubman Day, saying:

> Whereas an international tribute has been scheduled for March 10, 1990, to honour the bravery and compassion of Harriet Tubman, one of the famous "Conductors" of the Underground Railroad who, a fugitive slave herself, risked her life guiding blacks from slavery to places of freedom, including the City of St. Catharines; and Whereas the City of St. Catharines was the last station in Harriet Tubman's journey north, and served as a haven for the hundreds of blacks who remained in this area to become an important part of the social fabric of our community; and Whereas the British Methodist Episcopal Church at 92 Geneva Street was the place of worship and the source of strength for Harriet Tubman and her people, and continues today to be a place of worship and a repository of black culture and heritage for many of their descendants; and Whereas the British Methodist Episcopal Church is planning a dinner on Saturday, March 10, 1990 as well as other events to honour the extraordinary life of Harriet Tubman and her close association with their church;
>
> Now, therefore, I, Joseph L. McCaffery, Mayor of the City of St. Catharines do hereby proclaim Saturday, March 10th, 1990 as Harriet Tubman Day in St. Catharines, and I urge the citizens of St. Catharines to support the British Methodist Episcopal Church in their observances of this important occasion. (*Blacks in the Niagara Peninsula*)

88. *St. Catharines Journal,* Sept. 3, 1857. Lindsey's letter suggests that his leadership of the construction sparked some jealousy among other members of the congregation, notably James Harper, who accused him of having dipped into the building fund. Several members rallied in defense of Lindsey. *Toronto Star,* Feb. 8, 1998. In Niagara Falls, another BME chapel, also bearing many similarities to Southern churches, was erected at about the same time. Oliver Parnall, a prosperous black who only a few years earlier "swam the Niagara River to freedom," was a driving force behind the Niagara BME chapel. The story of Oliver Parnall remains a vibrant part of the oral history of the Niagara Falls black community and was recounted to the author by Mrs. Wilma Morrison. The quotation comes from an undated pamphlet jointly

circulated by the Nathaniel Dett Memorial Chapel of the British Methodist Episcopal Church of Canada and the Norval Johnson Heritage Library. In 1983, the Niagara Falls BME Church was renamed the Nathaniel Dett Memorial Chapel in honor of the African American composer, who was born in Niagara Falls, Ontario.

89. Thomas, *Niagara's Freedom Trail.*

90. *St. Catharines Journal,* Mar. 11, 1841. Owen A. Thomas emphasizes Merritt's role in establishing harmonious relations between whites and newly arrived blacks. See Thomas, *Niagara's Freedom Trail,* 44.

91. See Thomas, *Niagara's Freedom Trail,* 44–45. Membership is discussed in James Lewis, "Coloured Baptist Churches in Canada West," in *Blacks in the Niagara Peninsula.* Gray's letter appeared in the *St. Catharines Journal* on Mar. 11, 1841.

92. On Apr. 30, 1853, Lamb announced in the *St. Catharines Journal* that the black orator from Ohio, H. F. Douglass, would be speaking in the town hall that evening.

93. *St. Catharines Journal,* Aug. 18, 1853. Antislavery activists invoked higher law and rejected biblical justifications of slavery. At a meeting in 1852, it was resolved "that the enslavement of man is a flagrant sin against God and an outrage upon humanity not to be countenanced by civilized people who reverence the word of God or bear the Christian name." *St. Catharines Journal,* Apr. 22, 1852.

94. *St. Catharines Journal,* Aug. 20, 1840. On Apr. 9, 1852, the *St. Catharines Journal* stated: "On to-morrow evening a public meeting will be held in the Town Hall, when addresses on the evils of slavery will be delivered. Songs, by the colored choir, in favor of freedom, will enliven the business of the evening." *St. Catharines Journal,* Apr. 8, 1852. See also *St. Catharines Journal,* July 16, 1852. For antislavery resolutions passed by activists in St. Catharines, see *St. Catharines Journal,* Aug. 20, 1852.

95. Howe, *Report to the Freedmen's Inquiry Commission,* 77–78.

96. West and Grose quoted by Drew, *The Refugee,* 89, 87.

97. Howe, *Report to the Freedmen's Inquiry Commission,* 77–78.

98. During this period, there was significant division within the black community on this issue. Integrationists such as Mary Ann Shadd argued against separate schooling and believed that the black community's best interests would be served if its children attended public schools. Others, such as Henry Bibb, thought that because of the particular hardships and prejudice blacks had suffered under slavery, they needed time to develop on their own before integrating with the rest of the community. Knight emphasizes that racist whites sometimes seized upon separate schools as an argument for excluding blacks from common schools, saying that if blacks established a separate school in an area, then they no longer should be allowed to attend a common school. See Knight, "Black Parents Speak," 269–84.

99. Reports on school attendance in *Blacks in the Niagara Peninsula.* In some instances, the return of black students to integrated schools met with resistance from whites, proving that although racism in early Ontario may have been less extreme than it was south of the border, it certainly existed.

100. *Voice of the Fugitive,* Feb. 26, 1852, reprint in *Blacks in the Niagara Peninsula.*

101. *St. Catharines Standard,* June 8, 1989.

102. Wilson to Bibb, Feb. 26, 1852, in *Blacks in the Niagara Peninsula; Provincial Freeman,* Mar. 24, 1853; Drew, *The Refugee,* 30; Lewis, "Coloured Baptist Churches in Canada," in *Blacks in the Niagara Peninsula.*

103. Drew, *The Refuge,* 30.

104. In the 1850s, a black resident of St. Catharines wrote to Lamb that the black soldiers would be "freely and bravely rendered" if militia troops were needed. After observing black militia training in 1852, Lamb described the black unit as "imposing." *St. Catharines Journal,*

July 1, 1852, and June 6, 1856. Dick's Creek in St. Catharines was named in memory of Richard Pierpoint. Maggie Parnall, letter to author, Nov. 30, 2005.

105. Ernest Green, "Upper Canada's Black Defenders," *Ontario Historical Society Papers and Records* 27 (1931): 370–73. Thomas suggests that during the Rebellion of 1837 almost 1,000 blacks volunteered their services in support of the colonial government. Thomas, *Niagara's Freedom Trail*, 16–17.

106. Quoted in Green, "Upper Canada's Black Defenders," 372.

107. Donald George Simpson, "Negroes in Ontario from Early Times to 1870" (diss., Univ. of Western Ontario, 1971), 233; *St. Catharines Journal*, July 8, 1852. On the events, see *St. Catharines Standard*, June 8, 1989; Thomas, *Niagara's Freedom Trail*, 53–54; and Green, "Upper Canada's Black Defenders," 386–88.

108. Kate Harries, "Church Renews . . . Zion Baptist Hails Its Famous Pastor," *Toronto Star*, Sept. 14, 1998.

109. Dennis Gannon to Arden Phair of the St. Catharines Museum, Feb. 6, 2000, citing the *Lockport Daily Advertiser* of June 21, 1859, now in the archives of the St. Catharines Museum.

110. Undated pamphlet from Zion Baptist Church in *Blacks in the Niagara Peninsula*. Rochelle Bush, a local conservationist in St. Catharines, suggests that the Zion Baptist Church was actually "in financial ruin" when Burns became pastor. See interview in *St. Catharines Standard*, Sept. 20, 2003.

111. Hiram Wilson to William Lloyd Garrison, *Liberator*, Aug. 22, 1862. The estimate of the size of the congregation comes from Francis Petrie, *Niagara Falls Review*, Aug. 13, 1977.

112. Fred Landon, "Anthony Burns in Canada," *Ontario Historical Society* 22 (1923): 165; St. Catharines Zion Baptist Church pamphlet, in St. Catharines Public Library Special Collections. Hiram Wilson spoke of "Brother Burns" having made a good impression and "lectured widely" in various places in the *Liberator*, Aug. 22, 1862.

113. *Liberator*, Aug. 22, 1862.

114. Ibid. Song reprinted from an unidentified black newspaper published near Windsor, Canada West, in 1851, in *Blacks in the Niagara Peninsula*. The words were sung to the tune of "Oh! Susannah."

115. *St. Catharines Standard*, Sept. 18, 2000.

Epilogue

1. *Liberator*, Aug. 13, 1858.

2. *The Frederick Douglass Papers*, ed. John W. Blassingame (New Haven, Conn.: Yale Univ. Press, 1985), 3:3.

3. Anthony Burns, letter published in *Liberator*, Aug. 13, 1858.

4. *The Journal of Richard Henry Dana, Jr.*, ed. Robert F. Lucid (Cambridge, Mass.: Belknap Press of Harvard Univ. Press, 1968), 2:625.

5. Anthony Burns to the Baptist Church at Union, Fauquier County, Virginia, in Carter G. Woodson, ed., *The Mind of the Negro as Reflected in Letters Written during the Crisis, 1800–1860* (1926; New York: Russell and Russell, 1969), 661.

6. Ira Berlin, "Who Freed the Slaves? Emancipation and Its Meaning," in *Union and Emancipation: Essays on Politics and Race in the Civil War*, ed. David W. Blight and Brooks D. Simpson (Kent, Ohio: Kent State Univ. Press, 1997), 105–21.

7. *The Works of John C. Calhoun*, ed. Richard K. Crallé (New York, 1854), 4:542–49.

Index

Aberdeen, Lord, 92

Abolitionism/abolitionists, 67, 136n9, 139n79; alienation from other citizens, 36–37, 40, 42–43, 59, 143n48; Boston's reputation for, 35, 146n89; Burns's, 116, 118–19, 124–25; in Canada, 92–93, 99–100, 105, 118, 151n61; criticisms of Loring, 83–84, 146n105; denouncing slaveholders, 65, 72; divisiveness in, 40–42, 127n9, 133n24; effects of, 27, 37, 49, 65, 68–69, 71–72, 78, 117, 122, 145n86; effects of Burns's affair on, xiii–xiv, xvi–xvii, 83–84; effects of Burns's rendition in, 23, 45–48, 58–59, 61, 122, 145n86; on fugitive slave laws, 34, 36, 45–46; fugitive slaves as, 13; goals of, xvii, 30, 34; impotence of, 36, 45; increasing militancy of, xiv, 31–33, 37–38, 58, 80, 92–93, 123–24; international, xix, 81; New England Antislavery Society, 55; obstacles to, 51, 72, 107, 127n9; in politics, 26, 48, 136n24; portrayals of, 42–43, 72, 143n48; race and, xvi, xviii, 25; racial split in, xvi, 38, 55–56, 58–59, 61, 123; radical, 31–33, 42–43; resisting renditions, xi, 93; South overestimating influence of, 66–67, 82–83, 140n10, 146n89; Southern fear of, 80–81, 144n62; Southern newspapers criticizing, 68, 70, 72, 141n17; in St. Catherines, 107–8, 112, 116, 124–25, 154n93; tactics of, xi, 30, 40, 45, 51, 93, 127n9, 129n14, 154n93; as threat to law and order, 42–43, 45, 72; violence against, 31, 45; women as, 50–51. *See also* Antislavery sentiments; Emancipation

Acorn, 36–37

Adams, Charles Francis, 48

Adams, Elias, 109

Adams, John, 6, 10, 11, 34, 43, 81, 122

Adams, Samuel, 6, 10, 11, 34, 81, 122

Africa, in colonization proposals, 102, 142n42, 142n44

African Methodist Episcopal (AME) Church, 39, 110–11

African Methodist Episcopal Zion Church, 38, 39

Agency: Burns's downplayed, xiii, 56–57, 123; of Canadian blacks, xix, 118–19, 124–25

Agriculture: blacks' experience with, 107; in Canada, 90, 107; in elevation of blacks, 103–4

Alberti, George F., 89

Alcott, Bronson, 50

Allen, H. W., 64, 140n7

Allen, Richard, 110

American Party, 46–47

American Revolution, ix, xv, xviii, 11, 33, 34, 46, 56, 61–62, 119, 122, 123, 124, 148n10

Anderson, John, fugitive slave, 99, 150n35. *See also* Burton, Jack (aka John Anderson)

Anderson, Pastor John, 112

Anniversary Week, 8–9, 51

Antislavery sentiments: in Boston, xvi; in Britain, 87–88, 91–92, 98; in Canada, 91–92, 96–97, 148n11; effects of renditions on, xiv–xvii, 127n7; increasing, xvii, 127n7; purchase of Burns's freedom and, 53–54; South overestimating, xvii, 66–67, 124. *See also* Abolitionism/abolitionists

Appeal to the Coloured Citizens of the World (Walker), 72, 142n44

157